THE JEWS OF WALES

D1610618

THE JEWS OF WALES

A History

CAI PARRY–JONES

UNIVERSITY OF WALES PRESS

2017

www.uwp.co.uk
British Library CIP Data
A catalogue record for this book is available from the British Library

ISBN 978-1-78683-0937 (hardback)
978-1-78683-0845 (paperback)
eISBN 978-1-78683-0852

The right of Cai Parry-Jones to be identified as author of this work has been asserted in accordance with sections 77 and 79 of the Copyright, Designs and Patents Act 1988.

Published with the financial assistance of the Marc Fitch Fund

Typeset by Biblichor Ltd, Edinburgh

Printed by CPI Antony Rowe, Melksham

Contents

Acknowledgements

My research on the history of Welsh Jewry has occupied me for more than half a decade. The project began as a PhD thesis titled 'The History of the Jewish Diaspora in Wales' that was successfully defended at Bangor University in March 2014. I wish to acknowledge the important contributions made by my former PhD supervisor, Professor Nathan Abrams, as it was he who introduced me to this field of research. I would also like to thank Professor Andrew Edwards, who offered continual encouragement, guidance and support throughout my time at Bangor.

Many individuals have shared their expertise, insights and materials with me and have offered encouragement. I especially wish to thank Meic Birtwistle, Grahame Davies, Jasmine Donahaye, Colin Heyman, Glen Jordan, David Morris, Paul O'Leary, Huw Pryce, Esther Roberts, Einion Thomas, Diana Soffa and Stanley Soffa, as well as the assistance of archival and library staff in both the United Kingdom and the United States.

Various bodies have provided financial support for both my research and this publication. Major funding for my doctoral research came from the Arts and Humanities Research Council, while both the Royal Historical Society in London and the College of Arts and Humanities at Bangor University generously awarded me travel grants to attend archives and conferences in both the United Kingdom and the United States. I also wish to acknowledge the substantial financial support I have received from the Marc Fitch Fund towards the cost of publishing this work. I am grateful to all bodies for their vision and generosity in funding academic research.

I thank also my immediate family – Dad, Beca and Catrin – for the interest they have shown in my work and, more importantly, for always telling me that I could do it. Finally, I thank all the people at the University of Wales Press who have been involved in preparing this book for publication, particularly Dr Llion Wigley. It has been a pleasure to work with them.

I dedicate this book to the Jews of Wales, both past and present, and also to the memory of two special people who are no longer with us – my Nain, Elizabeth Alice Jones (1930–2017), who was extremely excited to see my doctoral work being published, and my mam, Meryl Elizabeth Parry-Jones (1953–96), who I know would have been behind me all the way.

List of Abbreviations

AAC	Academic Assistance Council
BMA	British Medical Association
BUF	British Union of Fascists
CAJEX	Magazine of the Cardiff Association of Jewish Ex-Servicemen and Women
CNS	Cardiff New Synagogue
CRO	Caernarfon Record Office
CUS	Cardiff United Synagogue
GA	Glamorgan Archives
HLUS	Hartley Library, University of Southampton
IWM	Imperial War Museum
JC	*Jewish Chronicle*
JYB	*Jewish Year Book*
LMA	London Metropolitan Archives
NWC	*North Wales Chronicle*
NLW	National Library of Wales
RCM	Refugee Children's Movement
SFNHM	St Fagans National History Museum
SWMF	South Wales Miners' Federation
TNA	The National Archives, Kew
WGA	West Glamorgan Archives
WL	Wiener Library
YMCA	Young Men's Christian Association

Map of Jewish communities established in Wales between 1768 and 1996

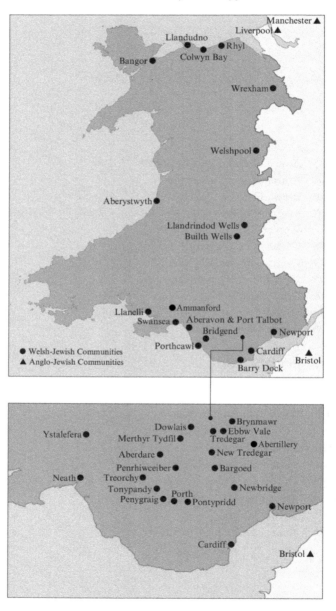

Manchester ▲
Liverpool ▲
Llandudno ●
Rhyl ●
Bangor ● Colwyn Bay
Wrexham ●
Welshpool ●
Aberystwyth ●
Llandrindod Wells ●
Builth Wells ●
Llanelli ● ● Ammanford
Swansea ● Aberavon & Port Talbot
Bridgend ●
Newport ●
Porthcawl ● Cardiff ●
Barry Dock ▲ Bristol

● Welsh-Jewish Communities
▲ Anglo-Jewish Communities

Ystalefera ● Dowlais ● ● Brynmawr
Merthyr Tydfil ● ● Ebbw Vale
Tredegar ● Abertillery
Aberdare ● ● New Tredegar
Penrhiwceiber ● ● Bargoed
Neath ● Treorchy ●
Tonypandy ● ● Newbridge
Penygraig ● Porth
● Pontypridd Newport ●
Cardiff ● Bristol ▲

Introduction

ALTHOUGH Jewish communities have been present in Wales since 1768, we have waited more than 250 years for the first nationwide historical study of the Jews in Wales to be written. This is largely because Welsh historians have traditionally associated religious belief and practice in Wales with Nonconformity (and Anglicanism to a lesser extent) and have thus tended to ignore the historical experiences of other religious minority groups such as the Jews.[1] This neglect should surprise no one, as for most of its history Wales has not been known as a nation of diverse faiths, however multi-denominational its Christianity. The religious census of 1851, for instance, revealed that 78 per cent of Welsh worshippers attended a Nonconformist chapel, and the predominance of Nonconformity up until the mid-twentieth century has led several scholars to brand Wales as a 'Nonconformist nation' or the Welsh as a 'Nonconformist people.'[2] As Paul Chambers and Andrew Thompson have pointed out, the story of Welsh religious history is 'not merely about Christian institutions.'[3], but nevertheless the historical presence of Jews and other religious minorities in Wales has been overlooked until relatively recently.[4] Their small numbers make it difficult to fit them into conventional narratives and analysis frameworks, and they have therefore been placed outside the dominant ways of thinking about the Welsh religious landscape.

If most Welsh historians have viewed the Jewish experience in Wales as peripheral or irrelevant to major trends in their field, the same is even more true in regard to historians of British Jewry, who have shown little, if any, desire to pay attention to the histories of Jews in British nations other than England. As the discipline's name, 'Anglo-Jewish historiography, suggests, historians of British Jewry have focused primarily on Jewish experiences in England, with the terms 'Britain' and 'England' often used synonymously, as in Sidney Salamon's work, *The Jews of Britain*, which offers an account of the Jews in England only.[5] This is hardly surprising given that Britain's more populous Jewish communities are to be found in English cities such as Leeds, London and Manchester. As Britain's largest Jewish centre, London has received the lion's share of attention, but studies of Jewish communities in the 'English provinces' have also been produced and are growing.[6] By contrast, the number of studies that focus on Jewish life in other parts of the United Kingdom remains small.[7] Undoubtedly this will continue to be the case until more works such as this are written, when 'British Jewish' rather than 'Anglo Jewish' should become the preferred term used by historians.[8] To help make this a reality, this book does not use the terms 'British Jewish' and 'Welsh Jewish' synonymously. Rather, it sees Welsh Jewry as a distinctive section of British Jewry, the other sections being Scottish, Anglo, Irish (to 1922) and Northern Irish (from 1922) Jewry.[9]

Regrettably, some historians are reluctant to change the terminology. Todd Endelman, for instance, is unwilling to discard the term 'Anglo Jewish' because:

> it is conventional to use the term 'Anglo-Jewish' to refer to Jews in Britain as a whole, including Jews in Scotland and Wales, even though they were not, in a strict sense, 'English' Jews. This usage is too well established to be dropped. Moreover, since the number of Jews who lived in Wales and Scotland was never large, folding them into 'Anglo Jewry' does not distort the overall picture.[10]

However, while the overall picture may not be distorted by folding Scottish and Welsh Jewry into Anglo Jewry, the process certainly distorts the picture of Scottish Jewry and Welsh Jewry. As Endelman clearly points out, Scottish and Welsh Jews are not 'English' and the particularities of their experiences would be lost if scholars took Endelman's advice. William D. Rubinstein uses the term 'Anglo' to describe British Jewry, but as Nathan Abrams reminds us, Rubinstein uses it in a linguistic sense, as the title of his work demonstrates: *A History of the Jews in the English-Speaking World: Great Britain*. The term is acceptable in this instance, for it is mostly accurate, (there are examples of Welsh-speaking Jews), but is an approach not widely shared by historians.[11]

More recently, some British-Jewish historians have been influenced by the school of 'New British History', offering a balanced account of Jewish history from all nations of the United Kingdom.[12] Although a section on Ireland (to 1922) and Northern Ireland (from 1922) is missing, the coverage of English-Jewish, Scottish-Jewish and Welsh-Jewish histories in John Campbell's 'The Jewish Community in Britain', for instance, demonstrates an attempt to move away from the Anglocentricity of British-Jewish historiography.[13] Indeed, other historians, such as Geoffrey Alderman and Raphael Langham, have published under the 'British-Jewish' banner, but their histories continue to focus on the Anglo-Jewish experience.[14] On the other hand, despite 'references ... to virtually the whole of the British isles', Harold Pollins's economic study of British Jewry is titled *Economic History of the Jews in England*, as he felt the 'Jews of the British isles' was too clumsy.[15] He is at least 'conscious that this is a dangerous step', however.[16]

Of course, the scholarly focus on Anglo-Jewish communities is justified to some degree for British Jewry has always been heavily concentrated in England. Still, something essential has been missed, for Welsh-Jewish communities have always been fundamental features in the British-Jewish landscape. Indeed, although most of Britain's Jews lived in major English cities, a significant number of Britain's Jewish centres were in fact Welsh (approximately thirty-six). It would be a mistake therefore to think that the full story of the British-Jewish experience can be told without considering the histories of Jewish communities outside of England, despite claims made by Endelman, who maintains: 'What happened elsewhere [in Britain], however piquant or arresting in human terms, reveals little about the main currents of Anglo-Jewish history.'[17]

Fortunately, not everyone shares this viewpoint and a pleasing sign is that the work in the field of Welsh-Jewish history, which has already been completed by Geoffrey Alderman, Ursula Henriques and Harold Pollins, among others, is now growing.[18] No nationwide history of Welsh Jewry has ever been published, however, and the smaller field of Welsh-Jewish history has itself been prone to the metropolitan bias expressed by Endelman, for much of it focuses on the experiences of south Wales Jewry.[19] Swansea, Wales's oldest Jewish community, and Cardiff, Wales's largest Jewish centre, have received the most attention, but studies of other communities in the region have also been produced – Tredegar's Jewish community in particular.[20] This is because its community was affected by the Tredegar riots of 1911 – the only major attack involving Jews in Britain between the 'Jew Bill' riots of 1753 and the rise of fascism in the 1930s.

Writing in the 1970s, Geoffrey Alderman was one of the first historians to examine the riots. Describing them as specifically 'anti-Jewish', he argued that they formed a unique dimension to the history of Welsh Jewry and emerged because Jewish immigrants were treated by the native Welsh as scapegoats for economic distress in early twentieth-century south Wales. Although non-Jewish property was also vandalised and no Jews were injured or killed during the riots, Alderman insisted that Jews were specifically targeted because they were regarded with animosity by the general population of south Wales. According to Alderman, 'the anti-Jewish element was central to the riots' since 'anti-Semitism in South Wales', particularly rich-Jew anti-Semitism, had a long history in the region. He also claimed that the riots were premeditated and that Jewish immigrants were unfortunate to have come to Wales, 'a land seething with religious bigotry'.[21]

Alderman's work has since been added to by a number of historians, all of whom conclude that the riots were driven by anti-Semitism (although Anthony Glaser once wrote that 'They remain something of an enigma wrapped up in mystery').[22] Some have disputed the riots' anti-Semitic nature, however, with the strongest contestation coming from William D. Rubinstein, who argued that they were not premeditated or specifically 'anti-Jewish', but simply the consequence of social and economic unrest. He suggests that the anti-Semitic element to the attacks was overexaggerated by both the leaders of Anglo Jewry in London and by the press to create a 'press sensation.' The non-Jewish Welsh, in his eyes, were incapable of such anti-Semitism since '*philo*-Semitism (admiration and support for Jews by gentiles) was virtually ubiquitous in Edwardian Wales.'[23] Alderman questioned Rubinstein's findings by stressing the validity of his evidence. He maintained that the riots were pre-planned and accused Rubinstein of carefully selecting and manipulating evidence to support his argument that Welsh society, and British society more generally, was characterised by philo-Semitism.[24] Although a consensus has yet to emerge, an insightful explanation has since been offered by Paul O'Leary, who argues that the riots do not fit comfortably within the confines of anti-or philo-Semitism. In his view, they were a classic example of the paradoxical nature of a 'tolerant society', which

> holds within it the possibility of a negative response to minorities as
> well as a hospitable one, on the grounds that a minority culture will

not be endured where it is perceived to threaten the values of the host society.[25]

Indeed, if the riots were driven primarily by fervent and long felt 'anti-Jewish' feeling amongst the non-Jewish Welsh, as Alderman suggests, then why were 'anti-Jewish' riots not a common occurrence in Wales? On the flip side, if Edwardian Wales was characterised by 'philo-Semitism', that is 'support and admiration for Jews', as Rubinstein writes, how do we explain the initial targeting of Jewish-owned shops and property by non-Jews?[26] It is also important to note that other immigrant and ethnic minority groups were victims of riots and hostility in nineteenth and early twentieth-century Wales, including the Irish in 1826 and 1882, the Chinese in 1911 and black seamen in 1919. Jewish immigrants were never consistently singled out for attack by the indigenous Welsh, as a casual reading of Alderman's work would suggest, nor was Wales a nation completely devoid of intolerant behaviour, as has often been assumed (discussed further in Chapter 4).[27]

As well as sparking an academic debate, the Tredegar riots have become synonymous with Welsh-Jewish history more generally, and as the late Leo Abse once noted, 'a well-worn tale.'[28] Indeed, most, if not all, Welsh history books that contain entries on Welsh Jewry are drawn to the riots, which, as Jasmine Donahaye points out, 'is presented as its sole distinguishing feature'.[29] Dai Smith's *Wales: A Question for History*, for example, devotes one sentence to Jews, noting that 'in 1911 in Tredegar, a 14-year-old Aneurin Bevan witnessed the shop-smashing that had, in part, an anti-Jewish element attached to its violence', while the only comment in Kenneth Morgan's *Rebirth of a Nation: Wales 1880–1980* to the Welsh-Jewish experience is 'Jewish landlords and shopkeepers were a popular target for working-class anger in August 1911.'[30]

References to Welsh Jewry have had an unfortunate and overwhelming sense of negativity and makes up a sad chapter in Welsh history. But is this the whole story of the Welsh-Jewish experience? Indeed, it is not, and there is more to Welsh Jewry than simply a history of suffering and hostility. Whilst in no way adopting a purely 'apologetic' and 'whiggish' interpretation, an approach most commonly found in the works of historians writing in the 'Roth Mould', this book discusses the successes of Welsh Jewry in addition to the difficulties.[31] Alderman once stated that 'too much [Jewish] communal history has been concerned with growth and achievement, not enough with difficulties and shortcomings.'[32] The reverse is true for Welsh Jewry. Too much has been written on the difficulties and shortcomings, and not enough on growth and achievement.

While debates about anti-Semitism have long taken centre stage in publications on Welsh Jewry, our understanding of the topic has also developed in other ways. Scholars such as Jasmine Donahaye and Grahame Davies have examined the literary, cultural and political exchanges between Jews and non-Jews in Wales, while others, including Neil Evans, have compared the histories of Jews with other ethnic minority groups in Wales.[33] More recently, architectural historian Sharman Kadish has explored the material landscape of Welsh Jewry, the synagogues of south Wales in particular.[34]

As mentioned earlier, although Jews were and are to be found throughout Wales, the histories of those who lived beyond the south have attracted little, if any, attention from scholars. Historical studies of Jews living away from established Jewish centres in Wales are non-existent and published works referring to north Wales's smaller communities are brief and largely factual, giving no sense of the texture of Jewish life in this region. For instance, the only mention of the history of Wrexham Jewry in a published work comes in W. Allister Williams's *The Encyclopaedia of Wrexham*, which devotes half a page to this community.[35] As a consequence, the history of north Wales Jewry has been doubly invisible – it has been overlooked by scholars exploring the Anglo-Jewish experience, as well as by those examining Welsh Jewry. As Abrams noted with regards to the small Jewish communities of Scotland, 'it is an unfortunate irony ... that we probably know more about the far-flung communities of the world than we do about those in our own islands.'[36] This comment is equally appropriate to Welsh Jewry. Indeed, until a study of all of Wales's Jewish communities is written, the history of Welsh Jewry, and British Jewry more generally, will remain incomplete.

This work attempts to rectify this omission by examining the histories of Jewish communities and individuals scattered throughout Wales, where such information is available. It serves as a reminder that there has been, and continues to be, a Jewish presence across Wales. Furthermore, most research on Welsh Jewry has concentrated on the period between the great migration of Jews from Eastern Europe during the late nineteenth century and the beginning of the First World War. There are examples of studies that look at Welsh-Jewish history beyond this period, but they are limited in numbers and scope.[37] This book endeavours to remedy these imbalances by exploring the history of Welsh Jewry from its humble origins to its current position in the early twenty-first century.

Sources and Methodology

Sources on Welsh Jewry are not extensive. At present, the fullest records are those of the Orthodox congregations in Cardiff and Swansea, though even those of the former are incomplete as many of its records were destroyed by a flood in 1981. As for the rest of the communities, the records are patchy and consist of the odd documents located in libraries and archives throughout Britain and the United States. Among the most valuable archival collections consulted were the chief rabbi's correspond-ence files, held at the London Metropolitan Archives, which helped shed light on the history of several of Wales's smaller Jewish communities and their relationship with the Chief Rabbinate in London. Alongside archi-val documents, extensive use was made of British-Jewish newspapers. Especially useful was the *Jewish Chronicle* (*JC*), which features reports of important events, correspondence and family notices relating to Jewish communities throughout the United Kingdom.

Jewish sources only tell part of the story however, and focusing solely on such material risks distorting historical reality, for it presents the expe-riences of communal leaders and those active in Jewish communal life as expressive of the Jewish experience in Wales as a whole. Yet not all Jews living in Wales identified with their nearest Jewish community and obtaining a true understanding of 'the Welsh Jewish experience' also requires the consultation of non-Jewish sources. Despite not focusing on Jewish themes and issues, local Welsh newspapers such as the *North Wales Chronicle* and the *Western Mail* were extremely useful for this purpose as they often reported on local Jewish communal and social affairs, as well as the activities of Jewish individuals and families whose names remain absent in community records. William Franklin, 'a Jewish hawker, residing at Berllan Bach, Bangor' features in the *North Wales Express* in January 1909, for instance, but nowhere is his name mentioned in sources that relate specifically to Bangor's Jewish community.[38] Local trade directories were also beneficial in providing information on Jewish traders and busi-nesses in Wales, but did not hold the same value when researching working-class Jews, for whom information was found in censuses amongst other sources. Another rich source for this study was the handful of published and unpublished memoir literature created by Jewish individuals who lived in Wales during the early to mid twentieth century.

Such a shortage of sources is not unique to Welsh Jewry. Much of Manchester Jewry's material has disappeared, but the work of the Jewish History Unit at the Manchester Polytechnic from the 1970s to the early 1990s to 'salvage the physical and documentary heritage of Manchester Jewry' has ensured that a number of records have survived.[39] To make up for the lack of written sources an enormous oral history project was established in Manchester so that the life histories of various Jewish individuals in the city, including immigrants, their offspring and refugees from Nazi-occupied Europe, were recorded. By 1984 the unit had put together a collection of over 400 taped interviews that are now housed at Manchester's Jewish Museum in Cheetham Hill.[40]

In contrast, little, if any, attempt, has been made until fairly recently to record the life histories of Welsh Jews. Although David Jacobs conducted interviews with a handful of Jewish individuals living in the south Wales valleys in the 1970s, studies of Welsh Jewry that draw on oral testimony are extremely rare. Ursula Henriques, for instance, justified the absence of oral testimony in her edited volume *The Jews of South Wales* by stating that at the time of publication in 1993 'most . . . of the families of the original Jewish immigrants [had] dispersed, taking their memories with them'.[41] Most does not mean all, however, and it is unfortunate that Henriques did not consult those Jews with memories of the late nineteenth and early twentieth centuries in south Wales, or their offspring, as well as Jacobs's recordings. As Tony Kushner once noted, historical studies of Welsh Jewry to date have provided their readers with a 'social history without [the voices of its] people'.[42]

This book aims to fill this gap by supplementing the written record with the voices of Jews who were interviewed by myself, as well as by volunteers of the 'Hineni' exhibition project, between 2010 and 2013.[43] It also draws on archived interviews from various institutions, including the Imperial War Museum and the British Library. By doing so, it seeks both to include and to examine the everyday experiences of Jews in Wales, as well as the small number of prominent figures, intellectuals and synagogue functionaries. The history of Welsh Jewry will undoubtedly be illuminated by the recollection of its people, for their voices will throw light upon the particular characteristics of Jewish life in Wales.

Although 'oral history is as old as history itself', the extensive modern use of the term did not appear until the rise of social history in the 1960s, when historians began to challenge the predominant history of the élite by offering the everyday person a place in history.[44] Its potential application to the social history of British Jewry was raised by Shaul Esh and Geoffrey Wigoder as early as 1962, and since then many British-Jewish historians have used oral sources in their work, including Jerry White and Rosalyn Livshin.[45] Despite this enthusiasm, the use of oral history has not gone unchallenged by scholars. One criticism is that oral history is subject to the fallibility of human memory.[46] Lynn Abrams, however, argues that 'This criticism [is] misplaced ... There is little evidence to suggest that people generally misremember events or experiences ... Even age does not appear to affect the veracity of human memory'.[47] Indeed, when conducting interviews for this study, I found that my informants were able to recall events from their lives in great detail, even those that occurred over half a century ago. Of course, people occasionally forget, but if such a problem occurs, aids such as photographs or personal documents can be used to retrieve memories. Moreover, if an interviewee's memory of an event is questionable, their testimony can be cross-referenced with contemporary sources.[48]

Another criticism of oral history is that it can be 'subjective'.[49] Yet criticising its subjectivity risks overlooking one of its great strengths, since oral testimonies, as well as providing information or 'more history' about groups whose written history is either missing or distorted, tell us about personal historical experiences. To cite an oft-quoted phrase of Alessandro Portelli, 'oral sources tell us not just what people did, but what they wanted to do, what they believed they were doing, what they now think they did ... Subjectivity is as much the business of history as the more visible 'facts'.'[50] Oral history is also intersubjective and includes the subjectivities of the interviewer themselves. Of course, it is the historian who selects interviewees for a project and the interviews are mostly driven by the questions asked, and then placed within what is considered to be an appropriate narrative framework. By interviewing Jews throughout Wales I have tried to recapture the everyday histories of Welsh Jewry, but inevitably both the oral and written sources in this study have been shaped in a way that reflects my concerns as a historian. Whilst I had every intention of allowing my interviewees to speak of their own perceptions, in the course of writing up I selected the parts of interviews that were of interest to this study.

In writing a history of Welsh Jewry, one of the main concerns was to achieve a fairly even geographical distribution of interviewees. Interview participants were selected using the so-called 'snowball method', where a list of interviewees from initial contacts led to an ever-widening circle of potential respondents. An additional concern when looking for interviewees was the question of identity –'Who is Jewish?' Identity scholars such as Stuart Hall have long asserted the fluid, complex, subjective and contested nature of identity, and Jewishness is no exception. *Halacha* (Jewish law) states that one can be Jewish through matrilineal descent or 'by choice', that is, through a conversion sanctioned by the *Beth Din* (rabbinical court) made up of three members who are fully observant of Jewish law. This, however, is a traditional and Orthodox viewpoint that has since been challenged by other branches of Judaism, such as the Liberal, Progressive and Reform movements which recognise the increasing reality of intermarriage, that is, Jews marrying non-Jews, and accept a patrilineal definition of Jewishness. While non-Orthodox movements also accept that a person can become Jewish through rabbinic conversion, such conversions are generally not recognised or sanctioned by Orthodox Jewry as they are not conducted in strict accordance with *halacha*.[51]

Moreover, while some Jews define their Jewishness in religious terms – they are Jewish because they practise Judaism – many non-religious Jews define their Jewishness in secular terms, with an emphasis on heritage, ethnicity or culture, or on elements of all three. With these differences in mind, scholars such as György Konrád have argued that the only defining characteristic of Jewishness common to all Jews is the propensity of a 'Jewish' person to self-identify as such – that is, 'what makes a person a Jew is saying they are one'.[52] Following Konrád's approach, this book defines 'Jewishness' in the broadest possible fashion to include all individuals who self-identify as Jewish, regardless of their *halachic* status or the degree of their religious and cultural observance. This book also adopts Alderman's definition of a Jew as one 'who was or is so regarded by his [or her] contemporaries.'[53]

The difficulty in identifying Jews was also apparent when researching archival material. While names in synagogue membership lists, marriage registers, burial books and on headstones in Jewish cemeteries are more than likely to be Jewish, those that appear in non-Jewish literature and sources such as local newspapers, trade directories and census returns are more difficult to identify.[54] This is because very few individuals were explicitly described as 'Jewish' in these sources, making it extremely challenging to identify a person's Jewishness outside a Jewish context. The identification of Jews in censuses was particularly challenging. Between 1841 and 1911 the standard census entry for an individual in Wales typically included their name, residential address, occupation, place of birth, nationality and from 1891 onwards the language they spoke (occupants were instructed to record whether they spoke 'English', 'Welsh' or 'Both'). In order to identify Jews listed in this material, I began searching for individuals and families with common Jewish surnames such as Cohen and Levy, those who were of Central or Eastern European origin (see Chapter 1) and those (primarily males) who were engaged in traditional Jewish occupations such as peddling, tailoring and watchmaking, a factor that will also be discussed further in Chapter 1.[55] Some people also noted languages other than English and Welsh in the census and since Jewish immigrants were the only group of people to likely put down Yiddish, Hebrew or 'Jewish' as a native tongue, identifying speakers of these languages (and their children) as Jewish is a reasonable assumption. For example, Michael and Annie Cohen of Cardiff were identified as Jewish in the 1891 census not only because of their Jewish-sounding surname, but because Michael was engaged in tailoring, a characteristically Jewish occupation, and they were both listed as Russian-born Hebrew speakers. Despite not listing Yiddish or Hebrew as their spoken language, Max and Johanna Levy of Bangor were identified as Jewish in the 1911 census because they had a traditional Jewish surname, were both Prussian-born and Max worked as a jewellery pedlar, one of the most common occupations for Jewish immigrant men in the nineteenth and early twentieth centuries.

Great caution had to be exercised when using this method, however, since not all Jews fitted neatly into all of these categories. Some were British-born, for instance, while others did not engage in traditional Jewish occupations or list their language as Yiddish or Hebrew in the census. Moreover, some Jewish immigrants living in Britain did not possess traditional Jewish names since the desire to become completely assimilated and integrated into British society motivated many to consciously adopt traditional British names or modify their Jewish and foreign-sounding names into British ones. Despite his not possessing a characteristically Jewish name, I concluded that Morris Henry Smith, a lodger living in Tredegar in 1911, was Jewish because he was Russian-born, a watchmaker (a trade typically associated with immigrant Jewish males) and resided with the minister of Tredegar's Jewish community,

Solomon Bloch. Smith's naturalisation file also reveals that his surname was originally Schmeres, and while name-changing was, for the reasons previously mentioned, also common amongst other immigrant groups in Wales and in Britain more generally, such as the Italians and the Irish, this combined with the other factors discussed makes a strong case for Smith's Jewishness.[56] Swansea-born Charles Dennis was also identified as Jewish in the 1911 census because his parents Daniel and Emma were both listed as Russian-born, his father was engaged in the traditional Jewish occupation of hawking and four of his siblings bore traditional Jewish names such as Leah and Myer. An obituary notice for Charles's father also appears in the *JC*, indicating that the Dennis family was almost certainly Jewish.[57]

To complicate things further, during the evangelical revival of the first half of the nineteenth century many non-Jewish Welsh families adopted Old Testament names that were often borne by Jews. These names include, for instance, Isaac, Samuel and Abraham but, as Cecil Roth has pointed out, 'Biblical names in the singular tend to be [non-Jewish] Welsh, and in the plural Jewish'. This is because Jewish surnames were traditionally patronymic, changing from generation to generation, rather than permanent, and the suffix '-s' was often added to the father's given name to denote that x was the 'son of' or 'daughter of' y. For example, if Samuel had a son named Abraham, that son would be named Abraham Samuels, but if Abraham had a son named Isaac, he would be called Isaac Abrahams. When Ashkenazi Jews (Jews from Central and Eastern Europe) were forced to adopt permanent surnames in various European states in the early nineteenth century, many chose to keep the patronymic surname that they then possessed. Whilst examining the 1891 census, I determined that Cardiganshire-born Mary Abraham, then living in Aberdare, and her son, John, were not Jewish not only because their Biblical surname was singular, but because they had characteristically Christian first names. Moreover, John worked as a coal miner and, despite the involvement of some Jews in this industry (discussed further in Chapter 1), it was not typically associated with Jewish occupational patterns.

Statistics

The challenge of identifying Jewish individuals poses problems in determining population numbers. The figures for this book are mostly taken from the *Jewish Year Book* (*JYB*), an almanack for British Jewry published since 1896. However, they are not entirely reliable for a number of reasons. Firstly, the *JYB* obtains its figures not from official data but by writing to individuals in the Jewish communities themselves. In 1936, for example, the Cardiff correspondent, Henry Samuels, received a letter from the joint editors of the *JYB* that stated 'I will be much obliged if you will let me know as accurately as possible the number of Jews in your city . . . If you are unable to inform us of the exact number, we will be much obliged for as close an estimate as possible.'[58] Thus the figures presented in the *JYB* are often based on guesswork. Secondly, the statistics are complicated by conflicting figures. Between 1965 and 1968, for instance, the *JYB* notes how the population of Cardiff's Jewish community almost doubled from 3,000 in 1965 to 5,000 in 1966, but then suddenly declined between 1967 and 1968 to 3,500. To add to the confusion, population numbers can also refer to seat holders, families or individuals. Finally, gaps and repetition appear in the statistics. Between 1941 and 1944, for example, no figures are provided 'due . . . to war exigencies', while the 'figures given' between 1929 and 1935 were 'approximately correct to 1929'.[59] It must also be remembered that self-identifying Jews who do not affiliate with a Jewish community, either culturally or religiously, as well as Jewish individuals and families who live away from organised Jewish centres, are not included in the *JYB*. Despite its various shortcomings, however, the *JYB* remains a valuable document since it is the only systematic compilation of population data dedicated specifically to British Jewry.[60] As well as the *JYB,* synagogue membership records must also be treated with some caution since they do not always reflect the true number of Jews living in that area or active in congregational life. Indeed, some members of Jewish congregations live away from the towns and cities where their synagogue is situated, but retain membership to support congregational activities financially, as well as to secure their burial rights.

Census data is complex and not fully accurate either. Although the 2001 and 2011 censuses of England and Wales and the parallel census in Scotland are the only ones to date to include a voluntary question on religion and feature a box labelled 'Jewish', they have failed to capture individuals who identify their Jewishness by ethnicity only.[61] This is because the ethnicity question is limited to nationality and skin colour and the option of including 'Jewish' in the write-in box may not have occurred to most of those concerned. Only 3.2 per cent of 'Jews by religion' in the 2001 census recorded their ethnicity as 'Jewish', for instance.[62]

Moreover, the situation is further complicated by the fact that many non-religious Jews may have ticked the 'Jewish by religion' box since no obvious alternative ways of declaring a Jewish identity were provided. Indeed, censuses may always underestimate a given Jewish population, since infamous historical events such as the Prussian 'Jew Census' of 1916 and the atrocities of the Third Reich have made some Jews, particularly the older generations, reluctant to disclose their Jewishness on any official government document.[63] Consequently, 'there is no such thing as a "true"' number when it comes to counting Jews' and the statistics included in this study serve as an estimate only.[64]

A Jewish Community in Wales?

There is or was not one Jewish community in Wales, but many, located primarily in the industrial cities and towns of the south such as Cardiff, Merthyr Tydfil and Swansea, followed by the smaller coastal towns of Bangor, Colwyn Bay, Llandudno and Rhyl in north Wales. Although Wales's geography is comparatively compact, one explanation for the development of numerous Jewish communities in the country is the makeup of the Welsh landscape itself. The topography of Wales, with its mountainous core, has essentially divided the country into two distinct parts, the north and the south, with communication links in both regions historically running parallel to each other from west to east. Indeed, particularly interesting is the relationship between north Wales's Jewish communities and their neighbouring Anglo-Jewish communities in Liverpool and Manchester for, as we shall see, the former operated almost as satellite communities to the latter and their social and religious practices were almost inextricably intertwined. Of course, such a relationship mirrors that of the population of north Wales more generally, since Liverpool, given its geographical proximity to the region (12 miles distant at its nearest point and 115 miles at its farthest) and the history of Welsh settlement in the city in the nineteenth century, has long been labelled the 'unofficial capital of north Wales'.

But what is meant by a 'Jewish community'? While the term is problematic and has traditionally been defined in Jewish culture as a *kehillah* (a congregation), a 'Jewish community' is defined here as a self-conscious and unified entity whose members interact in religious worship and/or social and cultural activities. It is not, however, necessarily defined by a geographical location or boundary, for as we shall see, most, if not all, of Wales's Jewish communities served Jews who for various reasons lived away from their population or spiritual centres. It is impossible to say how many isolated Jews associated themselves with their nearest Jewish community, though we know that many did.[65]

This book refers to many of Wales's Jewish centres as 'small Jewish communities.' But what is meant by a 'small Jewish community', and how 'small' is 'small'? According to Lee Shai Weissbach, there is 'no previously developed and widely accepted definition of what constitutes a small Jewish community'.[66] In its absence, he identifies 'small Jewish communities' as 'those with triple-digit populations' with 'reported Jewish populations of at least 100 but fewer than 1,000 individuals'.[67] This is because 'settlements of fewer than a hundred Jews were unlikely to have attained the critical mass necessary to constitute full-fledged communities'.[68] Weissbach was specifically referring to small Jewish communities in the United States and the same criteria cannot be used in identifying Wales's small Jewish communities. In terms of their overall history, the size of the communities ranged from twelve to 3,500, and thus many of Wales's Jewish communities do not fit Weissbach's 'triple-digit' model. Yet although approximately fifteen Jewish communities in Wales numbered less than a hundred Jews at their peak, they were all of sufficient size to form congregations with functioning synagogues, and their members pursued a Jewish way of life against all odds. This work therefore defines small Jewish communities as those with double- or triple-digit populations. Moreover, it is important to note that the size of a Jewish community fluctuates and it is never static. Therefore, a 'large' Jewish community may eventually become a 'small' Jewish community and vice versa. This was particularly true for Swansea Jewry, which grew from approximately 300 to 1,000 persons between 1896 and 1912, but numbered no more than 535 individuals from the late 1930s onwards.[69]

This book has six chapters. Chapter 1 outlines the history of Jewish migration and settlement in Wales, examining both how and why Jews came to the country. Chapter 2 discusses the particular patterns of religious and communal life in Wales's Orthodox Jewish communities, while Chapter 3 investigates the impact that Jewish persecution in Nazi-occupied Europe and the Second World War had on Wales and its Jewish population between 1933 and 1945. Chapter 4 explores the relationship between non-Jews and Jews in Wales during the nineteenth and twentieth centuries, a subject that the 1911 Tredegar riots have long been held to exemplify. Chapter 5 focuses on the importance of context and 'place' in history and explores the interaction between Jews and their Welsh surroundings, while Chapter 6 examines both the decline and the endurance of Wales's Jewish communities throughout the twentieth and early twenty-first centuries. The conclusion provides a summary of the core arguments made in both the introduction and the main body of the book. To assist nonspecialist readers, Hebrew and Yiddish terms are defined at first use, while a glossary of terms and definitions is provided at the end of the book.

I

Migration and Settlement

THE first documented Jewish settlers in Britain arrived in England in the wake of the Norman Conquest in 1066.[1] However, when Jews first made contact with Wales is more uncertain, since no settled communities were established prior to the eighteenth century. Jews in England resided first in London, but began to establish communities elsewhere in the country throughout the twelfth century. Significant Jewish settlements were founded in a number of English towns that lay close to the Welsh Marches such as Hereford and Bristol, for instance, but most scholars have seen such settlements as the furthest limits of Jewish westward penetration in the British Isles during this time. John Gillingham, for example, wrote that 'there were no Jewish settlements anywhere in Scotland, Wales, or Ireland', but they were found in England since 'English society had shared to the full in that fundamental socio-economic and cultural transformation of Europe. By contrast, Celtic society had not—or hardly at all.'[2] Patricia Skinner adds that 'had English rule spread faster to Wales, Scotland and Ireland, then the remit of the Jewish Exchequer [a department of the English royal exchequer charged with the supervision of all Jewish business] might well have extended to those territories too' but notes that there is some 'fragmentary evidence' for a Jewish presence in Wales before 1290, the year when Jews were expelled from England and English Crown lands in Wales for complex economic, political, and religious reasons.[3]

This 'fragmentary evidence' of a Jewish presence in medieval Wales is explored by Joe Hillaby who speaks not of 'communities' but of individual Jews found in the marcher lands of south Wales in the thirteenth century, who paid annual fees to the local lord for protection and residence. Using contemporary ministers' accounts and the fine rolls of

Edward I, he mentions the presence of five Jews, including Isaac and Vives son of Vives, who paid for annual licences in Abergavenny in 1256–7 and 1277 respectively; David, who died at Caerleon in 1278; and two Jews in Chepstow, one unnamed and the other called Peter, who were fined in the town in 1270/71 and 1283 respectively.[4] More recently, David Stephenson has supplemented these findings by pointing out a reference in the close rolls of Henry III to two Jewish moneylenders named Solomon of Haverford and Abraham who were collecting debts in Carmarthen in 1251.[5]

As well as Jewish individuals, a 1290 list of bonds belonging to Bristol Jewry reveals the existence of a Jewish family, three members of which were Josce of Caerleon and his two sons, Isaac and Aaron.[6] Although the toponym 'Caerleon' suggests that the family may have resided in the Welsh Marches, it is most likely, given that all three Jews appear in contemporary records only in the context of Bristol Jewry, that it derived from their commercial and financial interests in Caerleon and in south-east Wales more generally.[7] Joe and Caroline Hillaby speculate that the family may have once settled in Caerleon and eventually relocated to Bristol due to a lack of opportunities in south-east Wales,[8] but there is no existing evidence to support this claim. Similarly, there is no clear evidence to suggest that David, the Jew who died at Caerleon in 1278, was related to this family, as has previously been implied by Michael Adler and others.[9]

Other attempts at uncovering a Jewish presence in Wales during the Middle Ages have remained at best unconvincing. In 1903, for instance, Edward A. Lewis cited the late thirteenth-century charters of Edwardian boroughs in north Wales as evidence of Jewish settlement in the region.[10] However, while the charters of 1284 for Bere, Caernarfon, Conwy, Criccieth, Flint, Harlech and Rhuddlan state 'that Jews shall not sojourn in the same borough at any time', their clauses refer specifically to the exclusion of Jews rather than their expulsion.[11] The same can be said for the charters of Overton (1292) and Beaumaris (1296), which were both issued after the Edict of Expulsion given by Edward I in 1290.[12] Indeed, had there been previous Jewish settlement in north Wales one would expect the inclusion of an expulsion clause, as was the case with the charter for Newcastle upon Tyne (1234), which read: 'no Jew shall remain or have any residence in the said town either in our time or in that of our heirs'.[13]

Although Jews officially ceased to exist in England and English Crown lands in Wales between the expulsion of 1290 and their informal readmission in 1656, they were certainly not absent from English and Welsh society during this period. Drawing on contemporary ministers' accounts, William Rees finds an extraordinary reference to an unnamed Jew in the Carmarthenshire commote court of Maenor Deilo in 1386–7, which was then under the jurisdiction of Richard II's constable at nearby Dinefwr Castle.[14] Although Joachim Gaunse, a Jewish metallurgist and mining engineer from Prague, was involved in the copper-mining industry in Keswick in 1581, there is no evidence to suggest that he also developed Neath's copper-smelting works during this period, as Israel Abrahams and others have speculated.[15]

How soon after the mid seventeenth century the first openly practicing Jew emerged in Wales is difficult to ascertain. In his 1896 study of the history of Llandysul, William J. Davies mentions that a Reverend Edward Jones of the town married a 'rich Jewish lady' in the early 1700s, but provides no further information or evidence to support his claim.[16] Edward Jones's will dated 1744 reveals that his wife's name was Anne, but nowhere in this document is she described as Jewish or distinguished as such from her Anglican family.[17] Of course, Anne may have been a convert to Christianity, but there is no evidence of this. Furthermore, Neville Saunders notes that a list of lodge members at the Nag's Head and Star, Carmarthen beginning in 1725, 'contains the names of several Jewish free-masons, among them William Samuell, a glover by trade', but we cannot be certain that these men were indeed Jews.[18] What is certain, however, is that Jews were present in Wales in the mid eighteenth century, with the first Jewish community in the country established in Swansea in 1768.

Establishing Communities

The first known Jewish settler in Swansea was David Michael, a German-born migrant who came to the town in the 1740s. He was later joined by two other German-Jewish migrants named Mr Cohen and Mr Joseph and in 1768 there were enough Jews residing in Swansea for a 99-year lease of land for a Jewish cemetery in Townhill to be granted to David Michael by the Swansea Corporation, marking the formal beginnings of a permanent Jewish community in the town.[19] When Swansea Jewry first formed a *minyan* (a quorum of ten Jewish males traditionally required for Orthodox religious services) is uncertain but by the 1770s Wales's first synagogue was established in David Michael's House in Wind Street. It was situated 'at the back of his usual sitting-room', and 'was capable of containing thirty or forty persons'.[20] In 1789, the congregation moved to a room in the Strand and by 1818 the community, now numbering over one hundred Jews, was large enough to build Wales's first purpose-built synagogue.[21] Situated in Waterloo Street, it served Swansea Jewry until 1859 when a bigger synagogue, large enough to accommodate 228 people, was erected in Goat Street.[22]

Jewish immigrants continued to settle in small numbers and establish communities in other parts of south Wales over the next hundred years. A Jewish community was formally established in Cardiff in 1841, for instance, when the second Marquess of Bute donated land at Highfield for use as a Jewish cemetery. While no early records of Jewish congregational life in Cardiff are extant, we do know that some of the town's earliest Jewish residents included Levi Marks and his sons Michael and Solomon, who arrived in the 1810s and worked as pawnbrokers and jewellers, and that Cardiff Jewry originally worshipped in rooms in the town centre, including a room at the Cavalry Barracks in Union Street, 'a large room in Trinity Street' and a 'room in Bute Street', before acquiring enough funds and members to erect a purpose-built synagogue in East Terrace in 1858.[23] A Jewish community was established in Newport around 1859, though there is evidence of Jews residing in the town in the 1840s, including Samuel Polak, a clothes dealer and outfitter from Russia, and Abraham Isaacs, a Polish-born travelling salesman.[24]

Around the same time, Jews began settling and establishing communities in towns in the south Wales valleys. A small synagogue was built in Victoria Street in Merthyr Tydfil in 1848, serving a Jewish population of approximately forty, including Austrian-born Ephraim Harris and his Polish wife Anne, and Russian-born Joseph Barnett and his wife Hannah Leah, also from Poland, while a Jewish house of prayer situated in the Wainfelin district of Pontypool was consecrated in 1867 by a handful of Jewish families, including the Blooms from Poland.[25] Moreover, a Jewish community comprising a dozen families was established in Tredegar in 1873, with Polish-born pawnbroker Lewis Lyons elected as its president and a portion of his house in Queen Street adapted for use as a synagogue, while Jews settling in Pontypridd in the mid nineteenth century, including Polish-born brothers David and Charles Goodman, founded a synagogue there in 1867 to avoid the expense and inconvenience of having to travel to nearby Cardiff and Merthyr Tydfil for religious services (approximately twelve to fourteen miles).[26] Described as 'cosy' and 'little' by the *JC*, Pontypridd's synagogue accommodated up to fifty worshippers and was situated in a converted school-room 'near Penuel Chapel' in the centre of town.[27] A similar situation led to the construction in 1868 of 'a little synagogue' in Neath, funded by a Polish watchmaker named Lazarus Samuel and built so that the town's Jewish residents did not have to travel to nearby Swansea (approximately nine miles) for *Rosh Hashanah* (Jewish New Year) services.[28] Situated between Samuel's Buildings and the ruins of Neath castle and with accommodation for up to thirty worshippers, the synagogue was used only for the Jewish New Year services, a practice which continued until the 1880s.[29]

Although no Jewish communities were established in north Wales between the eighteenth and mid nineteenth centuries, there is evidence of a Jewish presence in the region during this period. The earliest Jews whose names are known were brothers Michael and Joseph Hyman, who were jewellery hawkers from 'foreign parts' in north Wales in the 1820s.[30] By 1828 Joseph was listed in a trade directory as a watch and clock maker in Bangor.[31] Others included John Aronson and his brother Solomon (from Prussia), who worked as jewellery pedlars in the region during the 1820s and set up a permanent watch and jewellery business in Bangor in 1828, 'in consequence of increased patronage' from 'the Nobility, Gentry, and the Public of North Wales'.[32] Solomon left for Liverpool in 1836, while John continued the business in Bangor, raising eight children with his wife, Maria, and became one of 'the most respectable residents of the neighbourhood'.[33]

As with other Jewish communities established in Britain between the late eighteenth and mid nineteenth centuries such as Liverpool, south Wales's earliest Jewish communities were established by poor immigrants or descendants of immigrants from central Europe. They came from various German states, parts of the Austrian Empire and from Posen, the region of Poland controlled by Prussia during much of the nineteenth century, and migrated to Britain to escape poverty and religious persecution in their homelands. Although conditions between the Central European states varied and began gradually to improve throughout the nineteenth century following the acquisition of equal legal rights by Jews (Jews were emancipated in Austria in 1867, for instance), Jewish life in Central Europe during the eighteenth and early nineteenth centuries was hard, with Jews facing restrictions on marriage, occupation, property ownership and residence, as well as being subject to high taxes. As a consequence, many fled their native lands to seek a better life elsewhere. Several thousand relocated to Britain, as it was considered to be a more open and tolerant society. From the seventeenth century onwards Jews in Britain were free to live, work and worship where they chose, and while popular anti-Semitism was by no means absent, British laws did not discriminate against Jews any more than against other religious Nonconformists (those who were not members of the Church of England, the Established Church), such as Catholics and Protestant dissenters. Like other non-Anglicans, Jews were barred from sitting in Parliament until the early to mid nineteenth-century; alternatives to the Anglican oath of allegiance, which had to be sworn when taking up public office, were offered to Nonconformists in 1828, to Catholics in 1829 and to Jews in 1858.

While persecution, discrimination and poverty were major factors in the decision of many Central European Jews to leave their homelands and migrate to Britain during this period, Todd Endelman reminds us that the 'complexion of the migratory flow changed' after the 1830s, when middle-class Jewish merchants from Central Europe began arriving in Britain 'because of its unrivaled mercantile and industrial pre-eminence', which was 'in part, a reflection of the social and economic transformation of German Jewry that was under way' throughout the nineteenth century.[34] The Jews of Dundee provide an example of this kind of migration; according to Nathan Abrams, they were merchants from Germany who settled there from 1840 onwards to purchase and export textiles to the continent.[35]

But why did Jews settle and establish communities in south Wales during this period? They did so mainly for economic reasons, as their arrival coincided with the beginnings of widespread industrialisation and urbanisation in the region. Jews were for the most part not directly involved in any of the principal industries established in south Wales during this period, such as coal mining and iron manufacturing. Working primarily as merchants and traders (discussed later in this chapter), they were attracted by the business and commercial opportunities provided by these burgeoning working-class centres. Thus, Jewish immigrants were drawn to Swansea when it became the copper-smelting centre of Britain from 1717 onwards, while it was the development of both Cardiff and Newport as coal and iron ports during the first half of the nineteenth century that attracted Jews to these towns. Jewish communities were established in the south Wales valleys towns of Merthyr Tydfil, Pontypool and Tredegar because all three had developed into significant ironworking centres by the early to mid nineteenth century. Indeed, Merthyr Tydfil, a backwater village of around five hundred people in the early eighteenth century, had by 1851 become the largest town in Wales, with a population of approximately 46,378 individuals, following the discovery of rich supplies of iron ore. Although Pontypridd did not become heavily industrialised during this period, remaining a market town, the opening of a station on the Taff Vale Railway from Cardiff to Merthyr Tydfil in 1841 certainly helped guide some early Jewish settlers to the town as they ventured into the south Wales valleys looking for economic opportunities.

As in south Wales, it was commercial opportunities that drew Jewish immigrants to north Wales, but while industrialisation was the attraction in the south, in the north it was the rural environment. Typically, the first Jews to come to north Wales had begun their lives in Britain in Liverpool and Manchester, two cities with significant Jewish communities.[36] They settled and worked for a time in these cities as petty traders and pedlars, before eventually heading west to rural north Wales (12 miles distant at its nearest point and 115 at its farthest) in search of an area with less economic competition. Leaving on a Sunday, they peddled in the north Wales countryside, selling all kinds of goods to rural households and villages, before returning to their homes in Manchester and Liverpool in time for the Sabbath. The Hyman brothers, for instance, were members of synagogues in Liverpool and Manchester, while the Aronsons had connections with Liverpool.[37] Journeys between the north-west of England and north Wales were often made by foot or horse-drawn cart, but by the 1820s steam packets began to run between Liverpool and Bangor and soon became the favourite mode of transport for Jewish pedlars.[38] Such a work pattern was not unique to north Wales Jewry, however. Kenneth Collins's research on Glasgow Jewry, for instance, has shown that Jewish pedlars from Glasgow travelled to villages in Ayrshire to sell their wares and returned home for the Sabbath, while Cormac Ó Gráda once noted that in Dublin, Jewish pedlars 'working outside the city typically returned in time for the Sabbath.'[39]

In addition to economic opportunities, it is possible that the rapid rise of Nonconformist denominations in nineteenth-century Wales – constituting 80 per cent of Welsh worshippers by 1851 – may have also encouraged Jewish immigrants to settle in the country because the Established Church, an institution with a long history of Jewish persecution stretching back to the Middle Ages, was not the dominant religious body in Wales as it was in England. Moreover, since the Welsh religious landscape was made up of a number of different Nonconformist denominations, it is possible that some Jewish immigrants believed that as followers of the Jewish faith, their religious practices were likely to be tolerated in Wales's religiously plural, albeit Christian, society.

Until the 1870s the Jewish population of Wales numbered no more than a few hundred individuals, but Jewish life had been established in the country and was primarily concentrated in the southern coastal towns of Cardiff, Newport and Swansea.[40] From the 1880s onwards the population of Welsh Jewry, and British Jewry as a whole, increased rapidly as Jewish immigrants began to arrive in great numbers from the Russian Pale of Settlement.

The Era of Mass Migration: 1881–1914

Between 1881 and 1914, an estimated 120,000 to 150,000 Eastern European Jews settled in Britain, raising the country's Jewish population from approximately 60,000 to 300,000.[41] The reasons for the mass migration from Eastern Europe were multifaceted and complex, and included a combination of anti-Semitic pogroms, persecutions and economic hardship. Tony Kushner and others have made it clear that although the pogroms that swept Russia during the 1880s, following the assassination of Tsar Alexander II in 1881 (for which Jews were blamed), forced many Jews to migrate, they were neither the main factor in nor the beginning of Eastern European emigration.[42] As we have seen, a small number of Russian Jews had arrived in Wales prior to 1881, as was true for the rest of Britain.[43] However, Jewish migration from Eastern Europe was far more pronounced after the 1880s, with most immigrants coming from the north-west part of the Russian Empire, an area that was not directly affected by antisemitic violence.[44] The number of Eastern European Jews migrating to the United States, for instance, rose from 200,000 in the 1880s to 300,000 in the 1890s. From 1900 to 1914 another 1.5 million arrived in America.[45]

There is no denying that there were instances of extreme anti-Jewish violence in Russia in the first decade of the twentieth century, including the pogrom in Kishinev in 1903 and those following the failure of the revolution of 1905, for which Jews, who were regarded as promoters of socialist and radical political ideas, were blamed. However, although these incidents caused many Jews to flee, Eastern European Jewish emigration was motivated largely, though not exclusively, by government occupational and residential restrictions that led to the economic deterioration of Russian Jewry. Between 1791 and 1917, Jews were only permitted to live and work in Russia's westernmost provinces, which became known as the Pale of Settlement.[46] The position of Russian Jewry fluctuated during this period, being highly dependent on the personality and policies of the ruling monarch. Alexander II (1855–81) permitted certain privileged Jewish merchants, skilled artisans, university graduates and their families to reside outside the Pale, but their position greatly deteriorated in the 1880s following the passing of a number of restrictive and discriminative laws against Jews by Alexander III in May 1882 in response to his father's assassination in 1881.[47] The basis of Jewish life in the Pale was the *shtetl* (a small Jewish town or village), but the new laws prohibited Jews from engaging in agriculture in rural areas or residing in towns or villages of fewer than ten thousand people. Jews were also prohibited from owning real estate or working as lawyers or in government were concentrated in the Pale's overcrowded cities, such as Warsaw and Minsk, where they typically turned to commerce and trade. Their situation was exacerbated by the rapid increase of the Jewish population in Russia, which rose from approximately 1,250,000 to over 5,189,000 between 1800 and 1897.[48] As the Jewish population of these cities increased, Jewish merchants and workers had to compete for a limited number of jobs, which led to most of them living in poverty. As a consequence, a vast number made the decision to emigrate to escape the economic tribulations of Tsarist Russia.

There were also Jews who had escaped military conscription or deserted the Tsarist army. Although the introduction of universal conscription in Russia in 1874, which required one son from each family to serve in the Russian army, was less stringent and discriminatory towards Jews than previous conscription laws, such as the Cantonist system implemented by Nicholas I between 1827 and 1856, which specifically targeted Jewish youth for military conscription, the prospect of serving in the Tsarist army for two years encouraged thousands of young men, Jews and non-Jews, to flee Russia.[49] Hyman Factor, for instance, was born in the province of Kovno, Russia in 1878, eventually settling in 1906 in Aberavon, where he was naturalised in March 1921. His application for naturalisation suggests that he left Russia to avoid military service. It reads:

> The applicant states that he was born at Salant, Russia on the 6 March 1878 ... He bears an excellent character in the neighbourhood of Aberavon, but he admits that he is regarded as a deserter from the Russian army.[50]

Other examples include Russian-born Solomon Krupp, a traveller in clothing residing in Llandudno in 1910, who left 'Russia before he reached the age for military service'.[51]

Such was the condition of Russian Jews between 1881 and 1914. Discriminated against, persecuted and victims of economic hardship and extreme anti-Semitic violence, they increasingly sought to leave their home country for other nations, taking advantage of cheap steerage tickets on steamships. It is estimated that 1.98 million Jews left Russia during this period, of whom 120,000 to 150,000 settled in Britain.[52]

Between the 1830s and 1914, Britain was the principal transmigration route for northern European migrants, Jewish and non-Jewish, en route to America.[53] This is because intense competition on Atlantic emigrant routes made it cheaper at times to sail first from Northern Europe to Britain rather than to make the trip directly.[54] This indirect route was also favoured by many Jewish migrants since it allowed them to stock up on kosher food (food that conforms to the regulations of Jewish dietary law) for the transatlantic crossing.[55] Although many Jewish migrants made the onward journey from British ports to America, some never left, and consequently a myth has developed that British Jewry, in the words of Harold Pollins, 'was built up of those who did not get to America'.[56] As Peter Braham commented:

> England was a land of transmigration for Jewish emigrants en route to the USA ... For some this transmigration merely meant disembarking at one British port before embarking at another ... but for others, perhaps because of lack of means, plans to travel to the USA were never realized and they settled in England.[57]

Yet there is no existing evidence to suggest that large numbers of Jewish migrants remained in Britain involuntarily due to lack of funds.

As Hasia Diner suggests, many Eastern European Jews made their trans-migration journey 'in steps', spending time in Britain working as pedlars before continuing westwards.[58] David Cesarani agrees, stating that 'it was economically rational to travel first to Britain and work to earn the rest of the money for the onward journey'.[59] This is further suggested by an article of 1886 from the Russian-Jewish newspaper, *HaYom*, which reads:

> their goal is America, and they stop en route in London. Sometimes they spend all they have . . . and have no means to travel further. Hence they remain here a short while until they learn a trade and save enough money to journey to the land of their choice.[60]

It is unknown how many Jews did their journey 'in steps', but the journey of Russian-born Joseph Policovsky is a case in point. Arriving in Britain at the turn of the twentieth century, he was listed in the 1901 census as a pedlar lodging in Llanelli. Five years later he married Sarah Berlovitz and they had three children in the town. Joseph eventually became a picture frame dealer and the Policovskys left for the United States in 1913, settling in Boston.[61] Why the Policovskys relocated to the United States is unclear, but this example demonstrates that some Jewish migrants spent a number of years in Britain before continuing their journey to America.

Some historians have also claimed that many Jewish migrants settled in Britain because they were either deceived by shipping companies into believing that Britain was New York or they were mis-sold tickets to America. According to Kenneth Collins, many Jews settled in Scotland because they 'were tricked into believing on their arrival in Leith or Dundee, that they had already reached America!', while Susan L. Tananbaum noted that 'Some paid for tickets to America, only to learn that they had disembarked on the Thames.'[62] Such claims are also embedded in the collective memory of British Jewry. Renee Woolf, for instance, recalled, that when her grandparents 'came to Llanelli, the captain told them they had come to America', but admits that the story may have been exaggerated.[63]

Indeed, as Nathan Abrams reminds us, 'The story of being deceived by unscrupulous agents or captains is a common one told among immigrant Jewish families, but one for which there is no actual evidence.'[64] Contemporary sources, for instance, allude to counterfeit tickets and steamship agents disappearing with money, but no mention is made of passengers being tricked into believing that they had arrived in America or being left stranded in Britain.[65] But why has this folklore emerged? Cesarani suggests that it was used as an 'alibi for opportunistic migration', to counteract 'the characterisation of the Jewish immigrant ... as "homo economicus"', while Abrams suspects that 'it is used as a cover for those who were simply sick of traveling on what must have been a horrendous journey'.[66] Indeed, the conditions of passengers travelling to Britain across the North Sea aroused much adverse comment. The *JC*, for instance, wrote in 1906 that 'our unfortunate coreligionists arrive in this country after a long and exacting journey ...A voyage as a steerage passenger across the North Sea in these conditions is a sufficiently cheerless and tiring experience.'[67] However, despite these unpleasant conditions, Jewish migrants who settled in Britain were not always individuals 'who were simply sick of travelling'. For many, Britain was the destination of choice. As Geoffrey Alderman has pointed out, the fact that there was an established Jewish community in Britain, which was able to make its way in a non-Jewish environment, must have been attractive to emigrants.[68] Britain was also appealing because, unlike Russia, Jews were offered religious, civil and political rights, as well as economic opportunities. This is suggested by the naturalisation file of Max Sefstone, who left Russia in 1891 and settled in Swansea. It states:

> I came to this country in the year 1891 in order to obtain a living, during the last 8 years I have managed to build up a business which I found it impossible to accomplish in Russia owing to the conditions of living in that country.[69]

Chain migration was also responsible for the movement of Jews to Britain, and there is ample evidence of Jews joining relatives in Wales. Between 1903 and 1904, for example, Lithuanian-born Dora Lipsett arrived in Merthyr Tydfil with her family to join her uncle, Herman Gittelsohn, who was a pawnbroker there, while Russian-born Morris Colpstein arrived in Newport in 1912 because his uncle offered him a job as a tailor.[70] At about the same time, Russian-born Raphael Fox ended up in Holyhead because his cousin Solomon Pollecoff had established a drapery business in the town.[71] Few Jewish families had the means to travel together, and it was typical for the husband to migrate first to save money to send for his wife and children. Romanian-born Samuel Samuel, for instance, settled in Ystalyfera in 1902, a year before his wife and three children arrived in south Wales.[72]

Connections with places of origin in Russia may have channelled Jewish migrants to specific towns in Wales. Aberavon in south Wales, for example, had five Jews from the Russian town of Salant, while seven Jews living in Swansea between 1908 and 1920 came from the town of Polangen.[73] Cardiff-born Jacqueline Magrill records that her father, Morris Lermon, 'went to New Tredegar [in 1907] where he knew' a Barnett Janner 'from Russia that had already gone there'.[74] He later moved to Cardiff, and over the years he was able to persuade his siblings from Russia to settle in his adopted hometown.

As well as suggesting that her grandparents arrived in Britain accidentally, Renee Woolf's story implies that they may have arrived in Llanelli directly off the boat. This is echoed by Channah Hirsch, who dedicated her memoir 'to the memory of the first wave of Jewish immigrants who landed, or got stranded, on the shores of Llanelli in the early 1900s'.[75] This, however, would have been a most unusual journey, since south Wales was not on the main migration route to Britain. In fact, most of the Jews arriving in Britain by sea came from Baltic ports such as Hamburg and would have arrived in the eastern ports of Grimsby, Hull, Leith and London, which were the main routes of entry for the Baltic trade. As Nicholas Evans discovered, out of five million European migrants who arrived in Britain between 1836 and 1914, over three million (or 60 per cent), did so via the ports of Hull and Grimsby.[76] Immigrants in transit then travelled by train across England to ports such as Liverpool and Southampton where they boarded ships bound for America.[77] Although it is impossible to map the journeys of all those who eventually settled in Wales, it appears that many Jews had resided elsewhere in Britain, typically in long-established Jewish centres such as Leeds, London and Manchester, and had travelled varied and complex routes to their final destinations. Two examples from Llanelli include Russian-born Barnett and Minnie Davies, who arrived in the town around 1910 after living in Liverpool and Swansea, and Peretz and Malka Sharff, who arrived in Llanelli in the early twentieth century via London and Merthyr Tydfil.[78]

Similar journeys undertaken by Eastern European immigrants form a part of the history of most, if not all, of Wales's Jewish communities. Polish-born Israel Garlick (b.1894) arrived in Britain with his parents in 1903 and spent seven years in Leeds, where he trained as a tailor's apprentice, before moving to Cardiff in 1912 to work as a pedlar selling incandescent gas mantles.[79] Similarly, Russian-born Barnet Harris settled in Liverpool with his family in the early 1890s, before relocating to Wrexham and opening a drapery store in the Central Arcade around 1904, while Russian-born Louis and Bertha Snipper arrived in Swansea in 1899 after sojourns in both London and Derby.[80]

Settlement and Growth

The arrival of Eastern European Jews transformed the Jewish population of Wales and that of Britain. As stated previously, the population of Welsh Jewry before the 1880s numbered no more than a few hundred but by 1917, according to the *JYB*, it had risen to an estimated 4,700. With this rise came the growth of existing congregations and the establishment of new Jewish communities.

Like earlier Jewish migrants, most of the Eastern European Jews settled in south Wales and the existing Jewish communities at Cardiff, Newport and Swansea witnessed a considerable increase in numbers. Between 1904 and 1914, for example, Cardiff's recorded Jewish population rose from an estimated 1,250 individuals to 2,025 and that of Swansea jumped from 400 to 1,000 in the same period.[81] The population of Newport's Jewish community climbed from 120 in 1904 to 250 eight years later.[82] But why were Jewish migrants attracted to these towns? Long a point of arrival for newcomers, all three towns offered the infrastructure necessary to support a traditional Jewish lifestyle. Cardiff, for instance, had one synagogue in East Terrace in 1881, but by 1904 the town boasted three synagogues, a Hebrew Board of Guardians and a Jewish Literary Society, while Swansea and Newport were both home to synagogues and various charitable institutions.[83]

Ultimately, of course, like most Jewish immigrants who arrived in the first half of the nineteenth century, what most East European Jews were seeking in these towns were commercial opportunities. The growth of Cardiff's Jewish community was related to the town's development as the largest coal-exporting port in south Wales and, in the final decades of the nineteenth century, in the world. Although the coal trade of Swansea and Newport was far smaller, both towns continued to flourish as export centres. By 1887, Swansea had become the international centre for trade in tinplate following the opening of the Metal Exchange, while Newport's docks continued to grow and were completed in 1892.[84]

Indeed, substantial economic and industrial growth characterised just about all the towns in south Wales in which Jewish communities were established. When Barry developed as a coal port at the close of the nineteenth century, Russian-Jewish merchants settled there to provide goods and services to the town's growing working-class population, among them Joseph Janner, a wholesale dealer and Abraham Hauser, a clothier and outfitter.[85] High Holy Day services were first held in 1904, but a formal congregation, serving approximately eight families, was not established until 1909.[86] Similarly, when Aberavon emerged as a thriving coal port in the 1890s, a small number of Russian-Jewish retailers moved there to make a living, including Jacob Kahn, a furniture dealer, and Raphael Levi, a draper.[87] By the early 1900s approximately seven Jewish families lived in Aberavon and a congregation was formally established in 1904.[88] Although a small number of Jews resided in Llanelli before the 1880s, its Jewish presence grew in the last decades of the nineteenth century owing to the town's development as a principal centre for the manufacturing and exportation of tin.[89] In 1902 Llanelli Jewry held High Holy Day services for the first time and began raising money for a synagogue building, which opened in Victoria Road in 1909 with room for up to two hundred worshippers.[90]

The link between economic opportunity and Jewish migration to Wales was most readily apparent in the south Wales valleys. As we have seen, Jewish communities were established in Merthyr Tydfil, Pontypool, Pontypridd and Tredegar before the 1880s, but Jews settled in the valleys in greater numbers from the last quarter of the nineteenth century, when the region witnessed a coal boom. A 'black klondyke', the valleys drew in migrants from all over Wales, the west of England and further afield during this period.[91] The Rhondda valley's population rose from 1,998 to 152,781 between 1851 and 1911, and by 1914 the south Wales coalfield employed approximately 223,000 miners.[92] Such a rapid rise in population created new towns and a growing consumer market, which was partially catered for by newly arrived Jewish traders and merchants. Indeed, many Jewish immigrants prospered in the region and encouraged others to follow them. In 1875, for instance, a 'Tred' wrote to the *JC* stating:

I refer to South Wales ... I can be borne out in my statements by anyone knowing the neighbourhood that there is room for no less than 500 Jewish families, for each and all to carry on a comfortable and prosperous living ... Merthyr, Aberdare, Tredegar, Rhymney and Rhondda Valleys, the centres of extensive coal and iron operations, afford the most ample scope for the struggling of our working community.[93]

Unlike other newcomers to the region, Jews typically did not seek work in the coal industry. Rather, like many early Jewish settlers in the valleys and in other regions of Wales and Britain, they started out as pedlars.[94] In the south Wales coalfield, they served a working-class clientele who lacked ready access to major commercial centres. They often sold on credit, making it affordable for working-class households to purchase consumer goods such as clothing, furniture and jewellery. Most pedlars travelled on foot, which limited both the quantity and the types of goods they could sell, but a number carried larger and heavier goods by horse and cart. For example, when Russian-born Israel Levy arrived in Newbridge at the turn of the twentieth century, 'he sold haberdashery and cloth from his horse and cart to miners's families in the valleys'.[95] Other examples of Jewish pedlars included Lewis Gordon from Russia, who worked as a traveller in general furniture in the Rhondda in the 1880s and Polish-born Enoch Hermann who, according to the 1891 census, worked as a travelling draper around Tredegar.

Peddling was an attractive occupation for newly arrived Jewish immigrants because it required little capital or training and not much command of the English and Welsh languages. Being self-employed also meant that Jewish pedlars could arrange their working schedules to accommodate Sabbath observance, though some were lax and transacted business on Saturdays.[96] Moreover, peddling reflected the economic pattern of Eastern European Jewish life, when severe economic restrictions limited many Jews to petty trading.[97] Although a lack of extant documentation means that evidence of occupational continuity is difficult to come by, some guidance is provided by Lloyd Gartner, who found that out of 9,047 newly arrived Eastern European Jews lodging at London's Poor Jews' Temporary Shelter between 1895 and 1908, 6,349 worked in trade and commerce before migrating.[98]

In the lore of British-Jewish history, peddling has been seen as the route whereby poor Jewish migrants moved into small or large business. Many pedlars in the south Wales valleys opened small stores. One was Russian-born Harris Himmelstein, who began life in Wales as a travelling draper in Dowlais. By 1911, he had saved enough money to open a watch-making and jewellery store at 47 North Street, Dowlais. In some instances, relatives would provide the capital needed to get started. The establishment of Solomon Zeidman's shop in Pontypool circa 1911 is a good example. His daughter, Judy Hornung notes how her father:

> opened a shop in Pontypool when he was seventeen, borrowed £100 from his father and paid it back within a year ... He was selling mainly working clothes, like boiler suits, flat caps; he even had hanging in the window the miners's lamps. And that was his shop there until 1923 when he and his brother moved to Cowbridge Road East, opened Zeidmans Limited, a big store which was there until my father died in 1965.[99]

As well as retail, contemporary trade directories reveal the dominance of Jews in the pawnbroking trade in south Wales. In the 1914 edition of the *Cardiff, Newport & District Trades Directory*, for instance, two pawnbrokers were listed in Brynmawr, both of whom were Jewish, while in Dowlais all four pawnshops were owned by Jews, as were six out of seven in Merthyr Tydfil and twenty-two out of twenty-six in Cardiff. Some of the names of Jewish pawnbrokers in south Wales at the time include Mrs J. Freedman and R. Freedman of Tonypandy, B. Roskin of Abercarn, H. Roskin of Cwm and Goodman Weiner of Nantyglo.[100]

There are a number of reasons that account for the near control of pawnbroking by south Wales Jewry. It was an occupation that had traditionally been linked with Jews since the Middle Ages, when they were marked out in most of medieval Europe by commercial legislation that restricted them to certain trades, such as finance and moneylending.[101] In addition, pawnbrokers were traditionally known as the 'poor man's banker', and with a rapidly expanding working-class population, south Wales proved attractive to Jewish migrants with previous experience in the business or those in search of economic improvement.[102] But the paradigm tells only part of the story, because not every Jew who came to the south Wales valleys, or to other parts of Wales, was a pedlar or a pawnbroker, and not every Jew moved up the economic ladder from petty merchant to shopkeeper.

Although atypical, semiskilled or unskilled Jewish workers were not entirely absent in nineteenth- and twentieth-century Wales. Some Eastern

European Jews in the 1911 census, including Morris Greenitz and Abraham Barsky, were listed as labourers for Guest, Keen and Nettlefolds Ironworks in Dowlais. Similarly, a number of Eastern European Jewish immigrants in the south Wales valleys worked in the coal mining industry.[103] They included Russian-born David Jaffe, a coal hewer living in Abertysswg in 1911, Barnet Cohen of Trealaw, who 'met with a fatal accident' in 1910 'while working the underground trams' and Russian-born Barnett Cohen, a timberman below ground who worked at Hopkinstown Colliery 'for about twenty years' before working as a hawker in fancy goods.[104] While some Jews had quite lengthy mining careers, others worked in the industry temporarily, most likely as a stopgap, either to 'earn enough money to set themselves up in business or help survive a period of financial stringency'.[105] One was Flintshire-born Joseph Cohen, who is listed in the 1891 census as a miner in Pontypridd, but by the 1901 census was working as a hawker in Swansea. Other examples included Ukrainian-born Sam Kraisman, who 'was employed as a miner in South Wales' at the age of twelve in 1908 before emigrating to Canada in the 1910s, and Walter Sendell of Trehafod, who worked down the mines for twelve months in the late 1920s before moving to London for work.[106] Jews in other parts of Wales also worked in essentially working-class occupations. Solomon Barnett of Buckley, the son of a Russian-Jewish hawker, was working as a miner in Flintshire in 1911, while Russian-born Abraham Glazier was an ironworker in Shotton, Flintshire, during the same period.

As was the case with the with the industrial towns of the south Wales coast, the arrival of East European Jews to the south Wales valleys led to a notable growth in some of the established communities of the region. Merthyr Tydfil's recorded Jewish population, for instance, increased from 300 to 400 between 1904 and 1920, while that of Tredegar rose from 60 to 160 between 1884 and 1912.[107] In 1895, Pontypridd Jewry was of sufficient size for a purpose-built synagogue, capable of accommodating nearly two hundred worshippers, to open in Cliff Terrace.[108] With the growth of the Jewish population came the development of new Jewish communities in the south Wales coalfield. Unfortunately, it is difficult to date the establishment of many of them precisely, since the records of most have been lost, while in many instances their formation was not announced in the *JC* or listed in the *JYB*. Jews such as Cornish-born Abraham Freedman and John Cohen from London settled in Aberdare from the 1860s, but a synagogue was not consecrated in the town until around 1887.[109] Jewish communities also sprung up in Brynmawr (1888), Porth (c. 1890), Tonypandy (c. 1894), Penygraig (c. 1900), New Tredegar (1903), Abertillery (c. 1904), Penrhiwceiber (1904), Ebbw Vale (c. 1906), Bargoed (c. 1915), and Newbridge (c. 1915), while the High Holy Day services for *Rosh Hashanah* (New Year) and *Yom Kippur* (Day of Atonement) were held, possibly for the first time, in Treorchy in 1897.[110] Contrary to the claim made by Geoffrey Alderman, no Jewish community was formally established in Rhymney.[111] Rather, it was home to one Jewish family, the Fines, and a few individuals such as Hyman French and Samuel Wallen, all of whom were associated with Tredegar's Jewish activities.[112]

A striking feature of Jewish life in the south Wales coalfield was the number of communities established, considering that the Jewish populations of most valley towns were relatively small and that synagogues were located only a few miles apart. Tredegar's Jewish community, for instance, numbered an average of 120 members during this period and was situated only two miles away from the Ebbw Vale Hebrew Congregation, which had only 80 members. Aberdare's Jewish community numbered no more than 90 individuals and was situated less than four miles away from the much larger Jewish community in Merthyr Tydfil, which had an estimated 300 members. But why were so many small Jewish communities established in this region of south-east Wales? The answer lies in the mountainous nature of the area, a topographical feature that made it difficult for Jews living in nearby towns to reach one another and organise themselves into a Jewish community.[113] Thus, while Ebbw Vale and Tredegar were only two miles apart, the Jewish residents of the two towns were situated in different valleys and separated from each other by a steep mountain. The difficulties faced by Jews travelling to a synagogue in a nearby valleys town during the early twentieth century is strikingly illustrated by Mordecai Boone, who grew up in Rhymney in the 1920s. He notes that the Boones

> were the only Jewish family there [in Rhymney], completely isolated. I can recollect my father getting us to go to *Shool* [Synagogue] on the Sabbath but we had to walk four or five or six miles, I don't know, over mountain tops and bogs and crossing streams, we used to be completely drenched when we got to Tredegar *Shool*.[114]

Although some made the arduous journey to synagogue, it must have been too difficult and tiring for most, and thus the population of the

Jewish communities of the south Wales coalfield remained small and scattered. This was a unique feature of Welsh Jewry, with no other region in the United Kingdom witnessing such a high concentration of Jewish communities in such a small geographical area (approximately sixteen communities within an estimated area of 169 square miles).

Smaller groups of Jews could also be found in other parts of south Wales. Jews gathered in Bridgend from the 1890s onwards as a result of its position on the Swansea to London railway line. According to the *JYB*, a congregation was founded in 1907, with Rev. L. Wolfe serving as minister until 1910. However, items in the *JC* suggest that the congregation had dissolved by 1913, possibly due to the absence of a minister. In that year Revd H. J. Sandheim visited the town 'with the view to re-establishing the congregation', but 'suitable accommodation for a synagogue and classrooms' was not obtained until 1927.[115] Moreover, the pages of the *JC* and *JYB* indicate that a Jewish community, numbering no more than about three families, existed in Ammanford between 1915 and 1921. There is no mention of a synagogue, but communal functions were held at the residence of Morris Cohen, the congregation's president.[116] Similarly, despite claims made by a variety of sources, there was no synagogue constructed in Ystalyfera.[117] Rather, it appears that Jews living in the industrial village were 'country' members of the Swansea Hebrew Congregation. They included Romanian-born Samuel Samuel, and Tobias Shepherd, a Polish-born *yeshiva* (rabbinical seminary) student, who lived in Swansea in the late 1880s before setting up as a furniture dealer in Ystalyfera around 1890.[118] Since the distance between Swansea and Ystalyfera (approximately thirteen miles) made it impractical to travel regularly to Swansea for synagogue services, a *minyan* was often formed at Shepherd's Ystalyfera home by Jewish men living in the village and those scattered across the Swansea valley, such as Israel Neft of Neath.[119]

Though there had been individual Jews in north Wales previously, Jewish immigrants did not migrate to the region in significant numbers until the last decades of the nineteenth century. North Wales proved attractive, as it had done to their predecessors, because it offered commercial opportunities, and word may have spread that Jews such as the Aronsons of Bangor were successful in the area. By the latter half of the nineteenth century the region also witnessed economic and demographic growth. North Wales's coastal towns, such as Colwyn Bay, Llandudno and Rhyl with their beaches and clean air, made them popular holiday destinations and travel was facilitated by the construction of the London and North Western line from Chester to Holyhead between 1844 and 1850. In Bangor, shipbuilding became an important industry and the opening of slate quarries in nearby Bethesda accelerated its growth and development. In 1850, over thirteen hundred houses were recorded in the city and Bangor was 'considered one of the most flourishing and improving towns in North Wales', eventually becoming a centre of higher education following the establishment of the University College of North Wales in 1884.[120] Industrial expansion in the coal, metallurgical and pottery industries also led to the growth of Wrexham in the nineteenth century, with its population increasing from 3,091 to 10,978 between 1822 and 1881.[121] As in south Wales, the development and growth of these towns created a demand for goods and services, which would have provided economic opportunities to the mainly poor, newly arrived Jewish immigrants.

North Wales's first Jewish community was formed on an informal basis in Wrexham. The first High Holy Day services were held in 1892 at a 'temporary premises' in Manly Road, but it was not until September 1894 that a formal congregation was established in Wrexham, with S. Myers elected as president and A. D. Epstein as treasurer.[122] Five months prior to this occasion a Jewish community was officially founded in Bangor, when a synagogue in the Arvonia Buildings in High Street was formally consecrated.[123] The founder of the congregation was Polish-born Morris Wartski, who arrived in Bangor in the early 1880s after living 'for a time in Liverpool'.[124] Beginning life in Bangor as a jewellery and drapery hawker, Morris opened a watchmakers, jewellery and drapery store at 21 High Street around 1895, before expanding his business to the nearby fashionable seaside resort of Llandudno in 1908. A year later, Wartski established a Jewish community in Llandudno and served as its first president.[125]

As well as attracting Jewish merchants who were drawn by the commercial opportunities afforded by the town's burgeoning tourism industry, Llandudno emerged as popular holiday destination for Jews from Liverpool and Manchester who were seeking a temporary escape from the hustle and bustle of city life. As early as 1871, a Joseph Aarons of Liverpool opened a kosher hotel 'in the crescent facing the promenade' to cater to kosher Jewish summer tourists.[126] Its success led to the opening of many other kosher guesthouses in the town, including Libau Villa,

Trevennel, Bodlondeb and Mazl House.[127] Although Ashkenazi Jews formed the greater part of Llandudno and British Jewry, a small number of Mizrahi Jews (Jews from the Middle East) resided in the town. Among them were Iraqi-born Yousif Murab (also known as Joseph) Gubay and his wife Lulu, who arrived in Britain with their children shortly after the First World War to escape the upheaval caused by the collapse of the Ottoman Empire.[128] They settled in Llandudno to take over the Oriental Stores on Mostyn street from Yousif's brother-in-law after he 'entered the textile business in Manchester'.[129]

Jewish holidaymakers from Liverpool and Manchester were also attracted to the north Walian seaside town of Rhyl, and by 1898 three kosher boarding houses had opened in the town.[130] A congregation had been formed two years earlier in September 1896, when 'twenty gentlemen and several ladies' attended a service conducted by both Morris Brodie of Market Street and a Revd Speiro in a room in Tudor Place.[131] According to the 1933 edition of the *JYB*, the Rhyl Congregation was still in existence, with the synagogue based in the Queen Chambers.[132] However, the 1935 edition states that the congregation ceased to exist about 1906.[133] Scanning the pages of the *JC*, it becomes apparent that from 1907 the Rhyl Hebrew Congregation had dissolved, probably because of 'a great fire' that destroyed the building housing the synagogue.[134] Without the funds to establish a new synagogue congregants moved elsewhere. To take one example, Morris Brodie, the congregation's founder, moved to Southport.[135]

At the end of the First World War, the recorded population of Welsh Jewry reached approximately 5,000 people, the vast majority of whom were Eastern European immigrants who had arrived in Britain during the previous half-century.[136] Their arrival swelled the population of Welsh Jewry, changed its demographic make-up (as we have seen, Wales was originally settled by Jewish immigrants from Central Europe) and greatly expanded the number of Jewish communities in Wales. Before 1880, seven Jewish communities had been founded, all located in south Wales, but by the end of the First World War approximately nineteen Jewish communities were to be found across Wales.[137]

Religious and Communal Life

JUDAISM is not a homogenous religion. Like other religions, including Christianity and Islam, it is made up of multiple denominations, all of which vary considerably depending on where in geographical and cultural terms they are practised. In Britain, Judaism is commonly divided into traditional Orthodox Judaism (including Haredi Judaism, commonly referred to as 'ultra-orthodox'), which holds that the laws of the *Torah* (the first five books of the Hebrew Bible) are binding and unchanging, and Progressive Judaism, comprising the Liberal 'left' and the Reform 'right', which traces its roots back to nineteenth-century Germany and maintains that Jewish law is not binding and should be adapted or modified to meet the needs of Jews in modern society.[1]

Between the late eighteenth and mid twentieth centuries, all of Wales's Jewish communities were organised upon Orthodox lines (a Reform congregation was established in Cardiff in 1948 and a Liberal group in mid-Wales in 1996; see Chapters 5 and 6). Despite all being of sufficient size and wealth to form congregations with a functioning place of worship, Wales's Orthodox Jewish communities were not identical in make-up, but differing settlements in many respects. By examining their synagogue histories and systems of religious leadership, as well as arrangements for Jewish educational and dietary facilities, we will see that the size, wealth, location and origins of these congregations were all significant factors in determining how religious and communal life unfolded in Wales's Orthodox Jewish centres.

Synagogues

Typically, when Jewish communities first formed in Wales, members immediately stimulated interest in organising a suitable and convenient place for worship. Of course, Jewish communities in Wales and throughout Britain were often initially too few in numbers and too poor to organise formal facilities for worship. Thus, as we have seen, it was common for early Jewish settlers to gather for prayers and services in very modest surroundings. In Bangor, for instance, Passover services were held in 1894 at the residence of Morris Wartski in High Street, while Llanelli's first services were held in 1902 in Harris Rubinstein's home.[2] In Port Talbot, services were initially held in Revd Folegrest's house and a room over the shop premises of Jacob Finkelstein, while in Brynmawr in 1889, 'Barnett Isaacs, the president, generously placed one of his houses at the disposal of the members' for services, which were later held in the Town Hall.[3]

Nonetheless, as the population of these communities increased and congregants gained a sense of greater stability, it was common for communities to build their own house of worship or convert a suitable building into a fully functioning synagogue. As Lee Shai Weissbach points out, it was important for Jewish communities to acquire adequate facilities of their own 'because it symbolized the permanence of a congregation'.[4] This was stressed by the Chief Rabbinate, particularly during the incumbency of Hermann Adler (1839–1911), who often encouraged Jewish communities throughout the United Kingdom to build synagogues because they symbolised confidence in a community's longevity and helped reinforce the notion that Judaism was a visible part of the local religious landscape.[5] During his pastoral tour in 1898, for instance, Adler visited Bangor, where he 'exhorted the congregation to build for themselves a suitable place of worship', while during a tour of south Wales in 1899, he suggested that Brynmawr Jewry should 'quit their present inadequate and comfortless abode and erect a permanent structure'.[6] Similarly, in a letter sent to the honorary secretary of the Tonypandy Hebrew Congregation in 1917, Chief Rabbi Joseph Hertz wrote that 'the fact that you have to be in part of a house for high holy service' is 'not very satisfactory', and suggested that the congregation find 'a more suitable place of worship'.[7] Thus, during the latter half of the nineteenth and early twentieth centuries, many of Wales's Jewish communities constructed their own synagogues.

As previously noted, Cardiff Jewry constructed its first synagogue in East Terrace in 1858, while Swansea's second purpose-built synagogue opened in Goat Street in 1859.[8] Newport Jewry's first purpose-built house of worship opened in 1871, while Merthyr Tydfil Jewry consecrated its third synagogue in 1877 to accommodate a growing community.[9] Elsewhere in south Wales, a synagogue was erected in Morgan Street by the Tredegar Hebrew Congregation in 1884, and by 1901 the number of Jews in Brynmawr had increased 'so rapidly' that 'a building for divine worship more suitable to their needs' was raised in Bailey Street.[10] Llanelli Jewry's purpose-built synagogue opened in Victoria Street in May 1909, while in 1911 the Ebbw Vale Hebrew Congregation converted a vacant chapel into a house of worship.[11] In 1921 a single-storey synagogue was erected by the Port Talbot Hebrew Congregation in Ty-Draw Place, when the community numbered about one hundred persons.[12]

The erection of a synagogue building was a costly undertaking and financing its construction was often a struggle for many of Wales's smaller Jewish communities. Indeed, in order to acquire their buildings, it was common for congregations to turn first to their own members for monetary donations and then to sources beyond their own communities. Money for Aberavon's synagogue building fund, for instance, was raised through dances organised by local fundraisers and by donations from Jewish families in the south Wales valleys, while Brynmawr Jewry solicited donations from other Jewish communities in the United Kingdom for the construction of their synagogue in 1900 by writing an appeal in the *JC*.[13]

The acquisition of a purpose-built or converted synagogue often burdened congregations with debt. Despite the generous financial assistance of 'many brethren in the Principality', Llanelli Jewry, for instance, faced a debt of £600 when their synagogue opened in 1909.[14] Four years later 'an urgent appeal' from the community appeared in the *JC*, stating that 'the bank has given a final notice of calling in the mortgage on the Synagogue' and 'unless a substantial reduction of the heavy debt of £576 is immediately forthcoming' the synagogue 'must be closed'.[15] To pay off the debt and increase revenue, it was decided to raise the weekly contributions of 'the already heavily taxed members', and terminate the services of the congregation's minister, Revd H. J. Sandheim.[16] Some congregations held fundraising events to help pay off the debt owing on their synagogues. In 1907, for instance, Brynmawr Jewry held a ball at the local Drill Hall 'for the purpose of liquidating the debt' on the synagogue, while a Jewish ball was organised by Ebbw Vale Jewry in 1914 'in aid of the Synagogue Mortgage Fund'.[17]

Despite their ardent desire to construct their own synagogue, many of Wales's smaller Jewish communities never did so. Indeed, there were no synagogue buildings built in north Wales and the region's small Jewish communities typically graduated from private residences to rented halls or rooms in commercial buildings. In this instance, the limited size of these communities, whose numbers ranged from twelve to eighty-five members, and their lack of financial resources were the main deciding factors. Indeed, Bangor's Jewish community was so poor and few in number in 1894 (around fourteen families) that they required financial support from co-religionists throughout the United Kingdom to help pay for a rented room they had 'fitted up for synagogal purposes' on the first floor of the Arvonia Buildings in High Street, which served as the community's house of worship for more than half a century.[18] Llandudno Jewry met for services in the Masonic Hall in Mostyn Street from 1909, and in 1948 converted a house in Church Walks into a synagogue.[19] Rhyl's Jewish community met for worship in a rented room above the 'Palace and Summer Gardens' building in Wellington Road from 1897 to 1900, and in a room at the Magnet Buildings, High Street, from 1900 to 1907, when the former rooms were 'no longer available'.[20] Similarly, Wrexham Jewry met for worship in five different rented locations between 1894 and 1930, including rooms above shops at 84 Bradley Road and 37 Rhosddu Road.[21]

A number of small Jewish communities in the south Wales valleys were never able to construct their own synagogue buildings, and throughout their existence their houses of worship were often located in terraced houses, a style of building that made up a large percentage of the region's material landscape. Aberdare's Jewish community, for instance, met for worship in a rented terraced house at 19A Seymour Street from 1887, before purchasing the building in 1902.[22] Although the Tonypandy Hebrew Congregation began a fundraising appeal in 1915 to construct a synagogue, it was never erected because congregants could 'not see the possibility of [its] upkeep ... with such small membership'.[23] Tonypandy Jewry initially met for services 'in Public Houses', but between 1912 and 1926 congregants worshipped in a rented a house at 7 Holborn Terrace, before relocating to a terraced house at 38, Eleanor Street.[24] Despite the laying of a foundation stone at Abertillery in 1910, a synagogue never materialised owing to a lack of funds.[25] Instead, the congregation established itself in the back room of 2 Newall Street, a terraced house belonging to a congregant, Harry Simons.[26] In addition to houses, other kind of buildings were used as synagogues by small Jewish communities in south Wales. In Bridgend, for instance, one was consecrated in the former council chambers building in Adare Street in 1927, while a rented 'room in an old inn' served as the synagogue for the short-lived Newbridge Hebrew Congregation in the early decades of the twentieth century.[27]

As well as serving as a place of religious worship, synagogues typically acted as the hub of Jewish social activity in a number of Wales's smaller Jewish communities. Whereas larger communities such as Cardiff and Swansea were, at one time or another, able to support communal buildings apart from synagogues, in most of Wales's smaller Jewish communities the synagogue was the only Jewish public building in town. Thus, while Cardiff Jewry opened a Jewish Institute in Upper Station Terrace in 1910 and Swansea Jewry met for communal and cultural activities in Cornhill House, Christina Street, from 1916 until 1956, the synagogue in Bangor was nearly always the place where social gatherings and communal functions took place.[28] Among the groups that met there were the Jewish Friendly and Zionist societies and the Local Study Circle.[29] A 'Jewish Literary and Social Society' met weekly at Aberdare's synagogue in the early twentieth century, while during the 1920s and 1930s Pontypridd's synagogues hosted Sunday night whist drives and dances.[30]

Indeed, synagogues in Wales's smaller Jewish communities typically served all of the community's needs and it was not unusual for purpose-built structures to include a *mikvah* (a bath used for the purpose of ritual immersion) in their design. Pontypridd's synagogue, for example, included a *mikvah* in its basement, while Llanelli Jewry's *mikvah* was located in a room to the left of the synagogue's main prayer hall.[31] Brynmawr Jewry had a *mikvah* that adjoined the synagogue, while Merthyr Tydfil's ritual bath 'was situated beneath the *shul* [synagogue]' in Church Street.[32] Swansea's Goat Street synagogue featured a small *mikvah* in the early 1900s, before relocating to Cornhill House in 1916 when more space was required.[33]

Whereas on-site *mikvaot* (plural of *mikvah*) were common features of smaller Jewish communities, larger Jewish centres such as Cardiff and Newport were in a position to negotiate with local authorities in order to erect publicly funded facilities in public baths and wash houses.[34] Cardiff's *mikvah*, for instance, was situated in the Guilford Crescent baths from around 1873, before relocating to the Empire Pool in 1959 when the former facilities closed, while Newport's *mikvah* opened in the Stow Hill Baths in the late 1890s.[35] However, some of Wales's smaller Jewish communities were unable to afford the luxury of a *mikvah*, nor were they large enough to warrant publicly funded bathing facilities. As a compromise, congregants wishing to obey the laws of family purity had to go to else-where. With no *mikvaot* in north Wales, for instance, congregants typically turned to Liverpool and Manchester.[36]

Burials

In much the same way as Wales's Orthodox Jewish communities strove to construct synagogue buildings to house their religious and communal activities, they also aspired to establish their own dedicated cemeteries, since Jewish law requires that Jews be buried in a separate burial ground that is consecrated in accordance with Jewish rites. As has been noted, Wales's oldest burial ground is in Swansea and dates from 1768 when a 99-year-lease of a plot of land in Townhill was acquired by David Michael. The cemetery was eventually purchased for the sum of twenty pounds in 1864 following a successful fundraising campaign, which drew in donations from the Chief Rabbi, Nathan Marcus Adler, and various British-Jewish communities such as Cardiff, Merthyr Tydfil and Liverpool.[37] Wales second-oldest Jewish cemetery can be found in Highfield Road in Cardiff, which, as noted in the previous chapter (p. 20), opened in 1841 following a donation from the second Marquess of Bute.[38]

Other Jewish communities in Wales established Jewish burial grounds in the latter half of the nineteenth century, but unlike those in Cardiff and Swansea, these were part of larger public cemeteries and demarcated by a fence, path or hedge.[39] This was mainly because they were established from the 1850s onwards, following various burial reform acts which led to the development of municipal cemeteries in Britain publicly funded by burial boards run by parish vestries. Indeed, as Sharman Kadish once noted, 'Victorian Britain was the great age of the public cemetery', and in the late nineteenth century Jews in Wales took advantage of the facilities on offer, as was did other British Jewries as well as non-Jews.[40] Newport Jewry, for instance, 'obtained a piece of land for the purpose of a Burial Ground' in Saint Woolos Cemetery in 1859, five years after the cemetery's official opening, while Merthyr Tydfil's Jewish community dedicated a cemetery in Cefn Coed Cemetery in 1865, six years after its opening.[41] In 1894 Pontypridd Jewry acquired a piece of ground at the Glyntaff Cemetery, having found that transporting their dead to Cardiff and Merthyr Tydfil for burial was too costly and time-consuming.[42] Similarly,

Brynmawr Jewry found it inconvenient to transport its dead to Merthyr Tydfil, approximately thirteen miles away, for burial and 'long felt the need of [their own] Burial Ground', which was eventually acquired in the town's municipal cemetery in 1919.[43]

Despite their ardent desire to bury their dead locally, some of Wales's Jewish communities were never able to afford the luxury of having their own dedicated burial ground and had to bury their dead elsewhere, often in the nearest Jewish cemetery. Jews from Llanelli, Neath and Port Talbot, for example, were buried in Swansea's Jewish cemetery, while Bridgend Jewry buried its dead in either Cardiff or Swansea.[44] The burial grounds of Brynmawr, Merthyr Tydfil and Pontypridd served 'a wide and scattered area' and Jews from across the south Wales valleys were buried in these cemeteries.[45] Moreover, no Jewish burial grounds were consecrated by any of north Wales's Jewish communities during the nineteenth and twentieth centuries. As in many other matters, the small size of these congregations and their limited finances were often the deciding factors. Due to their proximity to the larger Jewish centres of Liverpool and Manchester, internments traditionally took place in these two cities. Sophie Silver of Wrexham, for example, was interred in Rice-Lane Cemetery, Liverpool when she died in 1932, and Bessie Davie of Llandudno was buried in the Jewish section of Urmston Cemetery in Manchester in 1947.[46]

Congregations

While synagogues and dedicated Jewish cemeteries were the prime physical manifestations of a Jewish presence in Wales's towns and cities, the fundamental institution of Wales's Jewish communities was the local congregation. Throughout their existence, most Welsh-Jewish communities were home to only one congregation, because there were simply not enough numbers or resources to sustain more than one synagogue. However, for various reasons, some Jewish communities did support multiple congregations before the middle of the twentieth century. Among the major factors that led to the creation of multiple Orthodox congregations in the same community were disagreements and disputes relating to congregational affairs.[47] Despite numbering less than one hundred individuals, the Aberavon Hebrew Congregation split around 1907/1908 'as a result of a quarrel between members' over Sabbath observance.[48] Similarly, in Llanelli, the year 1915 saw the creation of the Llanelli New Hebrew Congregation, which emerged following 'a disagreement in the community as to who was the senior minister, Revd Solomon or Revd Jacover [sic]'.[49] The breakaway congregation sided with the latter minister and used a rented room in Castle Buildings, Murray Street, for its religious services.[50] Moreover, the 1899 edition of the *JYB* lists two congregations in Wrexham – the Old Synagogue in Bradley Road and the Wrexham New Congregation in Queen Street– revealing that the small community divided at some point in 1898.[51] How this situation arose is unexplained, but it may have been caused by conflicts of personality and internal disputes. Indeed, the original Bradley Road congregation appears to have been quite disorganised, as is evidenced by the number of alterations made to its committee between 1896 and 1898.[52] Nevertheless, the existence of multiple synagogues within these towns was short-lived, as it became apparent that their small communities lacked the critical mass and financial resources to sustain more than one congregation. Aberavon's split lasted no more than five years, for instance, while the rift in Llanelli Jewry went on for four years.[53] Wrexham's split was also short-term, lasting no more than a year.[54]

The likeliness of a community supporting more than one congregation for a lengthy period of time was also influenced by demographic factors, those communities that were able to support multiple congregations tending to be somewhat larger. In Cardiff, two congregations co-existed in the town between the late 1880s and the early 1940s, serving a Jewish community that grew from 1,250 persons in 1904 to about 2,300 individuals by 1942, while Swansea Jewry was home to two synagogues between the early 1900s and the 1950s, serving a community numbering around 1,000 persons.[55]

In Cardiff, the East Terrace congregation split in the late 1880s because of internal disputes between honorary members. According to the wardens of the congregation, Louis Barnett and Isaac Samuel, 'differences of opinion . . . in the management of communal affairs' arose in the spring of 1887, which led a group of congregants to secede and form 'a *minyan* in opposition'.[56] Calling themselves the Cardiff New Hebrew Congregation, the break-away group established a small synagogue at 5 Edward Place, while the old congregation remained in East Terrace until 1897, when, owing to an increase in members and the rising number of congregants living in the districts of Riverside and Canton, the synagogue relocated to an imposing purpose-built building in Cathedral Road.[57] The Cardiff New Hebrew Congregation even founded its own cemetery within the long-established Jewish cemetery in Highfield Road and constructed a wall to create two distinct burial grounds, a further sign of dissension between the city's two congregations.[58]

As the Jewish population of Cardiff expanded in the 1890s, an additional synagogue emerged to meet the needs of a divergent community. In 1899, a group of recently arrived Yiddish-speaking Eastern European Jewish immigrants established their own congregation, called the Beth Hamedrash and Talmud Torah.[59] Their motive for establishing a congregation of their own was the increasing acculturation of Cardiff Jewry, which, having been in existence for over sixty years, had become more English-speaking in composition by the late nineteenth century and had created a form of Orthodoxy that was better suited to a British milieu. Cathedral Road, for instance, adopted innovations such as English sermons, while both Cathedral Road and Edward Place introduced a shortened liturgy and placed an emphasis on maintaining decorum during services.[60] In contrast, the new arrivals from Eastern Europe were committed to traditional worship and study and a more fervent and expressive form of ritual observance. Therefore, 'to meet their requirements in religion and other matters', a splinter group erected their own synagogue in Merches Place in 1900 and appointed Revd M. Katz as its religious leader.[61] The congregation's existence was short-lived, however, a shortage of funds forcing it to amalgamate with Cathedral Road in 1904.[62] Both parties agreed that religious services could continue at Merches Place, but only on weekdays and Saturday afternoons, while Sabbath morning and High Holy Day services were only permitted to take place at the Cathedral Road synagogue.[63] The ultimate fusion of the two congregations took place in 1906 when the former president of the Beth Hamedrash and Talmud Torah, Benjamin Shatz, was elected treasurer of the Cathedral Road congregation.[64]

In the years following the First World War, Cardiff Jewry persisted in supporting two congregations, with the Cardiff New Hebrew Congregation moving its synagogue from Edward Place to a converted chapel in Windsor Place in 1918.[65] Calls to amalgamate the congregations were made in 1933 by members of Windsor Place, who were convinced that co-operation would strengthen Jewish life in Cardiff.[66] However, negotiations over amalgamation went on until the 1940s due to disagreements over *shechita* (ritual slaughter according to Jewish dietary laws), burial practices, the potential closure of the Cathedral Road synagogue and the fear that members of Windsor Place would dominate the affairs of a unified congregation.[67] Following pressure from Joseph Hertz, then Chief Rabbi of the United Kingdom, amalgamation was finally achieved in 1941, when the Cardiff United Synagogue was established with two houses of prayer, a communal council made up of representatives from both synagogues and a unified Jewish cemetery in Highfield Road.[68] Hermann H. Roskin of Windsor Place, 'an old advocate of amalgamation', was appropriately appointed the congregation's first president.[69]

In addition to liturgical acculturation, another issue that created tensions and eventually divided Orthodox communities in the late nineteenth century, particularly those that had been in existence for quite some time, was the class struggle that developed between Eastern European Jewish immigrant members, who were newly arrived, poor and working class, and long-established and assimilated congregants, who were largely middle class. In Swansea, for instance, it seems to have been a quarrel over the provision of kosher meat to immigrant members who had not subscribed to the congregation that led to a rupture in 1895.[70] Indeed, it erupted into a major dispute and resulted in 1896 in the formation by the Eastern European immigrants of a breakaway congregation called the Prince of Wales Road Minyan. Renamed the Swansea Beth Hamedrash in 1906, a year later the congregation erected a synagogue in Prince of Wales Road, Greenhill, then a poor immigrant area.[71] Some of the congregation's earliest members included Russian-born Morris Foner and Tobias Shepherd.[72]

Despite the existence of two synagogues in Swansea, the congregations were never completely divorced from each other. From 1909 onwards, for instance, the Beth Hamedrash paid the Swansea Hebrew Congregation twenty pounds per annum for the services of their minister 'on the occasion of any Births, Deaths or Marriages' and the right to bury their dead in the old congregation's cemetery.[73] Amalgamation attempts were made in the 1920s, but were unsuccessful because the Beth Hamedrash wished to 'remain an independent body'.[74] Yet, thirty years later, the Prince of Wales synagogue was abandoned owing to the gradual migration of upwardly mobile congregants westward to the suburban neighbourhoods of Sketty and the Uplands.[75] Adhering to the rule prohibiting driving on the Sabbath, congregants eventually found the three-mile walk from Sketty and the Uplands to Prince of Wales Road to be too arduous and from 1955 onwards they began attending the Swansea Hebrew Congregation's new synagogue, which was conveniently situated in Ffynone Road in the Uplands.[76] This transition was an easy one for most, since previous tensions between poor immigrants and wealthy acculturated Jews had ceased to exist by the mid twentieth century and with a combined population of approximately four hundred and sixty individuals, Swansea Jewry realised that they no longer had the critical mass to sustain two congregations.

Such divisions as occurred in Cardiff and Swansea were not a feature of most of Wales's other Jewish communities. As has been seen, this was primarily because most communities were too few in numbers to sustain multiple congregations, but it was also because many of Wales's smaller Jewish communities were generally more financially and religiously homogenous. Indeed, unlike Swansea and Cardiff, most of Wales's Jewish communities (with the exception of Merthyr Tydfil, Newport, Pontypridd and Pontypool) were established during the last decades of the nineteenth century, and composed entirely, or almost entirely, of poor Eastern European Jewish immigrants. They were the first to establish congregations in their towns, and thus there was no need to contemplate the liturgical traditions, practices and financial position of earlier Jewish settlers. This resembles experiences in the United States, where 'it was common ... to find a single congregation' in a community that 'was based primarily on the coming of Eastern Europeans'.[77] However, as the incidents in Port Talbot, Wrexham and Llanelli demonstrate, congregations established by Eastern European migrants during the late nineteenth and early twentieth centuries were not always free from conflict.[78]

Religious Leadership

Just as Wales's Orthodox Jewish centres endeavoured to erect their own synagogues, establish dedicated burial grounds, and form congregations, they also sought ministers to lead their communities in religious worship. Although the terms 'minister' and 'rabbi' are often used synonymously, very few of the ministers in nineteenth- and early twentieth-century Britain were given the title 'rabbi', since it was reserved during this period to the Chief Rabbi. Chief Rabbi Nathan Marcus Adler established this tradition to enhance his own authority and was reluctant that any minister, no matter how well qualified in rabbinical terms, should use the title.[79] This principle was initially upheld by his son and successor, Hermann Adler, but had begun to fade out by the turn of the twentieth century following pressure from Eastern European Jewish migrants and the council of Jews' College.[80] From the mid nineteenth to the mid twentieth century, rabbinical functions were heavily centralised in Britain and the majority of religious leaders who presided over Orthodox synagogues in Britain were appointed to congregations on the Chief Rabbi's recommendation under the title 'Reverend', in imitation of the Anglican clergy.[81] Many were graduates of Jews' College, a Jewish seminary in London that was founded by Nathan Adler in 1855 to train laymen to administer and preach within their congregations.[82] Those seeking rabbinical ordination could only secure it by relocating to the continent or by the official sanction of the Chief Rabbi.[83]

Traditionally, the religious staff of a well-organised Orthodox Jewish community includes a spiritual leader, a *mohel* (a person trained to perform circumcision), a *cheder* (classes for instruction in religion instruction and Hebrew) and a *shochet* (a trained and certified slaughterer); it is also desirable to have a *chazzan* (cantor) and a *shammas* (synagogue warden).[84] At the outset Cardiff Jewry lacked the numbers and resources to sustain an array of synagogue officials and its appointed ministers were thus required to perform multiple tasks. For example, the congregation's first spiritual leader, Revd Nathan Jacobs from Poland, was appointed around 1858 and acted not only as minister but also as reader, *shochet* and Hebrew teacher until he left for Newport in 1872.[85] During the final quarter of the nineteenth century Cardiff's Jewish population, as we have seen, grew rapidly, and by the 1890s the community was both well-established and wealthy enough to employ a range of religious staff. In 1893, for instance, Revd D. Wasserzug, a graduate of Jews' College, served as the Old Hebrew Congregation's minister and was assisted by the *chazzan*, Revd H. Caminitzki, and the *shochet*, Revd Harris Hamburg.[86] Born in Lithuania in 1867, Hamburg served the Cardiff Old Hebrew Congregation in various roles until his death in 1941.[87]

Unordained officials constituted only part of the religious leadership of Cardiff Jewry, however. Then numbering around two thousand individuals, by the end of the First World War Cardiff Jewry was prosperous enough to appoint its first officially recognised communal rabbi, Rav Asher Grunis.[88] Born in Poland in 1877, Grunis was ordained a rabbi by the *Beth Din* of Kalisch, and served as '*Rav* [ordained rabbi] of Wilezyn' for twenty-five years.[89] He received a call to Cardiff and with his arrival the city's Jewish community possessed a religious leader of importance whose status and *halachic* authority were widely recognised. Described as 'a great Talmudist', he served Cardiff Jewry until his death in 1937.[90] Two years later Moses E. Rogosnitzky of Nalibok, Russia, was appointed rabbi to the Cardiff New Hebrew Congregation, where he served until his death in 1945.[91] That year, his son, Rabbi Ber Rogosnitzky of Newcastle, was appointed *Rav* of the recently formed Cardiff United Synagogue, while Rabbi Ernest Wiesenberg of Kosice, Czechoslovakia, was appointed spiritual leader of the Windsor Place synagogue in 1946.[92] The latter left Cardiff in 1947 after accepting a pulpit in Sheffield, while the former served until his retirement in 1984.[93]

Cardiff Jewry was unique among Welsh-Jewish communities; no other community ever possessed an officially recognised rabbi. This is partly because the Chief Rabbinate refused to recognise the rabbinical titles of a number of men occupying British pulpits during the nineteenth and early twentieth centuries, but also because smaller congregations in Wales and throughout Britain were too few in number to afford the 'luxury' of a rabbi. Indeed, it was financially more convenient for smaller Orthodox congregations to recognise the Chief Rabbi in London as their spiritual head and make annual donations to the Chief Rabbi's Fund.[94] Despite the absence of officially recognised resident *halachic* authorities beyond Cardiff, it should be stressed that the majority of ministers or 'Reverends' who served Jewish communities in Wales were deeply religious, sincerely Orthodox and also very scholarly individuals.

Nevertheless, most ministers employed by Wales's smaller Jewish centres did not stay in their posts for lengthy periods. This was not a phenomenon unique to Welsh Jewry, but was also a feature of other smaller Jewish communities in Britain and the United States.[95] Between 1914 and 1942, for instance, the Aberavon and Port Talbot Hebrew Congregation was served by five ministers, whose average length of service was five years.[96] The situation was repeated in other Jewish communities in Wales. The *JYB* lists seven ministers serving the Brynmawr Hebrew Congregation between 1897 and 1940, while Pontypridd Jewry had ten different ministers between 1896 and 1926; on average, each stayed less than four years.[97] Similarly, Wrexham Jewry had nine ministers between 1898 and 1921, while Bangor had fourteen ministers between

1894 and 1943.[98] Although such a flux of religious leaders evidently had a negative impact on the stability of the formal religious structure of some of Wales's Jewish communities, it also meant that many of the country's Jewish ministers did not get the opportunity to cultivate relationships and long-lasting ties with members of the wider local community.

There were a number of reasons why many of Wales's smaller Jewish communities had trouble keeping their ministers for a lengthy-period of time, some of which derived from their small size, although others did not. With their limited numbers, small congregations found it especially challenging to pay their religious leaders competitive salaries, and because they were unable to afford to appoint more than one synagogue official, ministers were often required to perform multiple roles for little pay. Thus, in 1901, the Rhyl Hebrew Congregation advertised for a minister to act as *shochet*, reader and teacher with a salary of £52 per annum, while in 1903 the Aberdare Hebrew Congregation advertised a similar post with an annual salary of £65 per annum.[99] In contrast, the Hammersmith Synagogue in London, which initially appointed a minister in 1904 at £200 per annum, increased the salary to £250 because the former sum was considered 'a small stipend'.[100] According to the late Harry Cohen of Pontypridd, the congregation's ministers in the early twentieth century were 'jacks of all trades', they were 'the *chazzan*, the teacher, the *shochet*, the *mohel*' but weren't 'paid very much for doing all of this'.[101]

The Swansea Hebrew Congregation was sometimes able to appoint more than one official to provide these various services, but for most of its history the financial situation dictated that one individual undertook all of them. Indeed, most ministers were simply unwilling to perform these multiple roles for low pay and they left their pulpits for presumably better-paid ministerial positions elsewhere. Revd M. Isaacs, for instance, left the Bridgend Hebrew Congregation for Wolverhampton in May 1928 'on account of the poor wage' he received,[102] while Revd M. Franks of Barrow-in-Furness, who was appointed minister of the Bangor Hebrew Congregation early in 1922, had left by April that year because it was 'impossible for him to live ... on the salary' the congregation offered him.[103] Some ministers received financial assistance from the Chief Rabbi's Provincial Ministers' Fund, but they often found the amount to be insufficient. In 1926, for example, when the fund awarded Revd Hyman Goldman of Tredegar £16 5s., he asked for the sum to be raised to £30 as he found it 'really hard . . . to make a living with the small salary' he received from his congregation.[104]

In practice, few congregations ever dismissed an official, but sometimes the services of a minister had to be terminated as a result of a disagreement or a gross dereliction of duty. In Swansea, for example, Revd Simon Fyne was dismissed in 1906 because some honorary members were dissatisfied with his *cheder* teaching, and he made false allegations against the president Hyam Goldberg.[105] Similarly, Fyne's successor, Revd Herbert J. Sandheim, caused friction and disagreement within the congregation throughout his time in Swansea (in 1908, for instance, he incurred disapproval after asking to be exempt from reading the law in synagogue), and was forced to resign in November 1912 after it was discovered that he was heavily in debt.[106]

One of the main reasons for the high turnover of ministers in most of Wales's small Jewish communities was a desire to progress to what was perceived to be a more prestigious position in one of Britain's larger Jewish centres. Indeed, newly qualified ministers and those who were recent immigrants were more or less expected to begin their careers in smaller communities and then use the experience they acquired as a stepping stone to appointments in larger congregations. Jerusalem-born Revd Gershon Grayewsky, for example, served as Wrexham's minister from 1917 until 1918 and held a pulpit in Bangor for less than a year, before moving in 1919 to the larger Cathedral Road congregation in Cardiff, where he served as a *shochet* and reader until his death in 1975.[107] Similarly, Russian-born Revd Reuben Rabinowitz held pulpits in Whitley Bay, Brynmawr and Llanelli before assuming a rabbinical position at the Birmingham Central Synagogue, where he served from 1930 until his death in 1969.[108] Isaac Factor, who grew up in Port Talbot in the early twentieth century, recalled that 'many ministers . . . had their first positions with our community', including Revd Maurice Landy who left Port Talbot for London in 1942, eventually serving as rabbi for the Cricklewood Hebrew Congregation, where he remained for thirty-one years.[109]

Nonetheless, some of Wales's smaller congregations employed ministers who served long tenures and rose to prominence in their communities. In Llandudno, for instance, the Russian-born Revd Emanuel Berry served from 1910 until his death in 1944.[110] He did not earn a good salary, often asking the Chief Rabbi for financial assistance, but he remained in

Llandudno partly because he and his wife ran an Orthodox boarding house in the town, which brought in a sufficient income.[111] Similarly, Revd Abraham Snadow served as Newport's minister from 1910 until his retirement in 1964.[112] According to Snadow, 'the friendliness he first met' in the town 'which [had] been maintained by succeeding generations' is what 'really kept him there'. His congregants believed 'his own character . . . played a major role' and despite receiving a modest salary and being 'value for money', they appreciated the fact that he 'had never had one eye on the *Jewish Chronicle* communal vacancies column'.[113] Nevertheless, despite these examples, it was certainly unusual for smaller Jewish communities in Wales to employ long-serving ministers.

Given the scarcity of long-serving ministers, many of Wales's Jewish communities developed ways of functioning without resident religious leaders for some periods. For example, following Revd Grayewsky's departure in November 1919, Bangor Jewry went without a minister for nearly a year and relied on a lay member named Mr Reuben to conduct 'services each Sabbath and throughout the Holy Days'.[114] Some communities had to rely on ministers from larger congregations in the region. In 1905, for instance, Revd Simon Fyne of Swansea served as visiting minister to the Llanelli Hebrew Congregation, which was 'without any permanent minister' at the time.[115] Despite the crucial role played by lay leaders and visiting ministers in services, it was only when Wales's Jewish communities had an appointed and resident spiritual leader in their midst that they truly felt stable and secure in their religious activities. The fact that the Tonypandy Hebrew Congregation advertised for a minister in the *JC* at least three times between 1919 and 1920 is a testament to this thesis.[116]

Education

Of equal importance to the stability, security and longevity of a congregation, and to Jewish religion and culture more generally, was the provision of formal Jewish education for Jewish children, the future of Wales's Jewish communities. As was true in other parts of the United Kingdom, Jewish children in nineteenth and twentieth century Wales learned about their religion and culture through various formal means, including *cheder* classes attached to congregations (the Jewish equivalent of Sunday school), where students focused on religious education and learnt Hebrew, and

Jewish day schools, where Jewish children received both Jewish religious instruction and secular education under one roof. Despite the existence of Jewish day schools in London from the early eighteenth century onwards, only one Jewish day school, located in Birmingham, existed outside the British capital in 1845, the year in which Chief Rabbi Nathan Adler conducted a survey of Jewish religious instruction in Britain. No Jewish day schools were registered in Wales during this period and Jewish children typically received their religious instruction either at home or by a *cheder* teacher if one was available. For instance in 1845, with no Jewish school or *cheder* instructor available, the Cardiff community relied on laymen to provide Jewish religious instruction for their ten children.[117]

Before the passing of the Elementary Education Act in 1870, no national state-supported system of elementary education existed in England and Wales, with secular schooling provided primarily by religiously affiliated educational societies and paid for by parents and charitable subscribers. It was not compulsory to attend school before 1870, but if Jewish parents wished their children to receive a secular education, they sent them to Christian schools if no Jewish alternatives were available.[118] Concerned by the threat of proselytisation and the gradual breakdown of Jewish religious and cultural knowledge outside London, Chief Rabbi Nathan Adler sought to establish a Jewish day school in every Jewish community in Britain, no matter how large or small, where Jewish children would be taught both secular and religious subjects in a Jewish environment.[119]

In Wales, Adler's efforts bore fruit in 1866 when a Jewish day school opened in Merthyr Tydfil.[120] The school offered both religious and secular instruction, but appears to have been short-lived, as there is no further mention of it in the *JC*. Unfortunately, a lack of surviving records means that the precise reason for the school's closure is unknown, but it was probably a combination of a lack of funds and low student enrolment. Only twenty-three Jewish pupils attended the school, and to make up numbers 'a few children of Christian parents' were permitted to enrol.[121] It was the 'low state of . . . funds' that led to the closure of the Newport Jewish day school in 1873.[122] Housed in a purpose-built building next to the Francis Street synagogue (financed by voluntary donations) and 'open to all Jewish children, paying or not paying', it operated for less than three months.[123] Long-lasting Jewish day schools were typically located in centres with significant Jewish populations such as Birmingham and

Manchester, where the supply of students, financial support, and demand for religious and secular education within a Jewish environment were virtually continuous. However, with maximum populations of 250 and 400 persons respectively, Newport and Merthyr Jewry were too small to sustain full-time Jewish educational institutions.[124]

A co-educational Jewish day school opened in Cardiff in October 1866 on the initiative of the congregation's minister Revd N. Jacobs. Revd H. D. Marks of London was appointed its first teacher and its curriculum included lessons in Hebrew, history, English grammar, geography and spelling.[125] Revd H. J. Cohen of Jews' Free School, London, was appointed the school's first head teacher in August 1870, and by December of that year plans were underway to erect facilities.[126] The school's success was also short-lived, however, and in August 1871 it closed following Cohen's resignation over poor pay and his subsequent departure to Brighton.[127] Several attempts were made to re-establish a Jewish day school in Cardiff during the late nineteenth and early twentieth centuries, but they never materialised, since it was felt that the city's Jewish community, then consisting of under a thousand individuals, was 'too few in number' to sustain such an educational institution.[128] Moreover, the provision of state-financed, compulsory and nondenominational education for all children between the ages of five and twelve by local school boards following the passing of various education reform acts from 1870 onwards probably discouraged some Jewish parents in Cardiff from sending their children to an independent Jewish day school, especially those parents wanting to assimilate, who feared that a separate fee-paying Jewish school would foster a spirit of exclusiveness and also, as Alderman suggested, 'impede the process of social emancipation' that was brought about by educational reform.[129]

The Jewish day school movement in Wales was languishing by the turn of the twentieth century, and from then on the majority of Welsh-Jewish children attended local non-Jewish schools for their secular education and received their religious and Hebrew education outside school hours at their local congregations' *cheder,* as was the case with a large number of British-Jewish children. *Cheder* classes were established in Tredegar and Swansea in 1888, for example, while Hebrew classes were founded in both Bangor and Brynmawr in 1895.[130] The hours of tuition varied considerably between congregations and changed over time, but Jewish children in Wales typically received instruction for at least a couple of hours every week. In the 1890s, for instance, Bangor's *cheder* lessons were held on weekend afternoons and also on various weeknights, while in the late 1920s Bridgend's *cheder* classes were held for two-and-a-half-hours on Monday and Wednesday evenings and for two hours on Saturday and Sundays.[131] According to the late Lena and Leslie Burns, Jewish children living in Merthyr Tydfil in the 1900s and 1910s attended *cheder* 'every night … straight from school' and 'had very little leisure time' as a result, while Cardiff's Cathedral Road congregation held *cheder* classes each day of the week during the interwar period, with the exception of Friday night and Saturday.[132]

For Jewish families living at a distance from organised Jewish centres, there were nonetheless always some arrangements in place to provide for the religious educational needs of their children. Indeed, it was customary for some Jewish children to travel to their nearest Jewish centre for *cheder*. Joyce Arron (née Cohen) of Ammanford, for instance, recalled that during the 1940s and 1950s her father would drive her to Swansea (approximately seventeen miles) every Sunday for *cheder*, while during the same period Moses Stein of Amlwch travelled twenty miles by train to Bangor once a week for his *cheder* lessons.[133] It was also common for isolated Jewish families to arrange for ministers or teachers from nearby congregations to come to their homes to teach their young. During the 1920s, for example, Revd Berry of Llandudno travelled once a week to Conwy (approximately four and a half miles) to teach ten Jewish children, while during the 1940s and 1950s a *cheder* teacher from Cardiff named E. Fischer travelled to the Blacks' residence in Porthcawl every Wednesday to teach eleven children.[134]

In some instances, Jewish children living away from Jewish communities were provided with religious educational instruction by family members. For example, despite living only some two miles from the nearest *cheder* in Merthyr Tydfil, the family of the late Ben Hamilton of Dowlais thought the distance too great and insisted that Ben be taught by his father and grandfather. Although they were not formally trained to teach, Hamilton (b.1896) believed he 'had a first class Hebrew education' as he 'was incorporated into the love of Judaism and Biblical knowledge by the type of life [his] father and grandparents lived' in Eastern Europe.[135]

Yet not all Jewish families in Wales sent their children to *cheder* or made alternative religious educational arrangements. Jacqueline Magrill, who grew up in Cardiff in the 1930s, disliked her first few *cheder* lessons, after which her mother told her that she was not obliged to attend. Having never learnt Hebrew, Jacqueline felt disadvantaged in synagogue services as an adult and eventually regretted her mother's decision.[136] Cynthia Kahn (née Cohen), who grew up in a secular Jewish household in Penrhiwceiber during the 1930s and 1940s, was never sent to *cheder*. Unable to follow a service at the synagogue, Cynthia felt the lack of a religious education and at the age of sixteen began attending Hebrew and Jewish History lessons twice a week at the home of a 'very religious' layman named Sam Kahn (her future father-in-law).[137]

Assessing the quality of *cheder* education in Wales is complex, given that it varied from congregation to congregation and also differed from time to time. Sometimes the results were good, while other times they were poor. The same can be said for the gender make-up of *cheder* classes, as in the late nineteenth and early twentieth centuries many of Wales's Orthodox congregations, including the Cardiff New Hebrew Congregation and the Pontypridd Hebrew Congregation, appear to have adhered to Eastern European tradition by providing Hebrew and religious education to boys only, while others such as the Merthyr Tydfil Hebrew Congregation and the Abertillery Hebrew Congregation provided *cheder* lessons to both boys and girls.[138] While it remains unclear if these classes were coeducational or single sex, girls would not have been expected to learn Hebrew or the *Torah* to the same degree as boys, the future leaders of Wales's synagogue services.

The inconsistency in the quality of *cheder* instruction, particularly in smaller communities, was undoubtedly due to the high turnover of ministers, who, as we have seen, often doubled up as *cheder* teachers and differed in the extent of their Jewish learning and knowledge. Congregational religious classes were visited, usually on an annual basis, by outside educational authorities such as the Chief Rabbi, inspectors for the Central Council of Religious Education or learned ministers, and their comments demonstrate the variation in standards. In 1900, for instance, Mr S. Bloom examined the *cheder* classes of the Wrexham Hebrew Congregation and complimented 'the new minister and teacher' Revd L. Abrahamson 'on the improvement in the Hebrew education of the children', who were previously taught by Revd Lewis Smorgansky.[139] During his inspection of the Llanelli Hebrew Congregation's *cheder* in 1921, Rabbi Schechter of Manchester 'expressed himself greatly pleased with the high standard' of Revd L. Solomon and Mr J. Cohn's teaching.[140] However, a 1938 report on Revd Abelson's classes in Llanelli was less complimentary. The inspector 'found a lack of system and method' in his classes and commented on the deficiency of basic facilities in the classroom, such as a blackboard, 'an essential means of helping in the grasp of Hebrew'.[141]

Undoubtedly there were gaps between the departure of an outgoing minister and the arrival of his replacement, and in the interval Jewish education was either informal and often of low quality, or was not provided at all. For instance, when Hermann Adler inspected Merthyr Tydfil's *cheder* classes in 1899, 'he was not all satisfied with the progress made by the children' and blamed the poor result on 'the absence of a minister and teacher'.[142] In 1952, it was reported that Llandudno Jewry had 'been without a minister for some time' and that the children had 'had no [religious] instruction' for a number of months.[143] In the absence of a resident *cheder* teacher, some Jewish communities relied on travelling teachers. This occurred in Port Talbot during the 1940s, when a visiting teacher taught the children for a few hours once a month. This arrangement, however, was too irregular for some, and one long-term congregant remembers his religious education with great resentment: 'I would've liked to have learnt a lot more but I didn't have the opportunity'.[144]

Some Jews remember their *cheder* classes in very positive terms. Renee Woolf, for instance, recalled that the quality of Llanelli's *cheder* was very good during the 1940s and 1950s because the small number of children enrolled meant that pupils could be taught on a one-to-one basis.[145] The opposite was true for others. The late Harry Cohen described his *cheder* experience in early twentieth-century Pontypridd as 'bedlam' because the lack of facilities and teachers meant that 'children of a wide range of ages [were] taught at the same time'. Despite this inconvenience, he recalled that the Jewish boys of his generation in Pontypridd 'were extremely proficient' and were educated to such a degree that they were all capable of reciting the *maftir* (the last portion of the *Torah*) during Sabbath services.[146] However, even in larger Jewish centres such as Cardiff, *cheder* classes were not always of the highest quality. Reflecting on his childhood in Cardiff during the 1920s and 1930s, Leonard Minkes observed that the Windsor Place synagogue's *cheder*:

provided a prolonged but in certain respects, limited education. From the age of about 6–13, in three classes (infants, middle, top) . . . a largely repetitive but intensive education was given by trained and untrained teachers, in rather inadequate classrooms.[147]

In some instances, parents were not content with the *cheder* education provided by their local congregation and employed private tutors to help expand their offspring's Hebrew and religious knowledge. According to Channah Hirsch, Llanelli's *cheder* during the 1910s was not advanced enough for those Jewish families who 'came from towns renowned throughout the Jewish world as seats of learning – such as Grodno, Kovno, and Vilna in Lithuania', and thus they saved their money and employed rabbis to instruct their children privately.[148] Because of the high turnover of *cheder* teachers in Bangor in the 1930s, Isidore Wartski employed a professor of Semitic languages from the then University College of North Wales to teach his son Hebrew.[149]

Kosher

Just as Jewish communities in Wales sought to establish Jewish educational facilities that would meet both the religious and cultural needs of their young, they also sought to provide for the many other requirements of an observant Jewish lifestyle, including kosher meat. At the outset, the Jewish communities of Cardiff, Merthyr Tydfil, Newport and Swansea were all too small to sustain their own kosher butcher shops and arrangements were initially made with non-Jewish butchers to sell kosher meat slaughtered by the congregation's *shochet*. During the 1880s, for instance, two non-Jewish butchers, Frederick Whale of St John Street and W. H. Richards of Cowbridge Road, served kosher meat to Cardiff's Jewish community under the supervision of the *shochet*, M. Lewis.[150] Similarly, in the last decades of the nineteenth century members of the Swansea Hebrew Congregation purchased their kosher meat from non-Jewish butchers, including Abrahams of Swansea market, who were supervised by their *shochet*; while at the turn of the twentieth century Merthyr Tydfil Jewry obtained their kosher meat from Albert E. Bull's butcher shop in Victoria Street, where the meat would be *treibered* (prepared) by the congregation's *shochet*.[151]

Nevertheless, by the early twentieth century all four of these Jewish communities provided enough of a clientele for Jewish butchers trained in *shechita* to operate full-scale markets. Around 1910, a Jewish butcher from

London named Barnett Krotosky opened a kosher butcher shop in Wellington Street, Merthyr Tydfil, providing kosher meat to a Jewish population of about three hundred individuals, while his nephew, Louis Krotosky, opened a kosher butcher shop in Bridge Street, Newport, *c.* 1907, supplying about two hundred Jews with kosher meat until his departure in 1916.[152] Similarly, the four hundred or so Jewish individuals living in Swansea witnessed their first resident Jewish butcher in 1905, when Russian-born Jack Silver began selling kosher produce from a stall in Swansea market.[153]

The Krotosky family had kosher butcher shops in Cardiff as well as in Merthyr Tydfil and Newport. The first was established in Clare Street in 1901 by Joseph Krotosky (Barnett's brother), and the business was eventually run by various family members from a number of locations in the city, serving a Jewish population numbering 1,250 at its lowest and 3,500 at its greatest, until its closure in 1992.[154] At times the Cardiff Jewish population provided enough customers for more than one kosher butcher to operate in the city. These included Kosher Meat Supply in Tudor Street, which was owned by Lipka Gaist from about 1910 until her death in 1948, and Kayes (Kosher) Ltd., which operated from Frederick Street between the 1960s and early 1970s.[155] Indeed, such was the demand for kosher meat in Cardiff during the first half of the twentieth century, that the Jewish Institute and Social Club in High Street opened its own kosher restaurant in the 1930s.[156]

Although many of Wales's smaller Jewish communities had a large percentage of religiously observant Jews, the client base for kosher meat was limited. Thus, in many instances, no kosher butchers trained in *shechita* existed, and the purveyors of kosher meat were gentile butchers who made special arrangements to supply the Jewish community. For example, during the 1910s a local non-Jewish butcher in New Tredegar closed his shop to non-Jewish customers one day a week in order to supply Jewish families with kosher meat, while in early twentieth-century Waunlwyd, the late Simon Joseph noted that it 'was customary for [Jewish] husbands' in the locality 'to buy their [kosher] meat every Thursday' from 'a special section of the window' of J. P. Bishop's butcher shop in Cwm.[157] The actual slaughtering of livestock was done in a local abattoir by the *shochet* of the Ebbw Vale Hebrew Congregation, who then stamped the meat 'with a blue dye with the word "kosher" in Hebrew characters' and delivered it to the butchers.[158] During the 1910s and 1920s, a butcher in Pontypridd's market allowed the local minister (trained in *shechita*) to come to his stall once a week to serve Jewish customers, while both Bangor and Llandudno Jewry, the former from 1894 and the latter from 1910, made arrangements with local butchers to purchase a designated counter for kosher meats and to allow their community's *shochet* to come in and serve Jewish customers a few times a week.[159]

For those communities that were unable to support a full-time licensed kosher butcher or a *shochet*, or when their services were unavailable, there were nonetheless some arrangements in place to provide for the needs of Jews who observed the laws of *kashrut* (Jewish dietary law). Indeed, in places without a local kosher butcher or meat supplier, it was common for Jews to purchase their meat from other, often larger, Jewish centres. Throughout the twentieth century, some of the more observant families in north Wales had kosher food delivered by train from Liverpool or Manchester. Jack and Rebecca Pollecoff, for example, lived in Pwllheli from the 1930s until the 1970s and 'were sent . . . kosher meat from either Liverpool or Manchester' by train, while Paul Sugarman grew up in Rhyl in the 1930s and recalled that he used to go down to the railway station each Friday 'and get what they sent in from Manchester, like a kosher killed chicken'.[160] This was also the case for a number of Jews living in south Wales. According to Diane Marcus, kosher meat was sometimes sent to her family in Llanhilleth from London by train during the 1930s and 1940s. It was not the most efficient system, however, as the meat often did not arrive or had 'to be thrown out as it had gone off during the journey'.[161] Rather than arranging delivery, some Jewish families travelled to get their kosher meat. In early twentieth-century Ystalyfera, for instance, the Samuels took live chickens by horse and cart to Swansea to be slaughtered by a *shochet*, while in the 1940s and 1950s the Landys of Llanelli and the Cohens of Ammanford made weekly trips to Swansea to buy meat from Bessie Dulin's kosher meat counter in Swansea market.[162]

Charity

As was true of other British Jewries, another concern for observant Jews living in nineteenth- and twentieth-century Wales was the act of giving *tzedakah,* the responsibility to give aid, assistance and money to the poor and needy as outlined in both the *Torah* and the *Talmud* (a collection of ancient Rabbinic writings constituting the basis of religious authority in Orthodox Judaism). Since the mid nineteenth century, Britain has been home to numerous Jewish charitable organisations for the poor and destitute, the most prominent example being the Jewish Board of Guardians. Founded in 1859 to provide relief for impoverished Jewish immigrants living in London, by the turn of the twentieth century Cardiff, Merthyr Tydfil, Newport and Swansea had their own branches of the organisation or of similar benevolent societies 'to help the resident [Jewish] poor'.[163] Self-help charities such as these were not features of any other Welsh-Jewish community and their formation in centres that predate the mass migration of poor Eastern European Jews in the last quarter of the nineteenth century is not coincidental. This is because these organisations were founded and financed by long-established, acculturated and increasingly prosperous Jews, who felt compassion for the poverty of their recently arrived co-religionists. They were also reluctant to see poor Jewish immigrants becoming a financial burden on the state, fearing that this would imperil the image of British Jewry and provoke xenophobic hostility from wider British society.[164] Thus, the president of Swansea's Benevolent Association in 1900 was Isaac Seline, a Welsh-born Jew who ran a successful insurance agency in the town, while the president of Merthyr Tydfil's Ladies' Benevolent Society in 1904 was London-born Bertha Gittlesohn, whose husband Hermann was 'a well off' pawnbroker.[165] In Jewish communities made up almost entirely of poor Eastern European immigrants, such as Bangor and Llanelli, mutual aid organisations were established, where members donated a certain amount of money each week in order to receive financial benefits in times of hardship.[166]

As well as assisting Jewish individuals in need within their own communities, all of Wales's Jewish congregations, at one time or another, donated money to a variety of Jewish charities, both at home and abroad. In 1915, for instance, all the Jewish communities in existence in Wales at the time donated to the Fund for the Relief of the Jewish Victims of the War in Russia.[167] Similarly, during the 1910s and 1920s, the Jewish communities of Abertillery, Llandudno and Merthyr Tydfil collected donations for the relief of oppressed Jews in Poland, while Cardiff Jewry collected funds for such charities as the Foreign Jewish Protection Committee and the Fund for the Relief of the Jewish Victims of the War in Russia.[168] During the first decades of the twentieth century Tredegar Jewry donated annually to the Jewish Soup Kitchen in London and collected monetary donations for special appeals, such as the Manchester Victoria Memorial

Jewish Hospital Fund.[169] Raising money for causes that would benefit both local Jewry and the wider non-Jewish community within their vicinity, local health care and services in particular, was also of central importance to Wales's Jewish communities. In the 1890s, for instance, Merthyr Tydfil's Jewish community held annual services and fundraising events at the Church Road synagogue in aid of the Merthyr General Hospital (opened in 1888), while in the 1870s Cardiff Jewry held collection services in the East Terrace synagogue in aid of both the Cardiff Royal Infirmary and the Hamadryad hospital ship for sick seamen in Cardiff docks.[170] Indeed, although charitable giving must have been a financial strain for smaller Jewish communities, there is nothing to suggest that *tzedakah* was ever neglected by Welsh Jewry.

While the histories of Wales's Orthodox communities were similar in the sense that they all established synagogues, acquired ministers to lead their services, and provided social and religious facilities for their congregants, they were also significantly different in many ways. As we have seen, demographic and financial factors meant that larger communities were more likely than smaller ones to erect purpose-built synagogues for worship, appoint long-serving religious leaders and maintain certain facilities, such as kosher butchers. With a greater and more diverse Jewish population, Wales's larger communities were also more likely to sustain multiple congregations. Of course, Wales's smaller Jewish communities did occasionally split into sub-congregations, but their short-lived existence meant that cooperation and compromise were frequently crucial in these centres, more so than in larger communities. Given their close proximity to larger Jewish centres, some of Wales's poorer and smaller congregations also did without certain community-based amenities such as a *mikvah* because they could rely on the more populous and affluent neighbouring communities for these facilities.

3

Evacuation, Refuge and the Second World War

No area of modern Jewish history has received more attention from scholars than the persecution of German Jewry under Hitler during the 1930s and the destruction of six million European Jews by the Nazis between 1939 and 1945. Despite the plethora of published work on the topic, this period is arguably one of the most neglected areas within British-Jewish studies.[1] This is because the United Kingdom, unlike other European countries such as Hungary and the Netherlands, was never occupied by Hitler between 1939 and 1945, nor was its Jewish population deported to Nazi concentration and extermination camps, although this fate befell Jews living in the German-occupied Channel Islands, a dependency of the British Crown.[2] As William Rubinstein commented, 'Britain's was the largest European Jewish community to survive the Nazi Holocaust', and thus the study of the experiences during the Second World War of Jews in Britain, both refugees and permanent residents, has often been perceived by scholars as irrelevant.[3]

Although the Holocaust happened elsewhere, some scholars have recognised the significant impact that the persecution of Jews in Nazi Germany had on British Jewry, and British society as a whole, between 1933 and 1945.[4] A consideration of its impact on Welsh Jewry is, however, lacking in the growing literature on the subject.[5] Nevertheless, so ingrained is the association between Jews, Nazism and the Second World War in late twentieth- and early twenty-first-century society that no modern history of any Jewish community would be complete without exploring and addressing the effect of this period on its population. As we shall see, Wales's designation as a safe haven from Nazism meant that the country witnessed an influx of both Jewish refugees from Continental Europe and evacuated Jewish individuals and families from major British cities during the 1930s and 1940s, a migration pattern that proved to have a significant impact on both the demographical and the geographical make-up of Welsh Jewry, and of British Jewry more generally.

Jewish Medical and Academic Refugees

Between 1933, the year Hitler came to power, and the outbreak of the Second World War in 1939, over 60,000 Jews from Nazi-controlled territories such as Germany, Austria and Czechoslovakia fled to Britain for safety.[6] This mass-movement of Jewish refugees did not occur at once, however, but took place in several stages. Thus, to fully understand the history of Jewish migration from Nazi-occupied Europe to Britain throughout the 1930s, one must take account of both Nazi policy towards Jews and the British government's policy towards Jewish refugees, for both effectively dictated the pace of emigration and immigration.

For the first five years of Nazi rule, British government policy was, broadly, to restrict the admission of refugees to a modest number. Government officials were not insensitive to the plight of the refugees, especially when Nazi brutality outraged public opinion and provoked waves of sympathy, but British interests ultimately came first. In a period of continuing high levels of unemployment, the British government favoured the admission of refugees who would be an economic benefit to Britain. They preferred, for instance, people who had distinguished themselves in an artistic, scientific or technological field and/or those who might create new industrial enterprises.[7] Refugees who had sufficient financial resources to provide for themselves were also at an advantage. Those who were seen as having little to offer or who lacked any obvious means of supporting themselves financially were turned back at their port of entry by immigration officers.[8]

While Britain was important as a place of safety and staging-post for onward migrants and temporary exiles, it became a new home for a large number of displaced Jewish doctors, who were among the first victims of Nazi persecution.[9] As early as April 1933, for instance, restrictions were placed on the number of Jewish doctors in National Health Insurance practices in Germany and in the summer of that year the Nazis forbade Jewish doctors to cooperate with their non-Jewish counterparts.[10] Jewish doctors in the Third Reich also lost their role as experts and consultants and from 1933 onwards were no longer allowed to take part in professional training schemes.[11] Facing harassment and dismissal, thousands of Jewish doctors fled Germany during the 1930s in search of places where their skills might be valued, including the United Kingdom.

By 1939 an estimated 1,200 German and Austrian doctors, the majority of whom were Jews, resided in Britain, but on their arrival they faced formidable difficulties.[12] Indeed, during the 1930s the British Medical Association (BMA) opposed the admission of all but a select few 'refugee physicians of special distinction' on the basis that Britain was adequately supplied with doctors, that medical refugees would compete for employment with British graduates, and the fear that foreign doctors would subject British homes to foreign influences.[13] Although, as Tony Kushner points out, the Home Office believed this hostile attitude to be unreasonable, it was still unwilling to challenge the BMA's restrictive position.[14] As a result, it was extremely difficult for German doctors to settle in Britain – their German medical qualifications were invalidated, and they were required to study for two years before taking the British medical examinations.[15] A handful of medical refugees were admitted to the Welsh National School of Medicine in Cardiff, which offered a 'special scheme of instruction for refugee students'.[16] Between 1933 and 1934 twelve German students were enrolled and, following the Austrian Anschluss of 1938 and the Nazi invasion of Czechoslovakia in 1939, they were joined by seven Austrians and fifteen Czechs, including Austrian Jews Alfred Feiner and Edgar Rhoden.[17]

Of the many Jewish refugee doctors who sought refuge in Britain during the 1930s, only a small number were offered permanent positions in the United Kingdom. Although most were pressed to move on to other countries such as the United States, a handful settled permanently in Wales and carved out successful careers, including German-born Max Weis, who worked as a physician at the Rookwood Ministry of Pensions hospital in Cardiff from 1942 until his death in 1952; Leipzig-born Werner Bernfeld, who was appointed a venereologist in Cardiff City Hospital in 1955; and the already mentioned Alfred Feiner of Vienna, who worked as a general practitioner in Pontypridd between 1941 and 1977.[18]

As well as doctors, many German-Jewish academics lost their positions at German universities from 1933 onwards because of the Nazis' anti-Jewish policies. Fearing for their welfare, many sought refuge elsewhere. The international academic community quickly condemned the actions of the Nazis and many organisations were founded to aid displaced academics, such as the Academic Assistance Council (AAC), later renamed the Society for the Protection of Science and Learning, which was established in Britain in May 1933. Indeed, while the BMA fought to keep refugee doctors out of Britain, the AAC saw displaced German-Jewish academics of intellectual distinction as valuable assets to British universities. As Gerhard Hirschfeld once noted, this is not to deny the humane intentions of the AAC or of the British universities, but to suggest that the chances for refugee scholars were at their best when a coincidence existed of refugee need and British advantage.[19]

The AAC found considerable support from the Welsh academic community, with many Welsh scholars such as chemists Charles R. Bury of the University College of Wales, Aberystwyth, and Joseph E. Coates of the University College of Swansea facilitating the recruitment of refugee scholars and supporting fund-raising appeals towards at their respective institutions.[20] At Cardiff, enough funds were raised for Professor Werner Friedrich Bruck, a German economist of Jewish origin, to work at the University College of South Wales and Monmouthshire between 1934 and 1938.[21] Yet most displaced academics could only obtain temporary posts and were expected to re-emigrate like other refugees.[22] Thus Bruck left for New York in 1940, where he worked as a professor of political management at the New School for Social Research.[23] Indeed, of the small number of displaced refugee academics in Welsh universities, only Czech-born Erich Heller was to make a career in Wales after the war. After holding temporary positions as a German lecturer at the London School of Economics and the University of Cambridge, he was appointed head of the German department at the University College of Swansea in 1948 and became the first holder of the chair in German in 1950.[24]

Jewish Refugee Industrialists

Such a restrictive and selective policy was not limited to doctors and academics, however, but also applied to Jewish refugee businessmen and industrialists. As mentioned previously, the early 1930s was a period of mass unemployment in Britain, with over two million of the insured population out of work by 1935. While unemployment levels in Britain varied by region, it was especially high in areas that suffered a decline in traditional heavy industries, such as south Wales and the north-east of England. The government's response to the growing unemployment was to pass a Special

Areas Act in 1934 that sought to create jobs in depressed areas through the establishment of government-sponsored industrial estates.[25] In south Wales, a trading estate was established south of Treforest, a village situated approximately eleven miles north of Cardiff. In May 1935, the Commissioner for the Special Areas of England and Wales wrote to 5,000 British firms inviting them to consider setting up factories in one of the Special Areas. Of the two hundred that replied, only twelve were interested.[26] As there was a marked unwillingness on the part of British firms to go the Special Areas, the authorities began to show an interest in finding refugee businessmen who would agree to settle there and start up businesses.[27]

Although the Home Office lacked the powers to make the admission of refugee manufacturers dependent on any particular part of the country, it found ways of steering them towards the Special and other Depressed Areas. Resident permits, for instance, were to be issued more quickly for those settling in areas of high unemployment, while the factories were offered at a significantly lower rent than elsewhere.[28] Such incentives were highly appealing to Austrian-born Albert Pollock and his business partner, Joseph Krakauer, who established a leather gloves company called Burlington Gloves Ltd on the Treforest Industrial Estate in 1939.[29] For other refugee industrialists, it was south-east Wales's relative proximity to London (approximately 157 miles) that made Treforest an attractive area to start up a business. Despite having never been to south Wales before, German-born brothers Julius and Moritz Mendle established a plastic moulding business in Treforest in 1939 because it was closer to the British capital than the other Special Areas such as the north-east of England and the south-west of Scotland.[30]

The Treforest Industrial Estate officially opened in 1936, but Jewish refugee firms were not established there until 1938–9. This was because the majority of Jewish businesses in Nazi Germany were allowed to function until 1938, when the Reich interior ministry ordered the registration of all Jewish-owned companies and sold them cheaply to non-Jewish German businesses.[31] Jewish businesses in Austria and Czechoslovakia remained unaffected until the Austrian Anschluss of 1938 and the German occupation of Czechoslovakia in 1939. Having lost their businesses, thousands of Jewish businessmen and industrialists fled their homelands in 1938–9 to try and re-establish their firms abroad.

The businesses represented by the Jewish refugee firms at Treforest were extremely varied and included O. P. Chocolates, a chocolate and confectionery company owned by Oscar Peschek of Vienna; Embee Abrasive Materials, owned by brothers Paul and Alfred Mayer from Hamburg; Pearl Paints Ltd, a paint and varnish factory run by brothers Simon, Fritz and Willi Stern from Fulda, Germany; Metal Products Ltd, a light engineering company established by the Golten family of Prague; and Aero Zipp Fasteners Ltd, a zip-manufacturing company founded by Berlin-born Joachim Koppel, father of the émigré artist, Heinz Koppel.[32]

By May 1940, it was reported that fifty-five Jewish refugee firms were in operation at Treforest, employing 1,800 people.[33] As well as improving levels of unemployment in the area, the refugees were praised for introducing new industries to Britain, which reduced the import of a variety of goods and also increased the number of goods exported.[34] According to an article in the *JC*, Treforest's refugee firms played an important role in helping 'to cripple Nazi Germany's export trade'.[35] In fact, some of the Jewish refugee companies were deemed beneficial to the war effort, including the already mentioned Metal Products Ltd and Aero Zipp Fasteners Ltd, whose factories were requisitioned to create aircraft components for the Ministry of Aircraft Production, and Livia Leather Goods Ltd, founded by an Austrian Jew named Otto Brill, which produced 'leather covers for seats for RAF planes'.[36]

Kindertransport

For the first five years of Nazi rule, the British government's immigration policy was, broadly, to restrict the admission of refugees to those who would be beneficial to the British economy and the national interest. In 1938, however, this policy underwent a marked change. The turning point came in November that year, in the wake of a pogrom against Jews in Germany and parts of annexed Austria. The carnage of the night of 9–10 November 1938, later called *Kristallnacht* (night of the broken glass), sounded the alarm for a number of refugee aid organisations, both in Germany and abroad.[37] Indeed, almost immediately after *Kristallnacht*, a delegation representing both British-Jewish and Quaker groups, including the Central British Fund for German Jewry and the Friends Service Council, mobilised their forces to put political pressure on the British government to permit the entry of refugees from the Third Reich. Acknowledging that an 'open door' policy for all Jewish refugees was not possible, the Jewish organisations urged the British government to consider allowing large numbers of children into Britain.[38] The Home Office eventually gave way to pressure and in late November 1938 permitted an unspecified number of unaccompanied children under the age of seventeen to enter the United Kingdom from German-occupied lands.[39] The children were admitted on temporary travel visas provided that private citizens or organisations would guarantee to pay for each child's care, education and eventual emigration once the crisis was over.[40]

Following the British government's decision, a new nonsectarian organisation that would handle the bulk of the work involved in dealing with both Jewish and non-Jewish child refugees, the Movement for the Care of Children from Germany, was set up under the joint chairmanship of the Christian civil administrator, Sir Wyndham Deedes and the Anglo-Jewish Liberal politician, Herbert Samuel. Renamed the Refugee Children's Movement (RCM) in July 1939, the organisation sent representatives to Germany and Austria to establish the systems for choosing, organising, and transporting children to Britain, in what became known as the *Kindertransport* (children's transport). The first *Kindertransport* arrived in Harwich, England, on 2 December 1938, bringing around two hundred children, many from Jewish orphanages in Berlin.[41] The number of children who arrived in the United Kingdom under official auspices amounted to almost 11,000, of whom 9,354 (7,482 were Jewish) were brought over by the RCM.[42] While the majority of the refugee children were Jewish, the *Kindertransport* also rescued children whose parents were Communists or other political opponents of the Nazis. It was not only organisations that were involved in bringing refugee children to Britain. Some of the most famous examples of individually organised rescues included the efforts of Nicholas Winton, who organised the transport of 669 Jewish children from Nazi-occupied Czechoslovakia to Britain in 1939, and Jean Hoare, a Quaker who flew to Prague that same year and bought a large group of Czech refugee children, both Jewish and non-Jewish, to Britain.[43]

Once in Britain, the experience of refugee children varied considerably. Some arrived through private initiatives and went directly to the homes of their foster families or relatives and family friends, while those with no such connections were sent to reception camps like Dovercourt in Essex until they were suitably placed.[44] Potential sponsors frequently visited Dovercourt to pick out children and one of these was Revd Joseph Weintrobe, the minister of the Swansea Hebrew Congregation, who visited the camp in January 1939 following the formation of Swansea Jewry's Refugee committee in December 1938. He picked twelve Jewish boys, who arrived in Swansea in February 1939 and were cared for by members of the local Jewish community.[45]

Religious placement was a major resettlement issue that faced the RCM; that is, the question of whether Jewish refugee children be placed with non-Jewish foster families. Representatives of the RCM were initially divided on the question of accepting non-Jewish hospitality.[46] However, the lack of sufficient offers from Jewish households led to the acceptance of all homes, Jewish and non-Jewish, that met the necessary requirements.[47] As mentioned above, some Jewish refugee children were sent to live with relatives or family friends who provided the necessary sponsorship and financial guarantees. In most instances the children's Jewish upbringing continued uninterrupted, and there are numerous such examples from Wales, including Leipzig-born Anneliese Barth (née Baumann), who was sent with her younger sister to live with her mother's cousin in Cardiff.[48] Other Jewish children were fostered by Welsh-Jewish families previously unknown to them, including German-born Joseph Berg, who was sponsored by Pontypridd Jewry in 1938 and became an active member of the town's Jewish community; and German-born Ellen Davis (born Kerri Ellen Wertheim), who was fostered by a Jewish couple in Swansea in 1939. In her memoir, Davis recalls that her Jewish upbringing continued uninterrupted in Wales:

> Being a good Jewish family, we went to the [Goat Street] synagogue [in Swansea] on Saturday morning ... to say our prayers ... I felt at home hearing the prayers in Hebrew. It reminded me of Hoof where going to the synagogue had been so much part of my life. On Sunday morning in Swansea as at home, we went to *Chader* [*sic*] ... my Hebrew was good and the teacher could not fault my reading.[49]

With a large number of Jewish refugee children placed in Christian homes, the Chief Rabbi's Religious Emergency Council issued several pleas to host families not to convert Jewish children to Christianity. Some Christian families in Wales respected his wishes. For instance, Erwin Kestenbaum, a Jewish refugee from Czechoslovakia, was fostered by a Unitarian minister in Swansea named Revd Rosalind Lee and celebrated his *bar mitzvah* (a Jewish male's coming-of-age ceremony) at Swansea's

Goat Street synagogue in August 1939.[50] Other Jewish refugee children living with non-Jewish families in Wales, however, were forced to grow up without any Jewish learning or any real sense of their Jewish identity. For example, German-Jewish twins Susi and Lottie Bechhöfer (b. 1936) arrived in Britain on the *Kindertransport* in May 1939 and were fostered by a Cardiff Baptist minister and his wife. While the couple reassured the RCM that they would not baptise the girls, they were nevertheless sent to Sunday school, raised as Christians and renamed Grace and Eunice to erase all traces of their German-Jewish identities.[51]

Although the preferred form of refugee child resettlement was in foster homes, hostels became a common alternative for Jewish refugee children, particularly teenagers, who were harder to place. These collective homes for Jewish refugee children were established in many Jewish communities throughout Britain, including Cardiff and Newport.[52] Cardiff's Refugee Hostel was established in Cathedral Road in May 1939, while Newport's hostel was founded in 1940 and situated in a rented house in Chepstow Road.[53] While the hostels provided a place for the children to sleep and eat, they also accommodated for their religious needs. In Cardiff, daily religious services were held for the thirty-five refugee teenagers, while the twelve girls in Newport received Hebrew lessons and weekly Friday evening services.[54] Cathedral Road's refugee hostel closed in 1943, owing to financial difficulties, while Newport's hostel closed a year earlier following difficulties in securing a full-time matron to care for the girls.[55]

Hachsharot (agricultural training centres) were another form of resettlement for Jewish refugee children in Wales and in the rest of Britain during the Second World War. Organised by German-Jewish Zionist youth organisations such as Youth Aliyah and Bachad, *hachsharot* were originally set up in Germany in the first half of the twentieth century to train Jewish young for life and work in *kibbutzim* (collective communities traditionally based on agriculture) in *Eretz Israel,* the land of Israel (then situated in British Mandate Palestine). The deterioration of the position of Jews in Nazi Germany, particularly during the late 1930s, resulted in a decision to relocate all *hachsharot* situated in German territory to host European countries, including Britain, so that young Jews could continue their agricultural training uninterrupted and in a safer environment.[56] While approximately five hundred refugee children from Nazi-occupied Europe came to Britain on a *Kindertransport* sponsored by Youth Aliyah, many

Jewish adolescents brought to Britain by the RCM and by other means either requested to join a *hachshara* (singular of *hachsharot*), attracted particularly by the Jewish communal environment provided there, or were sent to one because there were no suitable foster homes in which to place them.[57]

Approximately twenty *hachsharot* were established throughout Britain between 1939 and 1945, two of which were founded in country houses in Wales as they had ample accommodation and land and were located in the relative safety of the Welsh countryside, an important considerarion when war broke out.[58] The largest of the Welsh *hachsharot* was the agricultural training centre at Gwrych Castle, Abergele, which operated between 1939 and 1941 following a donation by the castle's owner, Lord Dundonald, who offered it rent-free since the building had been derelict for over fifteen years.[59] A total of 180 refugee children from Youth Aliyah and Bachad were sent to Gwrych, where they divided their day between agricultural work and religious study.[60] The children also worked for local farms and businesses such as Edwin Roberts's farm in Tyddyn Uchaf, and Robert Jones's Printing Works in Abergele. According to Arieh Handler, a medical adviser at Gwrych, the children's satisfactory work resulted in a good relationship with the local population:

> [the children] had no difficulty in making friends with the locals, the shopkeepers, artisans and in particular with the farmers in the surrounding area. Many had no idea what we were doing in Abergele, who we were, where we came from and why we occupied Gwrych Castle ... As can be expected some of the employers in Abergele were interested in cheap labour. However, invariably the work carried out by the boys and girls was satisfactory. They were considered to be honest and trustworthy, and we received many applications for their services.[61]

Gwrych was abandoned in April 1941 due to the lack of agricultural work in the area and the remaining children were transferred to smaller, satellite *hachsharot* in Ruthin, St. Asaph and Rossett.[62] The Rossett training centre opened at Lane Farm in 1940 and was intended to operate as a self-supporting *kibbutz* (singular of *kibbutzim*). This proved to be financially impossible, however, and to alleviate the financial strain the refugee children were hired out as agricultural labourers to neighbouring farms, such as Wrexham Road Farm in Holt.[63] In 1940 a *hachshara* was also established by Youth Aliyah in Llandough Castle in south Wales, following a donation from the YMCA whose use of the estate as a junior transfer centre for boys, a type of agricultural reformatory for juvenile offenders, had ceased during the Second World War, following grant cuts by the Ministry of Labour, its financial supporter.[64] Situated near Cardiff, it enjoyed close relations with the city's Jewish community, with refugee children frequently being invited to participate in local cultural and religious activities.[65]

How many refugee agricultural trainees actually left Britain for Palestine is difficult to ascertain, but it appears that a large number never did. A survey conducted by the Association of Jewish Refugees in 2007, for instance, revealed that only five refugees resident at Gwrych Castle out of twenty-two surveyed emigrated to Palestine during or after the war. Twelve settled in the United Kingdom, while four emigrated to the United States and Australia.[66] One factor that restricted the number of those able to emigrate to Palestine was the limited number of immigration certificates available.[67] Other refugees either grew tired of agricultural labour and believed themselves to be ill-suited to kibbutz life in Palestine, or were simply not interested in emigrating. Berlin-born Herman Rothman, for instance, settled in London after his time at Gwrych Castle because he wanted to learn a profession, while Manfred Alweiss, also from Berlin, settled in Surrey after the war because he had become disenchanted with the prospect of kibbutz life in Palestine.[68]

'Enemy Aliens' and Internment

On 3 September 1939, the day Britain declared war on Germany, thousands of refugees, most of whom were German and Austrian Jews who had fled Nazi oppression, were living in Britain. As we have seen, they comprised a mixture of individuals, including among others academics, businessmen, children and doctors, who came to Britain to seek safety. Although originally labelled by the British government as 'victims of oppression', throughout the Second World War all German and Austrian refugees over the age of sixteen, Jewish and non-Jewish, as well as immigrants of German and Austrian origin who had lived in Britain for a lengthy period of time but had not been naturalised as British citizens, were transformed into 'enemy aliens' because they were subjects of countries with which Britain was at war. Italians living in Britain who had not been naturalised were also labelled 'enemy aliens' after Italy entered the war as an ally of Germany in June 1940.[69]

Between September and December 1939 one hundred and twenty tribunals were set up by the Home Office across Britain with the task of examining and dividing all 'enemy aliens' into three categories: A (to be interned); B (to remain at liberty, but subject to some restrictions); and C (to be exempt from internment and from restrictions). The vast majority of 'enemy aliens' were allocated to Category C (about 73,400), although approximately six hundred had been interned.[70] By the spring of 1940, however, with the apparently real and imminent threat of a German invasion, pressure grew upon the British government to order the mass internment of 'enemy aliens', as had been carried out in the First World War.[71] Males and females in Category B were interned in May, while the detention of all German and Austrian males in Category C was ordered in late June.[72] In all, by the summer of 1940 around twenty-eight thousand 'enemy aliens' had been interned, most of whom were Jews.[73] They were sent to camps in various parts of Britain, the largest of which was the Hutchinson Internment Camp in Douglas, Isle of Man.

Many Jewish refugees residing in Wales during the Second World War were interned as 'enemy aliens'. They included German-born Lothar Bernd Israel Bick, who settled temporarily in Cardiff with his family in 1939 before being deported to the Fredericton Internment Camp in Canada in July 1940, and German-born Eli Dror (b.1923), who came to Britain on the *Kindertransport* in January 1939 and later joined the *hachshara* at Gwrych Castle in Abergele.[74] In May 1940 Eli was sent to the Huyton internment camp near Liverpool and on 10 July he volunteered to board *HMT Dunera* (a passenger ship that carried approximately 2,543 'enemy aliens' to Australia) believing it was safer to take his chances on the high seas than to remain and be persecuted by the Germans if their expected invasion of Britain was successful.[75]

As already mentioned, the Jewish refugee industrialists who set up factories and businesses on the Treforest Industrial Estate in the late 1930s were praised by the British government in the summer of 1939 for their part in helping to revitalise the economically depressed south Wales valleys. However, in May 1940 these 'friendly aliens' who helped 'reduce unemployment' and 'cripple Nazi Germany's export trade', suddenly came under attack by the British authorities. According to a contemporary author with the pseudonym 'Scipio', nineteen of the refugee industrialists, Jewish and non-Jewish, were interned. Seventy-five individuals connected to the industrial estate were also ordered to move away from Cardiff because the city, owing to its docklands and position on the coast, was designated a 'protected area' throughout the war.[76] One of those included Nuremberg-born Wilhelm Jondorf, who ran a greeting cards company in Treforest named 'Cardiff Cards Ltd'. He was arrested in May 1940 and spent almost a year in internment camps, first at Prees Heath in Shropshire and then on the Isle of Man. His family were 'forced to move away' from Cardiff, and relocated to Abergavenny, where they lived for the remainder of the Second World War.[77] Some of Treforest's Jewish refugee industrialists were spared interment, however, because their businesses were deemed beneficial to the war effort. Julius and Moritz Mendle of Mendle Bros. Ltd, for instance, were not interned because their plastic moulding business made goggles for the air force during the war.[78]

Although the policy of internment was gradually reversed by the British government from August 1940 onwards, many people in Wales and throughout Britain continued to misunderstand the special position of Austrian and German Jewish refugees and were therefore unable to differentiate them from German and Austrian nationals, Britain's wartime enemies. Consequently, several Jewish refugees residing in Wales during the war years suffered from xenophobic abuse, including George Schoenmann of Vienna (b.1934) and Austrian-born Robert Krakauer (b.1935), who were both taunted as Nazis and German sympathisers by schoolchildren in Cardiff.[79] To avoid further discrimination, Robert's father, Joseph, anglicised the family surname to Gregory when he was granted naturalisation in 1946.[80] Some Jewish refugees attempted to avoid discrimination by denying their national identity. For instance, whilst living in Gwrych Castle Herman Rothman of Berlin told local Welsh labourers that he was Polish: 'I didn't tell them I was German, that was absolutely murderous, they would have killed me, so I told them I was from Poland'.[81]

Evacuation

In addition to Jewish refugees, Wales witnessed the presence of approximately two hundred thousand evacuated individuals between 1939 and 1945; among them were Jews, both British and non-British, who had been living in England. Enemy bombs had constituted a major threat in Britain since the First World War and from the early 1930s onwards the

British government feared that aerial bombing and the mass destruction of British cities and towns would be a major feature of warfare if the country were to be involved in another conflict.[82] To avoid such a catastrophe, plans were drawn up for an official evacuation of civilians living in urban centres such as Birmingham, Liverpool, Manchester and London to areas of the United Kingdom unlikely to be targeted by bombers. Most of Wales, including the industrial valleys, was designated a 'reception area' as it was assumed that the country was too far west and too rural to suffer from German bombing raids.[83] As Stuart Broomfield points out, 'this was probably a fair judgement to make' in 1939, but as the war progressed parts of Wales, particularly the industrial south-east, could no longer be designated as areas 'safe' from air attack.[84] Indeed, between June 1940 and March 1944 all three of Wales's largest urban centres – Cardiff, Swansea and Newport – suffered severe bombing. While approximately three million people, most of them children, were officially evacuated under the British government's evacuation scheme between 1939 and 1945, large numbers of families and individuals, both Jewish and non-Jewish, made their own arrangements to evacuate to designated safe areas, including those in Wales.

As with the *Kindertransport* children, the experiences of evacuated Jewish children in Wales varied widely. Some went with their schools or with their mothers, while others were evacuated individually or with their families. Many lived with Jewish foster parents or resided in an area with an existing Jewish community, while others, owing to the limited number of Jewish families in Wales able to act as foster parents, lived with non-Jewish families or away from an organised Jewish centre. As Tony Kushner wrote, 'evacuation was a very personal experience'.[85] In September 1939, Maurice Hesselberg was evacuated to Bangor with his school, the Liverpool Institute, and lived with a non-Jewish Welsh couple. Since about sixty of the evacuee schoolchildren were Jewish, members of the Bangor Hebrew Congregation established a kosher canteen in a hut donated by the vicar of St James's Church, Revd J. R. Davis and arranged weekly Sabbath morning services for them at the High Street synagogue.[86] According to Hesselberg, his foster parents respected his religious dietary requirements and they bought him meat every week from the kosher counter at the Vaynol Meat Stores in High Street (though they did not use separate cooking utensils).[87] The experience of other Jewish children evacuated to Wales was very different. In September 1940 Victor Sassoon was evacuated with his family from London to Llandudno, where they rented a small apartment for the duration of the war. Although they had left their Jewish surroundings behind in Stoke Newington, the Sassoons maintained a Jewish way of life in north Wales. They purchased meat from a kosher counter at a butcher's shop in Mostyn Street, attended services at Llandudno's synagogue, and celebrated Victor's *bar mitzvah* in the town in 1942.[88] In contrast, London-born evacuee Malcolm Eagle was billeted with a Baptist couple in Tonypandy in 1940, where in addition to *cheder* lessons, chapel services became part of his weekly routine.[89]

Concerns that Jewish children billeted with non-Jewish foster parents were conforming to Christianity and losing contact with their Jewishness were raised by leaders of south Wales Jewry at a conference held at Cardiff's Cathedral Road synagogue in June 1941. One speaker spoke of his concern that Jewish children were singing in chapel choirs, while another noted how 'the names of children called Cohen and Solomons' featured in a 'list of winners of a church examination'.[90] To prevent the alleged 'proselytizing zeal of non-Jewish foster parents', a hostel for Jewish evacuee children opened at Tan-y-bryn house in Cefn-coed-y-cymmer near Merthyr Tydfil in November 1941.[91] Accommodating up to forty-five children, the hostel was supervised by Revd Chaim Pearl of Liverpool, who, together with his wife Anita, provided religious and Hebrew education to the children.[92]

Given limited funds and accommodation, the Cefn-coed hostel was unable to accommodate a large number of south Wales's Jewish evacuees, and consequently Jewish children in the region continued to be billeted with non-Jewish families and participated in Christian activities. In April 1942, for instance, the *JC* reported that around twenty of the forty Jewish evacuees living in Abertillery regularly attended church or chapel services.[93] To improve the situation, *cheder* classes were organised and held three times a week at the Powell-Tillery Workmen's Hall and Institute, so that the children's religious education and their Hebrew lessons would continue uninterrupted during their evacuation.[94]

Throughout the Second World War, Wales's Jewish population rose quickly with the arrival of both evacuated Jewish children and families from England and refugees from Nazi-occupied Europe, who sought a safe haven in Wales. Unfortunately, the exact figure is unknown; the *JYB* kept no record of the population of British-Jewish communities between 1941 and 1945 'due ... to war exigencies'.[95] However, a sense of

demographic growth can be gleaned from reports in the *JC*. In September
1940, for instance, Llandudno's Jewish population had increased so much
that the synagogue at the Masonic Hall in Mostyn Street was too small to
accommodate local worshippers over the High Holy Days. Indeed, such
was the demand that overflow services had to be held at the schoolroom
of the Wesleyan Ebenezer Chapel in Lloyd Street.[96] With reference to
Bangor, the *JC* reported an 'increasing number of coreligionists in the
locality' in 1940 following the arrival of Jewish schoolchildren from the
Liverpool Institute and Jewish students from the University College of
London who were relocated to the University College of North Wales, in
addition to refugees and evacuated families such as Dutch-born Albert
Monnickendam and the Shafrans from London.[97]

In some instances, the influx of evacuated Jews in Wales during the
Second World War led to the resurrection of defunct Jewish communities.
Rhyl's Jewish community had disintegrated around 1907, but the arrival
of evacuated Jewish individuals and families from Liverpool and
Manchester, as well as Jewish servicemen stationed at Kinmel Park Camp
during the Second World War, led to a revival of Jewish life in the town.[98]
In 1941, there were enough Jews in Rhyl for a small synagogue situated
above Lloyd's Bank in Queen Street to be consecrated, with Revd Louis
Israel from Manchester serving as the congregation's first, and only, full-
time minister.[99] Also catering for evacuated Jewish families living in
nearby Abergele, such as the Burmans and Beelines of Liverpool, the
synagogue hosted five *b'nai mitzvah* (plural of *bar mitzvah*) and a wedding
between 1941 and 1943, and featured a recreation room for Jewish servicemen stationed in the area.[100]

As well as reviving defunct Jewish centres, the arrival of evacuated Jews
in Wales between 1939 and 1945 led to the establishment of new Jewish
communities. In late 1939, many Jews from Liverpool and Manchester
moved to the safety of Colwyn Bay on the north Wales coast and formed
a congregation in the town in 1940.[101] Congregants initially met for
worship in improvised spaces, including classrooms adjoining the English
Presbyterian Church in Conway Road, until a permanent synagogue was
secured in a Victorian house in Princes Drive by Mark Bloom, originally
from Manchester, in 1943.[102] Named 'Zion House', the synagogue catered
for around one hundred members and featured *cheder* classrooms and a
social centre that hosted dances and meetings for the town's Jewish
Literary and Social Society.[103] In 1942, Revd David Wolfson of Bangor

was appointed the congregation's first minister and was succeed by Revd Louis Kushell, who served as a part-time minister and reader from the late 1940s until his death in 1967.[104]

While the Jewish communities formed in Rhyl and Colwyn Bay during the Second World War remained in existence after hostilities had ended, many of them dispersed after the war. At the outbreak of war, for instance, students from University College London, many of them Jews, were evacuated to the University College of Wales, Aberystwyth, where they established a temporary synagogue at 5 King Street. They eventually returned to London in the summer of 1940, as the threatened bombing had not materialised.[105] Similarly, Jewish families evacuated to Builth Wells, including the Fligelstones of Cardiff and the Rashbasses of London, held religious services in a Baptist church in the town between 1941 and 1942, while evacuated Jews in Llandrindod Wells such as the Bolsom and Wix families from London held High Holy Day services at the Friends Meeting Hall in High Street and made arrangements for *cheder* lessons for over thirty evacuated children between 1940 and 1943.[106] At the end of the war, these Jewish families returned to their respective homes.

It is impossible to generalise about the treatment evacuated Jews received in wartime Wales, since individual and group experiences varied from place to place. As we have seen, various Christian congregations in Bangor, Builth Wells, Llandrindod Wells, Llandudno and Colwyn Bay offered their facilities for Jewish services, which suggests that relations with the local non-Jewish population were relatively harmonious. Indeed, a number of evacuated Jews had pleasant memories of their stay in Wales, despite their religious differences. For example, Ray Sopher of Manchester recalled 'everybody [being] very friendly' in Colwyn Bay because the locals sympathised with the plight of the evacuated individuals and families, while Frank Schwelb, one of the many Jewish students at the evacuated Czech School at Llanwrtyd Wells between 1943 and 1945, remembered 'with particular affection the Welsh people who welcomed' him and his classmates 'so warmly during [their] time of need'.[107] The good relations can possibly be explained by the fact that the Czech school reached out to local society. Townspeople were often invited to cultural evenings and school plays, for instance, while a number of the evacuated teachers and pupils regularly attended dances and other social events held in the town.[108]

Other evacuated Jews complained of anti-Jewish bigotry in some areas, however, particularly from individuals in towns and villages which had

had little, if any, previous contact with Jews. At the outbreak of the Second World War, London-born Ruth Fainlight was evacuated with her mother to 'a small coal-mining village in south Wales', and was stunned to find that a number of villagers refused to believe they were Jews because they had no horns:

> No one in the village seemed to have met or had any personal contact with a Jewish person before. We were told that we could not possibly be Jews ... Jews had horns. Early on in the school year someone reached up to feel my head. When I asked what was going on, the girl laughed embarrassedly and ran away. We did not have horns, so how could we be Jewish?[109]

Moreover, some individuals resented the influx of evacuated Jews to Wales, claiming that they were both burdensome and exploitative. In June 1941, for instance, Dr John Roberts of the Presbyterian Church of Wales wrote of his resentment of rich Jews from London and the north-west of England who evacuated to the north Wales coast, claiming that they were monopolising all available goods and local housing in the region.[110] His views echoed those of Welsh politician and academic William J. Gruffydd, who in 1941 published a scathing article about evacuated Jews living in north Wales that drew heavily on age-old anti-Jewish stereotypes of Jewish financial exploitation and greed. He wrote:

> North Wales is full of rich and crafty Jews who lap up all the resources of the country and leave the poor natives deprived and helpless ... is it not time for someone to protest openly against these Jews who have become a burden on Llandudno, Colwyn Bay and Abergele and the surrounding countryside? ... they have two main aims, and two alone – escaping from every danger in every place whatever the danger to other people, and carrying forward their old traditional manner of enriching themselves on the weakness of the gentile.[111]

The influx of evacuated individuals and families from England, both Jewish and non-Jewish, became a grave concern for a number of people in Wales, particularly those living in predominantly Welsh-speaking areas, who feared that their arrival would threaten the Welsh language and its culture. One of the most vocal speakers on the issue was the former leader of Plaid

Genedlaethol Cymru, Saunders Lewis, who once called evacuation 'one of the most horrible threats to the continuation and to the life of the Welsh nation that has ever been suggested in history'.[112] Such condemnations were later expressed by Lewis in his poem 'Golygfa mewn Caffe' ('Scene in a Cafe'), where he describes the unwelcome presence of evacuated individuals and families from England in Aberystwyth in 1940. With references to 'Whitechapel's lard-bellied women, Golders Green Ethiopians' (two areas of London with significant Jewish populations at the time) and 'kosher vinegar', Lewis clearly targeted evacuated Jews from London, whose presence in Wales, like that of evacuated non-Jews from England, was allegedly impinging on Welsh cultural life and values.[113] However, while there were at times strong feelings against evacuated Jews in wartime Wales, it is important to note that such resentment found little support and did not break into violence.

Jews in the Armed Forces

As well as receiving and aiding both refugees from Nazi-occupied Europe and evacuated Jews from England, Welsh Jewry played its part in the war effort by joining the armed forces. As was the case in the First World War, a disproportionate number of British Jews joined the forces during the Second World War– 17 per cent of British Jewry or 60,000 men and women compared to ten per cent of the British population as a whole.[114] The pressure faced by Jewish immigrants and their children to prove themselves devoted and loyal British citizens partly explains why the Jewish military war effort was so great. However, it is possible that a heightened sense of patriotism amongst second- and third-generation British Jews was also a factor. Typical is Harry Poloway (1915–2016) from Newport, who voluntarily joined the Royal Air Force in 1940 because he wanted to 'do his bit' for his country.[115]

While some Jewish men and women in Wales were called up for military and civil defence service between 1939 and 1945, many volunteered for duty and served with distinction. Among them were Marjorie Rivlin of Cardiff, who volunteered for the Women's Royal Naval Service; Captain Ronald H. Bernstein from Swansea, who volunteered to join the Royal Air Force in 1942, and was awarded the Distinguished Flying Cross in 1944 'for gallant and distinguished services in Italy'; Ammanford-born solicitor Sylvia Cohen, who was awarded the Medal of the British Empire for providing voluntary services for the armed forces legal aid scheme; and Sergeant Philip D. Phillips of Newport, who joined the Territorial Army in 1938 and served with the Royal Artillery in France and Germany throughout the Second World War.[116]

It is estimated that around 2,000 British-Jewish servicemen and women were killed during the conflict of 1939–45, and Welsh Jews were among the casualties.[117] The Cardiff United Synagogue, for instance, lost twenty-five of its congregants in battle, including 17-year-old Steward L. Phillips of the Merchant Navy who 'drowned at sea' in December 1944.[118] Members of other Welsh-Jewish communities were also killed in service, including 34-year-old aircraftman Israel P. Benjamin from Merthyr Tydfil, who was reported killed in action in May 1942 and Sergeant Henry E. Jacobs of Newport, a wireless operator and air gunner for the Royal Air Force Volunteer Reserve, who was reported killed in action in October 1941.[119]

Providing that their application was approved by the Military Intelligence Branch of the War Office, refugees were granted permission to enter the British armed forces in November 1939. Many were eager to join the fight against Hitler, though at first they were only allowed to serve in the Auxiliary Military Pioneer Corps (renamed the Pioneer Corps in 1941), an unarmed military unit that provided general labour for the British army.[120] Although this was a setback for those wishing to fight Nazism, from 1940 onwards joining the Pioneer Corps became an attractive option for many refugees as it meant an early release from internment.[121] During the war some 4,000 Jewish refugees enlisted and among them were some who resided in Wales or had been sent there to work.[122] They included Stephen Dale, born Heinz Spanglet in Berlin in 1917, who joined the Pioneer Corps in 1942 and was assigned to fix draining pumps in various locations in Wales, such as the defensible barracks in Pembroke Dock and an engineering camp in Aberaeron.[123] Though they were non-combatants, some of the pioneers were engaged in dangerous tasks, such as deactivating bombs and land mines. With little, if any, experience in such operations, explosions often claimed the lives of many. In April 1942, for instance, three Jewish refugees – Corporal Heinz Abraham and Privates Ludwig Rosenthal and Heinz Schwartze – were killed by an explosion during a training exercise on landmines at the defensible barracks in Pembroke Dock.[124]

Enlisting in the Pioneer Corps provided refugees between the ages of sixteen and fifty with an opportunity to demonstrate their loyalty to and support for the Allied cause, and from 1942 onwards Austrian and German refugees were permitted to enlist directly into technical units and the Special Forces. As the war progressed they were admitted to all branches of the British armed forces and played an increasingly important part in Britain's war effort.[125] Given their knowledge of the enemy culture and their fluency in German, some Jewish refugees from Germany and Nazi-occupied Europe were specially selected by the British Army for secret commando operations. In 1942, for instance, Lord Louis Mountbatten, then head of Combined Operations and of German extraction himself, devised a plan to form a clandestine British commando force, consisting largely of German and Austrian refugees who would work as interrogators and military intelligence experts in enemy territory. Formed in autumn 1942, the group was officially named No. 3 Troop of No. 10 (Inter-Allied) Commandos (nicknamed 'X-Troop' owing to its secrecy), and was led by a Cambridge language graduate from Caernarfon named Captain Bryan Hilton-Jones.[126] One hundred and thirty men, 86 of whom were German-speaking refugees, were recruited and billeted in the secluded seaside village of Aberdyfi in Gwynedd, where they adopted British sounding names (to disguise their German/continental origins) and underwent strenuous training in the mountains of Snowdonia for nine months.[127] Enrolment in the troop was purely voluntary and it appears that revenge against Nazism, a regime that aimed at destroying them, motivated most, if not all, of the refugee soldiers to join. Jewish soldier Ian Harris (formerly Hans Hajos) from Vienna, for instance, 'couldn't wait to fight the Nazis' because he 'knew they would have killed [him] and [his] family if [they] had stayed in Austria'.[128]

Ultimately the troop never fought as a unit; many were deployed alone or in small groups in and behind the front line in the islands of Crete and Sicily and mainland Italy.[129] The troop disbanded in 1944 and its members were attached to other military units just prior to D-Day. Of the forty-four men of No. 3 (Miscellaneous) who landed on the shores of Normandy on 6 June 1944, twenty-four were killed or wounded and three listed missing.[130] The Jewish casualties included Austrian-born Eugene Fuller (Eugen von Kagerer-Stein), who was accidentally killed by an American bomb on 13 June 1944, and German-born Ernest Lawrence (Ernst Lenel), who, on 22 June 1944, disappeared while on a solo patrol to identify German units.[131]

Of course, this is not to suggest that all Welsh Jews or Jewish refugees residing in Wales were supportive of Britain's war efforts or warfare more generally during the first half of the twentieth century. It is impossible to be certain how many of them were opposed to war during this period, but we know that, like a number of non-Jews in Wales some were strongly pacifist in orientation. Kate Bosse-Griffiths, for instance, the Lutheran-raised German novelist and scholar who fled Nazi Germany in 1936 after being persecuted for having a Jewish mother and settled in the Rhondda in 1939 following her marriage to a non-Jewish Welsh-speaking academic named J. Gwyn Griffiths, was a staunch pacifist due to her religious convictions as well as her own personal experiences of violence and persecution.[132] Together with her husband, Kate was active in pacifist and literary circles, including *Cylch Cadwgan* (Circle of Cadwgan), in south Wales during the Second World War, and in 1943 she published a pamphlet on the history of German pacifism on behalf of the Welsh-language pacifist society, Heddychwyr Cymru.[133]

The pacifist convictions of the Ystalyfera author Lily Tobias and her Polish-Jewish family had been partly informed by their politics (they were staunch socialists and saw the First World War as an imperialist conflict in which workers had to fight on behalf of the ruling classes) and partly by their religious principles (Judaism's objection to violence is based on many Biblical and Rabbinical texts). The family's patriarch, Tobias Shepherd, had fled from forcible conscription by the Tsarist army in the late nineteenth century,[134] and while many Welsh Jews, including Lionel Freedman of Merthyr Tydfil and Reuben Auban of Swansea, fought on the front line during the First World War as volunteers and conscripts, Lily Tobias's brothers, Solomon, Joseph and Isaac, were three of approximately 5,000 British conscientious objectors (Jewish and non-Jewish) to suffer imprisonment between 1916 and 1918, when they refused to be conscripted into the military on political and religious grounds.[135]

The years between 1933 and 1945 saw a remarkable transformation in Welsh Jewry. With the arrival of Jewish refugees from Nazi Germany and Nazi-occupied Europe, the period witnessed the first, and final, mass migration of Jews to Wales in the twentieth century. Like their Eastern European predecessors, the German and Central European Jewish refugees contributed greatly to both the established Jewish population of Wales and to Wales as a whole. Although they were also Ashkenazi Jews, they were generally more assimilated, better educated and wealthier than their Eastern European counterparts, and their arrival contributed to both the diversification and the embourgeoisement of the indigenous Jewish communities. As we have seen, the business acumen many of them possessed was of particular benefit to the economically depressed region of south Wales. A number of Jewish refugees in Wales, and Welsh Jews more generally, also contributed to the British war effort either on the home front or in the armed forces.

Initially, Jewish refugees were warmly welcomed by the Welsh population, but as war approached many Austrian and German Jews in Wales were treated with suspicion, as were a number of evacuated Jews from England. The presence of the latter further augmented Wales's Jewish population and resulted in the establishment of five wartime Jewish communities. While the return of evacuated Jewish families to their home towns and the onward migration of refugees to other countries such as the United States, both during and immediately after the war, led to the eventual decline and demise of some of these communities, a number of displaced Jews stayed and came to call Wales 'home'. Typically, it was those refugees and evacuated individuals who had established businesses or found employment in Wales before or during the war who stayed on. In 1963, for instance, the *JC* commented that 'very few of the [refugee] firms who were at Treforest before the war have in fact left Wales', while Philip Shafran, who was evacuated to Bangor with his family during the war, stayed there after 1945 because he had established a successful delicatessen business on the High Street.[136]

4

Jewish and Non-Jewish Relations in Wales

T HE history of race and ethnic relations in Wales is surrounded by
myths. In particular, Wales has often been perceived by both the
Welsh and the non-Welsh as a nation that is devoid of racial prejudice and
intolerance.[1] There are a number of reasons for this. According to
Charlotte Williams and Neil Evans, it stems primarily from the late nineteenth-century myth of the *gwerin* (common folk), the idea that Wales,
unlike England, was composed almost entirely of working-class people
who were brought together by religion (Nonconformity) and formed a
united, democratic and empathetic nation.[2] The relatively low concentration of ethnic minorities in Wales and the widely held notion that racial
prejudice and intolerance are only significant in areas of Britain with high
ethnic minority settlement, such as England, and particularly London,
have fostered this idea.[3]

The myth of Welsh tolerance also stems from the perception of Wales
as an 'internal colony' of England, first proposed by Michael Hechter in
1975.[4] There is a long-held belief that the Welsh, having been economically and culturally 'oppressed' by the English for centuries, are inclined to
empathise with other oppressed people and minorities.[5] As Sandra Betts
and Charlotte Williams point out, 'the Welsh national character is
portrayed as anti-imperial, tolerant and internationalist, by contrast with
the English, who are perceived as colonialist and racist'.[6] This suggestion
has, however, has been disputed by many scholars who have examined
Welsh contributions to the British imperial project and come to consider
Wales a core part of the empire rather than a colonial dependency.[7] In
Wales the 'significant other', in terms of self-definition, has long been
England and the English, and as a result the country's longstanding cultural
diversity and its relations with migrants and ethnic minorities, in

particular its experiences of intolerance and racial prejudice, have remained largely unexamined until relatively recently.[8]
This is especially true with regard to Jewish and non-Jewish relations in Wales. Of course, the one exception is the Tredegar riots of 1911 which, as Jasmine Donahaye rightfully points out, has 'in the absence of analysis of other aspects of Jewish history in Wales . . . come to erroneously represent Welsh-Jewish experience and [non-Jewish] Welsh attitudes to Jews . . . more generally'.[9] Since 1911, no further rioting involving Jews is reported to have occurred in Wales, yet casual reading of the available literature can leave a strong impression that the history of the relations between Jews and non-Jews in Wales has been unremittingly negative and hostile.[10]
The Tredegar riots have received the lion's share of attention and historical research needs to move beyond this event and examine the history of relations between Jews and non-Jews in Wales in a wider context.[11] In doing so, we will see that these relations were/are complex and do not fit comfortably within the confines of 'philo-Semitism' or 'anti-Semitism', which is how the subject has been scrutinised by historians until now.[12] These interpretations, however, are far too monolithic, as the history of non-Jewish and Jewish relations, in Wales and elsewhere, is not wholly consistent and does not easily fit into the categories of pro- or anti-Jewish. Drawing on the work of David Cesarani, Bryan Cheyette and others, this chapter examines relations between Jews and non-Jews in Wales through the lens of 'Semitic discourse', an approach that addresses the complexities, ambivalences and context of Jewish and non-Jewish relations, which, as Cheyette once wrote, allows scholars to avoid 'essentializ[ing] Jews as uniquely timeless, unchanging victims', as well as 'position[ing] the history of anti-Semitism outside of the social, political, and cultural processes which gave rise to this history in the first place'.[13] Using Cheyette's theoretical model, this chapter stresses that non-Jewish and Jewish relations in Wales were not fixed, but ever-changing, fluid and context-dependent.
The idea of 'tolerance' also deserves further consideration in this context, because 'tolerance', like 'Semitic discourse', is never absolute; it is a conditional acceptance that paradoxically holds within its reach the possibility of responding both negatively and positively to difference. As Paul O'Leary reminds us, 'toleration presupposes a defined power relationship' whereby minority cultures are 'endured' rather than 'embraced'

by the majority.[14] Thus, while a tolerant society may permit cultural or ethnic 'outsiders' the right to practise their beliefs and customs freely, this acceptance can easily be reversed should the majority feel that their values are being undermined.

A Reverent Curiosity

It is difficult to pinpoint exactly when the indigenous Welsh first came into contact with Jews. As noted in Chapter 1, Jews have been present (and officially absent) in Wales since the Middle Ages, but as most of the country's Jewish communities were not established until the mid to late nineteenth century, it is likely that most non-Jews in Wales would not have encountered Jews until the latter period. Grahame Davies speculates that Welshmen involved in the Third Crusade between 1189 and 1192 were 'likely to have encountered Jewish communities' in the Holy Land, but admits that there are no extant passages from the period 'dealing with the Jews'.[15] Indeed, while Christian Wales would have been familiar with Jewish figures from the Bible, particularly after 1588 when the entire Bible was translated into Welsh for the first time, there may have initially been suspicion among locals when Jewish migrants began to arrive in the nineteenth century, as many had never seen Jews before. By and large, however, surviving evidence suggests that Jewish settlers in nineteenth- and early twentieth-century Wales were treated by their indigenous Welsh neighbours with reverential curiosity.

Indeed, many reports from the Welsh-Jewish communities, particularly at the end of the nineteenth century and the beginning of the twentieth, note the presence of interested or curious non-Jews at synagogue services and other events. During the consecration service of Bangor's synagogue in 1894, for example, it was noted that 'the synagogue was filled by the members, visitors from adjacent towns, and several Christians', while in 1873 the laying of the foundation stone of Newport's Jewish school-rooms was attended 'by a number of Gentiles' who were 'interested in the ceremony'.[16] Similarly, the *JC* reported that during the *Kol Nidre* (opening prayer of *Yom Kippur*) service in Brynmawr in 1899 'a large number of Christians stood outside the temporary synagogue . . . listening in respectful silence to the chaunting [*sic*] of the prayers'.[17] Moreover, the foundation stone ceremony at Llanelli's synagogue in July 1908 was attended by a number of non-Jews, including a

Revd D. E. Rees, who was 'interested in the ceremony' because 'he was well acquainted . . . with the Jewish people through his Bible'.[18]

Jewish weddings were also reported with breathless curiosity in local Welsh newspapers. In 1856, for instance, the *Cardiff and Merthyr Guardian* described a 'very imposing' Jewish wedding in Merthyr Tydfil that 'attracted a good deal of attention' from non-Jewish locals, while the *North Wales Guardian* noted that 'the first Jewish wedding celebrated in Wrexham' took place 'in the presence of a large number of onlookers'.[19] Similarly, in 1912 the *Carnarvon and Denbigh Herald* featured a lengthy article on the Jewish wedding of Willie Crystal and Pauline Goldman in Caernarfon. Being 'the first ceremony of its kind ever celebrated in the town', the event 'created unusual curiosity' with 'hundreds of people assembled to watch the arrival of the wedding party to the Guild Hall'. At the reception, Isidore Wartski of Bangor noted that 'he was very glad to find so many of their . . . neighbours present, as it showed there were no feelings of animosity, but of good fellowship'.[20] Indeed, such examples demonstrate that although the indigenous Welsh were curious about their Jewish immigrant neighbours, they were respectful and tolerant of their religious customs and traditions.

Reactions to Jewish Concerns

As well as tolerating Jewish cultural and religious activities, a large number of non-Jews in Wales were sympathetic to and supportive of Jewish issues, particularly the persecution of Jews in Eastern Europe during the late nineteenth and early twentieth centuries, which produced energetic protests in Wales against the oppression of Russian Jewry. Protest meetings against the 'terrible persecutions of the Jews in Russia and to express public sympathy with the sufferers' were held in Cardiff and Merthyr Tydfil in 1882, for example, while in 1905 many of Swansea's non-Jewish residents generously supported a charity appeal to provide shelter for Jewish families affected by the pogroms in Odessa.[21] Moreover, in response to the Beilis affair of 1913, when a Ukrainian Jew was falsely accused of ritual murder in Kiev, a number of non-Jews in Swansea sent 'letters of protest' and 'sympathy' to the town's Jewish community.[22]

Neither was the virulent anti-Semitism and oppression of Jews in Nazi Germany overlooked by the non-Jewish Welsh. The Nazi boycott of German Jewish businesses in April 1933, for example, led to two mass protest meetings in Pontypridd and Swansea.[23] According to the *JC*, the presence of 2,000 people at Pontypridd's meeting 'undoubtedly' showed that 'the whole of the Welsh Valleys were aroused in sympathy with the German Jews'.[24] Non-Jewish organisations throughout Wales also displayed their sympathy by inviting local Jews to speak about the persecution of Germany Jewry under Nazism. In 1938, for example, Port Talbot's Jewish minister, Revd Maurice Landy, addressed the local Young Methodist Guild on 'The Position of German Jews from 1933 to 1938', while in March 1940 Bangor's Jewish minister, Revd David Wolfson, spoke to the local branch of the international Christian movement, 'Toc H', where 'deep sympathy was expressed by several [non-Jewish] speakers with the persecuted Jews in Germany and Poland'.[25]

At the same time as the non-Jewish Welsh were openly condemning the Nazi persecution of Jews, Britain was plagued by the activities of Oswald Mosley's British Union of Fascists (BUF), one of the largest and most well-known British movements hostile to Jews during the twentieth century.[26] Although the BUF came to south Wales in 1934, scholars are in general agreement that the party made little headway in the region.[27] Indeed, BUF meetings and rallies held in south Wales were often not well attended and great disapproval of them was expressed by the local population. When Mosley addressed a meeting in Pontypridd in May 1936, for instance, 'a special force of 250 police was drafted in . . . to protect the Fascists', while a month later a large anti-fascist rally took place in Tonypandy, where blackshirts were mobbed by a crowd of two thousand people.[28]

The main impetus behind the anti-fascist campaigns in south Wales was provided by working-class organisations, particularly the Communist Party, which opposed the BUF's far right policies, but the BUF's anti-Jewish stance was certainly disapproved by many non-Jews in south Wales.[29] For example, former Cardiff councillor G. N. W. Thomas delivered a speech against the BUF in October 1936, in which he 'defended the Jews, and said Parliament should pass an Act to stop any person maligning any section of the community'.[30] Similarly in December 1936, the *JC* applauded Cardiff County Council's decision to forbid the BUF from using any 'expressions of hostility to the Jews' at their meetings in the city, while in August 1936 the Merthyr Watch Committee objected to Fascist meetings on the ground that 'local Fascists had threatened respectable citizens, Jews and non-Jews, with personal violence'.[31] The following year, L. J. Cumming, the district leader of the BUF in south Wales, resigned because of the party's increasingly anti-Jewish position.[32]

Nonetheless, the concentration of the BUF's speeches on anti-Semitism and the passive support they received from a small number of Cardiff shopkeepers (most likely due to the BUF's claims that Jewish tradesmen were competing economically with their British counterparts) led the city's *JC* correspondent, Henry Samuel, to call for a 'well-organised [Jewish] Defence Committee to deal with local anti-Semitism' to be formed in September 1936.[33] No such committee materialised, however, because it soon emerged that the BUF had little support in Cardiff. For instance, following the low turn-out 'of some thirty people' (of whom around thirteen were Jews) to hear BUF member 'Mick' Clark speak in Cathays Park in June 1937 and the audience's lack of enthusiasm for his anti-Jewish remarks, Samuel reported that 'I don't think we have much to fear in this city from . . . a fast-diminishing group of Blackshirts'.[34]

Politics and Sport

Perhaps the ultimate manifestation of the acceptance of Jews by non-Jews in Wales was the participation of the former in the political and civic life of the towns and cities in which they resided. Indeed, almost every Welsh-Jewish community could claim at least a few congregants who became councillors, mayors and the like. In Bangor, Isidore Wartski, a councillor for fifteen years, served as the city's mayor between 1939 and 1941, while Russian-born Morris Cohen was elected chairman of Ammanford council between 1925 and 1939.[35] Similarly, Brahem Freedman of Swansea and Lionel S. Abrahamson of Newport were elected councillors in 1896 and 1898 respectively, while Henry Cohen was re-elected to the Aberdare Urban District Council in 1923.[36]

The pattern of political service established by Jews in early twenti-eth-century Wales continued throughout the century. Vicki Lazar of Llandudno became mayor of Aberconwy in 1978, for instance, while Jack Pollecoff served as Pwllheli's mayor between 1967 and 1969.[37] In 1987 Julius Hermer was elected Cardiff's first Jewish mayor, while Labor Dennis of Burry Port, a cinema-owner, was chairman of the local urban district council in both 1949 and 1966.[38] More recently, Mark Michaels was made mayor of Montgomery in both 2006 and 2012, while Cedric Rigal was elected both mayor of Conwy and Constable of Conwy Castle in 2012, the first Jew in Wales to hold the dual title.[39]

As well as being involved in local government, Jews have served as members of parliament for Welsh constituencies, with three Jews to date having served as Welsh MPs:[40] Cardiff-born Leo Abse, Labour MP for Pontypool and Torfaen between 1958 and 1987; Burnley-born Alex Carlile, Liberal and Liberal Democrat MP for Montgomeryshire between 1983 and 1997; and Lancashire-born Alfred Mond, son of German-Jewish industrialist Ludwig Mond and managing director of the Mond Nickel Company in Clydach between 1902 and 1923, who served as Liberal MP for Swansea Town and Swansea West between 1910 to 1923, and Carmarthen from 1924 to 1928 (he became a Conservative in 1926).[41]

Although Abse and Carlile faced no problems in being elected MPs, Mond's political career in Swansea was not without difficulties. During the 1910s his German-Jewish identity came under attack, particularly from his political opponents. Indeed, to understand fully the hostilities Mond faced, one must place them in the context of the Germanophobia that hit Britain before and during the First World War, as well the Jewish-Bolshevik conspiracy theory that was one of the results of the 1917 Russian Revolution. During Mond's re-election campaign in 1918, for instance, the *South Wales Daily Post*, then owned by the Unionist candidate for Swansea Town, David Davies, accused him of trading with the German enemy and also claimed that he was secretly funding the Bolshevist cause as part of the global plan of international Jewry to dominate the world.[42] Although Mond was inundated with letters of support, such unfounded claims resonated with some of Swansea's residents, with Mond receiving both anti-German and anti-Jewish remarks from members of the public during his election campaign.[43] Swansea Jewry was appalled by these 'shameful attacks', but in the midst of these ugly conflicts it is important to remember that Mond successfully fought and won his elections in the 1910s.[44] His loss of Swansea West to a Labour candidate in 1923 was not due to anti-Semitism, as some have speculated, but reflected the wider political landscape of south Wales at a time when the majority of Liberal seats, particularly in the south Wales coalfield, gave way to the rising Labour party.[45]

As well as their heavy involvement in the political life of the Welsh towns and cities in which they settled, the historical record suggests that Jews faced little or no problems in becoming members of non-Jewish social and sporting clubs in Wales – further testifying to their successful integration and acceptance by the non-Jewish Welsh. In early twentieth-century Tredegar, for instance, S. Louis Harris was elected secretary for the Tredegar Literary and Scientific Society, while during the same period Julius Prag of Merthyr Tydfil was appointed president of several organisations, including the Liberal Club and the local Chamber of Trade.[46] Many Jews also held high positions in their local business clubs, including glazier Charles Arron, who was elected president of the Aberavon and Port Talbot Chamber of Trade in both 1970 and 1971, and Matt Cohen, who acted as president of the Pontypridd Rotary Club during the 1950s.[47] Welsh Jewry was particularly proud of its involvement in Freemasonry, an organisation that had long barred membership to Jews in Continental Europe and America, and often announced the appointment of their coreligionists to the position of Worshipful Master in the *JC*. Such examples included Joseph Simons and his son S. Simons of Abertillery, who were installed as Worshipful Masters of the Gwent Lodge in 1918 and 1926 respectively, A. I. Freedman of Merthyr Tydfil, who was the third Jew 'within about ten years' to attain the position of Worshipful Master of the Loyal Cambrian Lodge when he was appointed in 1908, and Phillip Pollecoff, who was elected 'Worshipful Master of the St. David's Lodge of Freemasons in Bangor in 1924.[48]

Historians have long recognised the important role played by sport in promoting the social inclusion (or sometimes exclusion) of ethnic minority groups. As Paul O'Leary and Neil Evans commented with reference to ethnic minorities in Wales, 'sport has been a means of socializing individuals' and 'is fundamentally about the drawing of boundaries between those who are considered members of the group and those who remain outside'.[49] Whereas numerous examples exist of Jews being barred from membership of sports clubs in British cities such as Manchester, Glasgow and London, the existing evidence suggests that Jews were generally welcomed and readily accepted by Welsh sports clubs.[50] During the 1930s, for instance, both Louis Littlestone of Pontypridd and Muriel Lermon of Cardiff played for their local golf clubs, while Joe Lazar was elected captain of Llandudno's golf club in 1964.[51] Rebecca and Jack Pollecoff were elected captains of Pwllheli's golf club in 1948 and 1961 respectively, while Maurice Simons was elected captain of the Pyle and Kenfig Golf Club in 1960 after thirty years of membership.[52] Moreover, Izzy Cohen of Ammanford and Hyman Corrick of Swansea both played for their local rugby clubs during the interwar period, while Phyllis Barnet of Bargoed played for the local tennis club, winning several competitions during the

1930s, including the Junior Welsh Tennis Championship in both 1931 and 1933.[53] Welsh Jewry occasionally established its own sports clubs (Cardiff and Newport Jewry formed their own cricket teams in the 1920s, for instance), but there is no evidence to suggest that they were founded in response to anti-Semitism. Rather, they were an expression of community identity and were established on the same lines as other local teams, some of which were organised around particular churches or neighbourhoods.[54]

Although Welsh-Jewish participation in professional sports has been minimal (possibly due to Jewish tradition, which traditionally favours learning and intellectual accomplishments over sporting pursuits), those who did take part met no barriers in developing a sporting career in Wales.[55] Brothers David and Evan James, born to a Jewish mother and non-Jewish father, played rugby for Wales in the 1890s, for example, while Anthony Simons played rugby for the Glamorgan Wanderers before being elected president of Pontypridd's Rugby Club in 1975.[56] More recently, Cardiff-born Joseph M. Jacobson and Israeli-born Dekel Keinan both played for Cardiff City FC, the former between 2006 and 2007 and the latter from 2011 to 2012, while Israeli footballer Itay Schechter played for Swansea City FC between 2012 and 2013.[57] Welsh Jews also faced little or no problem in being elected to and taking up positions as sport administrators. Brothers Philip and Louis Fligelstone of Newport, for instance, were respectively appointed president of the Welsh Amateur Swimming Association and chairman of the Glamorgan County Cricket Club in 1951, while Myer Cohen of Cardiff, a former president and chairman of the Welsh Hockey Association, was elected chairman of the Welsh Games Council in 1978.[58] Similarly, Abraham Freedman, a former Welsh Rugby Union referee and chairman of Swansea Town Football Club, was elected president of the Welsh Football League in 1947 and re-elected in 1962.[59]

However, despite these examples of successful integration, there is no denying that Welsh Jews occasionally faced discrimination fuelled by the insecurities of certain members of the indigenous Welsh middle class, who feared that by associating themselves with upwardly mobile Jewish immigrants they would undermine 'the inherently exclusive milieu of British "clubland"'.[60] Thus, a professional man 'was told to resign' from a country club in Cardiff in 1934 after several weeks of membership because 'he was a Jew', while twenty years later the owner of the Victoria Club in Cardiff declared that 'Jews were not wanted' because her late husband wished for 'no Jewish members'.[61]

Tolerance

How should we explain the relevant tolerance displayed towards Jews in nineteenth- and twentieth-century Wales? There are several possible and interrelated explanations. First, most of Wales's Jewish communities were never significantly large, and all formed a small percentage of the population of the towns and cities in which they were situated. Thus, Cardiff's Jewish community at its peak in the 1960s made up a mere 0.01 per cent of the city's population, while Bangor's Jewish population formed no more than roughly 0.02 per cent of the city's total population.[62] Although Nathan Abrams is correct in pointing out that 'small numbers ... do not guarantee tolerance', the small size of Welsh-Jewish communities did mean that Jews living in Wales were more likely to come into contact and interact with non-Jews on a regular basis than those living in towns and cities with neighbourhoods that were overwhelmingly Jewish in character. Jews 'lived cheek by jowl with non-Jews' from the very beginning, and consequently became known to local society as individuals.[63] For Michael Howard, the small number of Jews in Llanelli meant that the Jewish community was more integrated and less ghettoised than in towns and cities with larger numbers of Jewish residents.[64] Similarly, Rona Hart believed that the small number of evacuated Jews from England who settled and lived in Colwyn Bay during the 1940s and 1950s formed a distinct but non-ghettoised community. Living amongst non-Jews, Rona took on the role of a Jewish ambassador, teaching her non-Jewish neighbours about Jews and Judaism, and thus breaking down any suspicion and ignorance that may have previously existed.[65] In many instances, non-Jews have reported getting along very well with their Jewish neighbours. Typical is the recollection of the author W.C. Elvet Thomas, who wrote of his close childhood relationship with his Jewish neighbours in Canton, Cardiff, in the 1910s:

> They were Orthodox Jews ... Every Friday night, when it became dark, we could see them lighting the candles – their custom to show that the Sabbath had begun ... Feasting was often part of the celebration, and because they were of a generous nature no feast occurred without plenty of fruit and delicacies passing over the garden wall for us ... It is often said that the Jews are miserly but we found them otherwise.[66]

Moreover, Tom Devine argues that Jewish hostility was largely absent in Scotland because most Jews did not compete directly with Scots or others in the labour market, and the same can be argued for Wales to some degree.[67] As we have seen, unlike other immigrant groups in Wales such as the Irish and the Chinese, the vast majority of Jewish migrants were not looking for manual work. Rather, they worked in commercial and skilled trades, such as tailoring and watchmaking (roles they had traditionally occupied in Eastern Europe), and provided consumer services for a predominantly non-Jewish population, which allowed them to interact with customers, as well as contribute to the local economy of towns and villages across Wales. In Bangor, for instance, the Shafran family established a delicatessen store in 1939, which was a first for the city and frequently seen with a long queue of people outside, while in Llandudno Joe Lazar ran a successful and popular department store and was a highly respected and recognised member of the wider community, so much so that when he died in 1985, over six hundred people attended his memorial service.[68] This is echoed by many Jews in Wales, including Herman Jaffa, the then editor of *CAJEX*, who noted in 1961 that the 'good relations with our Gentile neighbours' in south Wales 'is due in no small measure to our conduct in personal and business behaviour'.[69]

It may also be that the Jewish tradition of self-help and charity projected a respectable image of the Jewish community to the wider non-Jewish population, and thus pre-empted any suggestions that Jews were financially burdensome or an encumbrance on public welfare schemes. This is suggested by J. Ronald Williams in his 1926 sociological study of Merthyr Tydfil, in which he writes:

> They [the Jews of Merthyr Tydfil] have been law-abiding citizens and give great assistance to charities and public causes. Their contribution to local life exceeds what one would expect from a small community . . . Although they have never lived in colonies they are strongly united and have always helped those in distress so that no Jew has ever become a charge upon the local Guardians.[70]

Perhaps too, Jews and non-Jews in Wales, particularly those of the latter who are Welsh-speaking, share both a 'cultural empathy' and a perception of themselves as cultural minorities; an identification, which, as Donahaye has recently pointed out, gained momentum during the late nineteenth and early twentieth centuries, when nationalistic thinkers sought to emphasise Wales's particularity within Britain.[71] Such an identification was also highlighted by Welsh Jews during this period, with the *South Wales Jewish Review* featuring a report in 1904 on the performance of D. Emlyn's oratorio 'In Captivity' at that year's National Eisteddfod in Rhyl, which highlighted the speech of the MP for Denbighshire West, John Herbert Roberts, who noted that the subject of the piece – the captivity of the Jews in Babylon – 'had always stirred the hearts of Welshmen' because

> The national life of Wales had passed through many similar phases of experience that fell to the lot of the children of Israel, for they had been kept in isolation for many centuries; but now they had emerged with new hope, broader sympathies, and a wider outlook upon human affairs.[72]

Donahaye dismisses the sincerity of this identification from a Jewish perspective, suggesting that it was conscientiously highlighted by Jews to secure support and reassurance from the host community during a period when pogroms in Russia were increasing and anti-alien feeling, which climaxed with the Aliens Act of 1905, was gaining momentum in Britain.[73] Whatever the truth, such sentiments were also expressed by Jews in times of stability, which suggests that this invented tradition of cultural empathy was genuinely felt by some. In 1963, for instance, Lionel Simmons of Cardiff wrote an article for the *JC* entitled 'The Welsh and Ourselves', which dwelled on the affinities between Jewish and indigenous Welsh culture:

> To say that Welshman and Jews have much in common is a gross under-statement: culturally, spiritually and socially the similarity of the two peoples is remarkable . . . Over the centuries the Welsh . . . have clung stubbornly to their traditional way of life, habits and customs, refusing to be swamped by the dominant environment . . . Like the Jew, he is intensely proud of his heritage, his kinsmen and the Land of his Fathers . . . Like the Jew, he is often the butt of detractors and revilers . . . Common nobility through common sufferance is matched by similarity of temperament.[74]

Finally, non-Jewish Welsh tolerance towards Jews may be attributable in part to the emphatically Old Testament focus of the Nonconformist denominations that made up the greater part of Welsh religious affiliation from the late eighteenth century to the mid-twentieth; this resulted in Jews being perceived with pious admiration as the 'People of the Book', while there was also a perception of the Nonconformist Welsh as descents of the lost tribes of Israel.[75] Although scholars are in agreement that there was nothing specifically Welsh about this affiliation (indeed Abrams notes that it was also a feature of Scottish and American Protestant movements), some, including Grahame Davies, have understood this affinity to constitute an element of an ancient and 'sustained' tradition of a 'Welsh identification with Jews', part of what Dorian Llywelyn once termed the 'Welsh-Israelite' tradition.[76] Nevertheless, as Donahaye rightfully notes, Llywelyn understood this tradition to be an ancient Welsh spiritual and religious identification *as* Jews rather than *with* Jews, and points out that a tradition of 'Welsh identification with Jews' was an invention of a 'more recent vintage', arising in the early twentieth century 'to meet the needs of a contemporary [nationalistic] agenda' that sought to create 'an image of the Welsh nation as a repository of moral purity'.[77]

The most well-known and often-cited example of this Nonconformist affiliation with the Old Testament in early twentieth-century Wales was Prime Minister David Lloyd George, who was raised a Baptist in northwest Wales and later approved the Balfour Declaration of 1917. In a speech to the Jewish Historical Society of England in 1925, Lloyd George stressed that it was the Old Testament basis of his religious upbringing and education in Wales that prepared the ground for his sympathy and support of Zionism:

> It was undoubtedly inspired by natural sympathy, admiration, and also by the fact that, as you must remember, we had been trained even more in Hebrew history than in the history of our own country. I was brought up in a school where I was taught far more about the history of the Jews than about my own land ... five days a week in the day school, and ... in our Sunday schools, we were thoroughly versed in the history of the Hebrews.[78]

This tradition of affiliation between Welsh Nonconformists and the Hebrew Bible did not occur in isolation, however, and was also expressed by Jews in Wales, both past and present. Reflecting on her childhood in early twentieth-century Tredegar, Millie Harris wrote that 'the local [non-Jewish] people were very religious; they respected us [the Jewish community], and always reminded us that we were "the People of the Book"', while the late Ben Hamilton of Merthyr Tydfil stressed that 'Welsh people ... [are] more closely akin to the Jew than probably other people, in their respect of their great affection for the Old Testament'.[79] Similarly, in 1923 Isidore Wartski of Bangor wrote to the Chief Rabbi, claiming that 'Welsh people have a reverence for the "People of the Book" that is perhaps unique'.[80] Although unique in many ways, as we have seen, this religious engagement with Jews was not a strictly Welsh phenomenon, nor was it part of an ancient tradition of Welsh identification with Jews, as some have claimed.

As well as a familiarity and engagement with the Old Testament, the pro-Jewish sentiment adopted by many Welsh Nonconformists was reinforced by their opposition to any form of religious persecution (from which they themselves had suffered).[81] In her novel *My Mother's House* (1931), for instance, the Welsh-Jewish writer Lily Tobias describes a pro-Jewish Welsh schoolteacher as 'a conscientious Nonconformist, whose [liberal] principles approved the freedom of another faith'.[82]

Nevertheless, despite evidence that this affiliation has been shared by Jew and non-Jew alike, Geoffrey Alderman and others such as Jonathan Campbell have challenged its sincerity by drawing our attention to the objection of Nonconformists in Blackwood to expressing sympathy with Jewish shopkeepers affected by the 1911 Tredegar riots.[83] According to Alderman:

> when the Monmouthshire Welsh Baptist Association, meeting at Blackwood ... on 6 September, was asked to pass a resolution express-ing sympathy with the Jews, *several* ministers of religion and others took exception to the motion; one delegate argued that 'Resolutions did more harm than good, and they encouraged the Jews. There were about 100 Jews at Tredegar now, and if they had many more resolu-tions they would have 500 there'. The resolution was indeed allowed to drop.[84]

Yet Alderman fails to explain why several Baptist ministers 'took excep-tion to the motion'.[85] The Monmouthshire Welsh Baptist Association did not refuse to express sympathy with Jews because its members were anti-Jewish, as he implies, but because 'the premises of Nonconformists were also looted'.[86] Furthermore, Alderman fails to acknowledge that the anti-Jewish remark made by the one delegate was 'greeted with dissent and loud cries of "Withdraw"' from the floor.[87] However, that such a comment was made in the meeting does alert us to the fact that Nonconformists were not always tolerant of Jews and that the attitude of the former to the latter was considerably more complex than one of 'support and admiration', as Rubinstein has previously suggested.[88]

Tensions and Hostilities

The Jews with whom Nonconformists chiefly identified were the ancient Hebrew people of the Old Testament. Therefore, when examining relations between Jews and non-Jews in Wales it is important to distinguish between what Donahaye has termed non-Jewish responses to 'biblical Jews' and 'post-biblical, historical Jews'.[89] This is because giving prominence to the former does not guarantee a positive attitude to the latter. Although the affiliation between Nonconformists and the Hebrew Bible certainly predisposed many Welsh people to take a positive interest in their Jewish contemporaries, religious admiration did, in some cases, give way to prejudice and intolerance. As mentioned previously, in 1941 W. J. Gruffydd, 'a convinced Nonconformist' and 'a Liberal in his political sympathies', attacked evacuated Jews living in north Wales during the Second World War in his periodical *Y Llenor*, claiming that they were both cowardly and financially exploitative.[90] Similarly, the 1899 travelogue *O'r Bala i Geneva* (From Bala to Geneva) by the Calvinistic Methodist Liberal, Owen M. Edwards, draws on the age-old stereotype of the avaricious and economically exploitative Jew. Following an encounter with Jews in Heidelberg, he wrote:

> Can one justify the hatred of the nations of the Continent towards the Jews? I have thought a great deal before replying – yes, without a doubt. For one thing, their presence has been an obstacle on the road to developing commerce.[91]

More ambivalent in his attitude towards Jews was David Lloyd George. Although his Nonconformist upbringing led him to feel an affinity with the 'People of the Book', Lloyd George was not always accepting of Jews. Along with many other public figures, he readily believed the conspiracy theory that promoted the belief that the Boer War was being fought to protect the profits of cowardly Jewish gold- and diamond-mine owners, declaring in a speech given at Carmarthen in 1899 that the war was fought on behalf of Jewish capitalists who 'ran away as soon as the conflict commenced' and lived 'in the best hotels in Cape Town' where they held 'costly banquets' and displayed 'the richest of diamonds'.[92] A decade later Lloyd George described Edwin Montagu, the under-secretary of state for India and the second Jew to serve in the British cabinet, as a 'dirty coward. Men of that race always are', after Montagu suggested that the National Insurance Bill of 1911 be abandoned.[93] However, anti-Jewish insults such as these were never present in Lloyd George's remarks about his Jewish solicitor Rufus Isaacs, revealing that his acceptance of Jews was conditional. Indeed, there is much truth in Geoffrey Alderman's claim that 'Lloyd George was philo-semitic only when it suited him', with his anti-Jewish sentiments typically surfacing when he felt challenged and threatened by the ethnic 'other'.[94]

Apart from Lloyd George, at least three other examples have been adduced by Alderman to support his argument that there was a long and deep-rooted tradition of anti-Semitism in Wales: the attack on *shechita* in Llanelli in 1904, the 'Jewess Abduction Case' of 1869 and the alleged 'blood libel' at Pontypridd in 1903.[95] Concerning the first, Alderman stated that the attempt to prohibit *shechita* in Llanelli in 1904 was a sign of the 'sheer prejudice [of the non-Jewish Welsh] against the Jewish religion and those who practised it'.[96] The case, however, was raised because of a genuine concern for the welfare of animals and the safety of those using the local abattoir, rather than from motives of anti-Semitism. This is revealed by an article from the *South Wales Daily Post*, which stated:

> steps should be taken to prevent unnecessary pain to animals killed by the Jews at the slaughterhouse. As present they do not stun the animal before its slaughter, but tied it in a most peculiar fashion, which rendered it most dangerous ... to the other people at the slaughter-house ... The chairman (Mr D. H. Edmunds) said he had great respect for these people, and their persuasion, but would not agree to allowing them to carry on acts of cruelty and risking other people's lives.[97]

The alleged 'abduction' and 'forcible' conversion of an eighteen-year-old Jew named Esther Lyons by a Cardiff Baptist minister and his wife in

1868 has been grossly exaggerated by Alderman and Anthony Glaser to support their arguments that Welsh dissenters were coercive in their conversionist actives and therefore religiously intolerant towards Jews.[98] Although Alderman rightly states that Esther Lyons's father took the Baptist minister and his wife to court in 1869, when both were 'found guilty of enticement', he ignores the fact that this verdict was later overturned on appeal in 1870 'on the ground that the evidence was insufficient'.[99] It is clear from a letter that appeared in the *Cardiff and Merthyr Guardian* in August 1868 that Esther Lyons left home voluntarily and consented willingly to her conversion. Although it emerged that the letter was partly written for her, she later insisted 'that they were all [her] own thoughts and sentiments':

> It ill becomes me to enter into a public discussion with my father, but thus much I may publicly declare, that no one has ever made the slightest attempt and still less coerced me to leave my father's house … of my own accord I left his house, and … I have found in Jesus of Nazareth the Saviour of my soul, and have been baptized in His name.[100]

Indeed, the whole affair appears to have been exaggerated by a father who, as Ursula Henriques observed, 'was obviously torn by grief at the loss of his daughter' and ashamed 'that she should be a "*Meshummad* [Apostate]"'.[101]

Reports of a 'blood libel' in Pontypridd were published in the *JC* by an anonymous correspondent in 1903 and it seems that some historians, including Alderman and Henriques, have taken these allegations at face value. Nevertheless, a 'blood libel', which accused Jews of kidnapping and murdering Christian children in order to use their blood as part of Jewish religious rituals, never occurred in Pontypridd. Rather, a rumour circulated that a non-Jewish servant girl employed by a local Jew named Myer Fishout 'had been taken by force into the synagogue, wrapped in a sheet and insulted'.[102] Concerned by what they had heard, a group gathered outside Fishout's house to discuss the matter, some of whom allegedly threatened and verbally insulted any Jew who passed by. Police were called in and the affair quickly died down after the girl admitted that 'she was to go the synagogue and to appear as Jesus "only for a lark"'.[103] Although not caused by any profound contempt for Jews, the incident undoubtedly caused tensions between the town's Jewish and non-Jewish populations.

The fact that non-Jews thought it amusing to mock Jewish religious beliefs served as a reminder that, for all their acceptance as fellow citizens, Jews were slightly out of place in an overwhelmingly Christian milieu. The late Harry Cohen summed up the feeling of Pontypridd Jewry during the early twentieth century by observing succinctly that 'whilst there was no overt anti-Semitism' in the town, Jews 'felt a bit out of place of the community at large'.[104]

Between the 1880s and early 1900s the issue of Jews being 'out of place' in British society became highly politicised when the arrival of between 120,000 and 150,000 poor Eastern European Jewish immigrants gave rise to heightened anti-alien activity in Britain, particularly in East London where over 100,000 Jews resided. Complaints were made that Jewish migrants arrived penniless and dirty, spread diseases, were a burden on the rates and that their concentration in one area led to increased rents. In a period of economic depression, they were also accused of competing with the indigenous population for employment.[105] Anti-alien feeling surfaced as a movement in London in 1886 and culminated in the Aliens Act of 1905, which controlled and restricted immigration into Britain from areas outside the British Empire. Although the act did not apply specifically to Jews, it was primarily designed to stem the influx of Jews from Eastern Europe.[106] The small number of Jewish migrants in Wales during this period meant that the 'alien question' was arguably less prominent there than in London, but this is not to suggest that anti-alien activity was completely absent in late nineteenth- and early twentieth-century Welsh society.

As mentioned previously, although most of Wales's Jewish migrants worked in trade during the late nineteenth and early twentieth centuries and therefore did not compete for employment in the industrial sector, a small number, particularly in the south Wales coalfield, were engaged in primary industry. While Jewish immigrant labourers appeared to have been tolerated for the most part, during periods of heightened xenophobia and paranoia, such as those that occurred in Britain at the turn of the twentieth century, their presence was enough to cause resentment among some of Wales's indigenous labourers.[107] In early 1903, for instance, over two hundred Eastern European Jewish migrants settled in the Gellifaelog district of Merthyr Tydfil and the employment of many of them in the local ironworks was heavily criticised by a reader of the *Western Mail*, who wrote to the editor complaining that:

During the last few months hundreds of foreign Jews, etc. have arrived at Dowlais and Merthyr, and are ousting our own countrymen from various positions in the works, owing to their adaptability and willingness to work for something next to nothing, and the management do not care who they are, providing they can make a good percentage out of their labour.[108]

By the summer of 1903, resentment towards Jewish migrant labourers went beyond malicious attacks in the local press and erupted into open violence when Jewish immigrant employees of the Guest, Keen and Nettlefolds Ltd ironworks in Dowlais were attacked by non-Jewish workers, a number of whom were Irish.[109] The reason for these attacks is not entirely clear-cut. According to contemporary newspaper reports, the Jewish labourers were not attacked because they worked longer hours or undercut wages, since it was found that they worked similar hours and received the same pay as other workmen.[110] However, a letter sent to the *JC* by a Jewish resident of Merthyr Tydfil reveals that a party of Jewish labourers at Dowlais were expected to leave for Canada on 24 August, but failed to do so because the Jewish Board of Guardians did not receive confirmation from the Canadian authorities.[111] Perhaps local workmen or unemployed labourers were waiting to replace these Jewish workers and were angry when they discovered that they were unable to commence their employment. Indeed, an article in the *Merthyr Express* of 12 September 1903 reveals that a contingent of both unemployed militiamen from the Boer War and local workmen were prepared to take the place of these Jewish workers once they departed for Canada.[112]

Although it has been previously stressed that Jewish immigrant traders found niches in the local economy and contributed to the economic prosperity of towns and villages across Wales, there were occasionally times when their non-Jewish counterparts believed that their influence in the retail trade had become too pronounced, an attitude that typically surfaced during periods of social and economic uncertainty. In 1903, for instance, against the backdrop of a burgeoning anti-alien campaign in Britain, a group of indigenous Welsh shopkeepers in Llanelli approached the local council demanding that Jewish immigrants be excluded from the local market to protect their livelihoods and business interests.[113] The council's response is unknown, but it is important to note that this kind of opposition was not being argued upon anti-Semitic lines. Rather, the emphasis was upon a defence of the employment of the indigenous Welsh, which was perceived as being threatened by immigrants who happened to be Jewish.

As well as being on the receiving end of anti-migrant activity, Jews in nineteenth- and twentieth-century Wales occasionally encountered age-old, anti-Jewish stereotyping which, in common with many analyses of Semitic discourse and tolerance, was not an inherently fixed attitude, but a contextual one, typically surfacing when Jews, the ethnic 'other', appeared to be undermining the security and position of the non-Jewish Welsh, the majority population. As has become clear from the writings of W. J. Gruffydd and O. M. Edwards, one prevalent Jewish stereotype present in Wales was that of the grasping, exploitative and avaricious Jew. The origins of this can be traced back to the Middle Ages when European Jews were prohibited from owning land or practising a large number of professions, and were channelled into a narrow range of commercial and middleman occupations, such as moneylending.[114] The position of Jews in the process of moneylending was greatly strengthened by regulations imposed by medieval rulers, who granted them special rights to impose high interest rates. Unsurprisingly, arrangements of this kind fomented popular resentment towards Jews and gave rise to the stereotype of a rapacious, calculating and 'money-mad' people.[115] When such an image first emerged in Wales is unclear, but there are references in Medieval Welsh poetry that use the word 'Jew' in a derogatory manner to denote avarice or callousness. For instance, in his poem '*Rhag Hyderu ar y Byd*' ('Against Trusting in the World') Dafydd ap Gwilym (*fl.* 1340–70) writes of a lover who was cheated of his wealth by an '*Eiddig leidr, Iddew gwladaidd*' ('Jealous thief, a rustic Jew'), while another poem '*I Iesu Grist*' ('To Jesus Christ') also describes Jews as deceiving thieves: '*Iddeon, lladron rhy dwyllodrus*' ('Jews, thieves too deceiving').[116]

The stereotype of the avaricious and cunning Jew gained further credence over the centuries and entered the minds of later generations by the way popular English-language fiction depicted Jewish characters, such as Shakespeare's Shylock, the grasping moneylender who showed no mercy towards gentiles in *The Merchant of Venice* (1596–8), and Charles Dickens's Fagin, the covetous Jewish criminal in *Oliver Twist* (1838). Indeed, the image of the Jew as Shylock flared up occasionally in south Wales during the late Victorian and early Edwardian periods owing to the large number of Jewish migrants engaged in the pawnbroking business.

Although south Wales's Jewish pawnbrokers fulfilled a vital economic role for the working-class population, enabling them to raise money quickly in times of need, their business activities occasionally bred resentment when customers were forced, through necessity, to pledge valuable items at high interest rates to meet pressing financial difficulties. On such occasions, Jewish pawnbrokers were often portrayed by non-Jewish customers as Shylocks, greedy money-grabbers preying on the poor. In 1879, for instance, an anonymous complainant from Aberdare wrote to the *Western Mail* claiming that he had been financially victimised in a local pawnshop owned by 'an avaricious race of men' and 'sanguinary Shylocks'.[117]

Amid all the manifestations of casual stereotyping in Wales, there were also occasional expressions of more flagrant and extreme anti-Jewish attitudes, especially in times of social or economic distress. For instance, in response to the local housing shortage in Merthyr Tydfil in 1903, Hugh Jones, a member of the Merthyr Board of Guardians, wrote to the local press, complaining that Jewish landlords were exploiting the situation by charging extortionate rents for their own financial gain. While Jones's complaints are best understood in the context of increasing anti-alien activity and paranoia in Britain during the early twentieth century, they undoubtedly drew on age-old stereotypes of Jewish financial greed. Jones described Merthyr Jewry as an 'octopus' spreading 'its tentacles in all directions' (a reference to Frank Norris's novel *The Octopus: A Story of California* (1901), which offers a repellent example of the money-obsessed Jew) and claimed that Jewish financial machinations led to the Boer War: 'The German and Russian Jews in Johannesburg embroiled our country in the South African tangle and exploited our empire to satisfy their greed for gold'.[118]

Economic anti-Semitism singled out financial greed as an inherent quality of the Jew and this stereotype certainly featured in the campaign against company unions at the Bedwas Colliery in 1936. During the dispute, much of the miners' frustration was directed against the colliery's Jewish owner, Samuel Instone, who sought to replace the radical South Wales Miners' Federation (SWMF) with the 'non-political' South Wales Miners' Industrial Union.[119] While some of the anger unleashed by the miners may have been justified, it was articulated in the most vitriolic and anti-Semitic of terms. Set against a landscape of economic depression, many miners believed they were being oppressed by an exploitative Jewish capitalist and suggested '[smashing] the Jewish shops [in the locality] because Instone was a Jew'.[120] No such attack occurred, however, as Arthur Horner, the president of the SWMF, took it seriously enough to raise the matter at a coalfield conference, where he threatened to resign if Bedwas workers started any anti-Jewish activity.[121]

More distasteful, and arguably more rooted, were the anti-Jewish senti-ments that appeared in the writings of Saunders Lewis, one of the founders of the Welsh Nationalist Party (Plaid Cymru).[122] An English-born, Welsh-speaking convert to Roman Catholicism, Lewis's political views were heavily influenced by nineteenth- and early twentieth-century right-wing French nationalism, and like many on the right in the interwar period, including T. S. Eliot and Hilaire Belloc, he subscribed to the unfounded conspiracy theory that rootless international Jewish financiers were controlling the economic affairs of nations for their own financial gains.[123] Lewis expressed this belief in various writings during the 1920s and 1930s. In 1926, for instance, he wrote that it was 'Jews who [shaped] the economic ideas of the modern world, men like Marx ... and Mond, men who have not inherited a single tradition of country and commu-nity'.[124] Moreover, in 1933 he praised Adolf Hitler for fulfilling his promise 'to completely abolish the financial strength of the Jews in the economic life of Germany', while his 1939 poem 'Y Dilyw' ('The Deluge') notes of the alleged role played by New York Jewish financiers, with 'their Hebrew snouts in the quarter's statistics', in causing the 1929 Wall Street Crash.[125]

Saunders Lewis's anti-Jewish remarks have received considerable atten-tion from scholars over the last three decades, with the most recent contribution coming from Richard Wyn Jones, who situates Lewis's atti-tude towards Jews under the banner of anti-Semitism, noting somewhat apologetically that he was a man of his time, his 'crude ethnic prejudices, and anti-Semitism in particular, were part of the cultural currency of the era'.[126] Yet, Lewis's attitudes towards Jews were much more complex than this. They were inconsistent, fluid and contextual, and best understood in the context of Semitic discourse.[127] While Donahaye rightfully notes that 'Lewis's hostile statements about Jews seem particularly to concern the stereotype of the international Jewish financier', he appears to have main-tained a clear distinction between his attitude towards Jewish capitalists and Jews more generally.[128] Indeed, although he praised Hitler in 1933 for confronting German-Jewish financiers, that same year Lewis also condemned the general persecution of Jews by the Nazis because 'inno-cent [Jews] were undoubtedly suffering alongside the harmful', i.e. Jewish capitalists.[129] Moreover, the growing intensity of German persecution of Jews in the late 1930s led Lewis to state in 1939 that Nazi Germany's anti-Jewish laws were 'contrary to all principles of justice', while in 1942, as reports on Nazi mass killings of Jews began to reach the allies, Lewis complained of the 'new atrocities committed against the Jews' in Poland.[130] Indeed, the horrors of the Holocaust appear to have changed Lewis's views on Jews completely and from 1945 onwards he abandoned his earlier hostile statements concerning the stereotype of the international Jewish financier in exchange for feelings of sympathy.[131] In 1945, for instance, he described Hitler's 'attack on Jews and his constant belief that the Jews controlled the policies of Russia, England and the United States' as 'something akin to madness'.[132] Thus, to label Lewis as a full-fledged anti-Semite is misleading.

Although Lewis's economic anti-Semitism was never officially adopted by Plaid Cymru, the Welsh Nationalist Party has not been immune from tensions with Jews, particularly when it comes to the party's stance on Israel. While Plaid's published literature from the 1950s and 1960s showed great admiration for the Israeli success in reconstituting the Hebrew language, believing it could be emulated with the Welsh language in Wales, the party's positive attitudes towards Israel began to change in the 1970s in response to the country's engagement in war with its Arab neighbours (Plaid's leader, Gwynfor Evans, was a pacifist) and its occupation of Palestinian territory (the West Bank and Gaza) in 1967. Indeed, despite describing himself as 'a Zionist for most of [his] life ... attracted above all by the revival of the Hebrew language', Gwynfor Evans admitted in 1976 that his party had become 'disturbed by the attitude which Israel had adopted towards the Palestinians and, on occasion, towards her other Arab neighbours'.[133] The party became a focus of anti-Israeli activity, a perception further reinforced when Plaid attempted in 1976 to foster trade links with Libya, a government notably hostile to Israel, as well as the revelation that only one Plaid Cymru MP out of three was listed as pro-Israeli in a 1978 parliamentary survey.[134]

A series of further activities deepened the tension. In 1995, in the run up to the signing of the Oslo interim agreement, which called for an Israeli withdrawal from a small part of the occupied Palestinian territories, concerns were raised in the British-Jewish press when Israeli settlers in the West Bank were described as 'dangerous racists' at Plaid's annual conference.[135] Seven years later, the party's call to boycott Israeli goods in response to the Israeli government's decision to construct a barrier separating Israel from the West Bank caused a stir amongst some members the British-Jewish community, evidenced by the reporting of these events in the front pages of the *JC*.[136] While Plaid's attitudes towards Israel may be construed by some as anti-Semitic (the party is attacking the Jewish ancestral homeland and is therefore anti-Jewish), there is no evidence to suggest that its history of anti-Israeli activity was fuelled by any specific hatred towards Jews or opposition to the existence of Israel. Rather, evidence suggests that the party's anti-Israeli stance, as in the case of many others who criticise Israel, was driven by its disapproval of the Israeli government's policies and actions in the latter half of the twentieth and early twenty-first centuries, its handling of the Israeli-Palestinian conflict in particular.

Anti-Israel sentiments have also been present in Welsh universities and were particularly apparent during the 1970s, following the UN's resolution of 1975 which declared Zionism to be a form of racism. In 1976, several student unions in British universities barred Zionist speakers, including those at the University College of North Wales, Bangor and the University College of Swansea.[137] Although Bangor and Swansea were adamant that they had 'not taken a stand … which could be construed as anti-Semitic' and that they were 'against the political policy of Zionism, not against Jews', the appearance of an article in the latter university's student newspaper that year, which warned of the 'Zionists' plot to conquer the world', certainly drew parallels with the conspiracies found in early twentieth-century anti-Semitic literature such as the *Protocols of the Learned Elders of Zion*.[138] Many British Jews were deeply upset by these events, as is manifested by their extensive coverage in the *JC* and the large number of complaints received from the Union of Jewish Students.[139]

As well as anti-Israeli activity, Welsh Jews were not immune from tension or troubling incidents more generally during the latter half of the twentieth century. In the 1970s and 1980s, for instance, the Jewish cemeteries in Brynmawr and Swansea's were vandalised, but the absence of anti-Jewish graffiti in Brynmawr and the fact that non-Jewish cemeteries were also attacked in Swansea during this period led local Jewry and the police to conclude that the incidences were not anti-Semitically driven.[140] Although right-wing extremism has been minimal in Wales, it has never been absent.[141] In August 1947, for instance, in response to the hanging of two British sergeants in Palestine by the Irgun group, the home of Cardiff's

JC correspondent, Henry Samuel, was daubed with the message 'Jews – Good old Hitler'.[142] Fifty-five years later, Swansea's synagogue was attacked in what was believed by the police and the National Assembly Against Racism to be 'a racially aggravated attack' and the work of neo-Nazis, owing to the destruction of religious items such as *Torah* scrolls and the presence of graffiti referring to Nazi atrocities against Jews.[143]

What conclusions can be drawn about non-Jewish and Jewish relations in Wales? While non-Jews in Wales have certainly not been immune from anti-Jewish prejudices over the years, the surviving records suggest that overt anti-Semitism was not a major feature of Welsh-Jewish life. Indeed, Wales was not a violent place for Jews and anti-Jewish attitudes have been an elusive, low-key affair, perhaps best understood as minor anti-Semitism or, to borrow the words of Geoffrey Field, an anti-Semitism 'with the boots off'.[144] As we have seen, the Jewish community's relations with the wider non-Jewish community in Wales were largely positive and their civil liberties and security were never put in serious jeopardy.

However, the presence of 'minor' anti-Jewish sentiments does reveal that the toleration of Jews was never absolute in Wales. Indeed, while Jewish immigrants generally integrated well into Welsh society, hostility towards them did surface occasionally. But when were non-Jews in Wales most likely to be intolerant of Jews? As O'Leary reminds us, intolerance towards minorities typically increases when they are perceived to be threatening the values and lifestyles of the dominant majority, and although intolerant acts were certainly not daily occurrences in Wales, they tended to surface during periods of great social change, uncertainty and distress, such as an economic depression or a war.[145] This was undoubtedly the case for many Jewish immigrants in south Wales during the first half of the twentieth century, who, as we have seen, encountered anti-Jewish stereotypes and a resentment of them as middlemen in business and/or competitors during times of financial struggle and economic uncertainty. Feelings of paranoia and xenophobia spawned by the insecurities of the First World War also meant that well-integrated and long-respected Jewish figures in Wales such as Sir Alfred Mond felt the sting of intolerance intermittently during the 1910s.

5

Jewishness and Welshness

As mentioned in the introduction, in his study of British-Jewish history, Todd Endelman incorporates 'Welsh Jewry' under the banner of 'Anglo Jewry'. Endelman justifies this decision by stating that 'since the number of Jews who lived in Wales . . . was never large, folding them into "Anglo-Jewry" does not distort the overall picture.'[1] Perhaps it does not distort the overall 'Anglo-Jewish' picture, but folding the Jews of Wales into 'Anglo Jewry' is, as Jasmine Donahaye points out, another kind of distortion because it 'erases the particularity of Welsh Jewish experience' and asserts the English-Jewish experience as the definitive one.[2] This chapter corrects the distortion by exploring how Jews have responded to Wales and how Welsh dimensions have shaped both the experiences and the identities of Jews living in Wales. In doing so, it highlights the important role played by 'place' in the unfolding of Welsh-Jewish – and also British-Jewish – history.

The Welsh Language

Perhaps the most notable factor in distinguishing the experiences of a number of Jews in Wales from Jews in England is their encounter with the Welsh language. As we have seen, many of the first arrivals in the late nineteenth and early twentieth centuries were commercial travellers who were looking for business opportunities throughout Wales. Like their English counterparts, most of them conducted business in English, but regional linguistic variations also made for many different experiences of Jewish peddling in Wales. In Welsh-speaking regions of Wales, such as the north-west, Jewish pedlars would have acquired some knowledge of Welsh. Russian-born Jacob Sugarman, for instance, worked as a travelling clothier in north Wales during the interwar period and 'got to learn to speak Welsh by going in and speaking to the farmers.'[3] Jewish pedlars also acquired Welsh in certain parts of south Wales with high levels of Welsh-speaking ability, including the western valleys. Monty Black, a travelling salesman from Swansea, spoke Welsh to his customers who lived in 'farms across the Black mountain from Brynaman.'[4] In some instances, the children of Jewish pedlars acquired some Welsh in school and brought it home to teach their parents. Born in 1906, Nay Joseph of New Tredegar recalled teaching his father, a travelling draper, 'certain things in Welsh such as *pais*, petticoat, stockings, *sanau*, window, *ffenestr* . . . so that he could go to the . . . Welsh people . . . and [say] '*ti moyn* (do you want) a *pais* (a petticoat)? *Ti moyn sanau* (do you want stockings)?'[5]

These early Jewish pedlars were most often aspiring merchants and, having accumulated sufficient income, some set up businesses and resided in predominantly Welsh-speaking towns. Like their competitors, these small Jewish retailers provided a personal service to their customers, which, in some instances, required them to learn Welsh. One example is draper Phillip Pollecoff of Bangor and his wife, Amelia. The *North Wales Chronicle* reported in 1947 that:

> Mr Pollecoff is well known throughout North Wales, and he now possesses two of the largest businesses in North Wales – Bangor and Holyhead . . . In his early days he learned the Welsh language before English. Mrs Pollecoff has played a very great part in developing the business, she has learned the Welsh language very thoroughly, although she was born in Liverpool and resided there until her marriage.[6]

Some Jewish-owned stores in south Wales also conducted business in both Welsh and English. Hilda Howard (née Kershion) was born in Russia in 1911, but grew up in Llanelli and spoke Welsh fluently. Following their marriage in 1940, she and her husband, Bernard, bought and expanded an existing drapery business, running three shops in Llanelli and Carmarthen. Her son, Michael, recalls that his mother 'certainly spoke Welsh to a lot of customers in the shop'.[7] Another was Bernard Bernstein, a draper from Merthyr Tydfil. During the 1940s and 1950s the Bernsteins operated a fabrics stall at the Abergavenny market, where Wendy Bellany remembers her father speaking Welsh to the family and how delighted he was to meet Welsh-speaking Jews.[8] Some professional Jews who lived and worked in towns and villages across south Wales also had to acquire a working knowledge of Welsh. Simeon Cohen, for instance, 'had to learn Welsh' when he worked as a general practitioner in 1920s Treorchy 'because a lot of his patients . . . didn't speak English'.[9]

Nonetheless, while Welsh was used by some Jews as a language of business and of intercourse with the wider Welsh-speaking population, it never became the language of the Jewish home nor was it passed down to the next generation. The language of the home for the first Jewish settlers would have been a mixture of Yiddish and English, but over time English predominated. Despite speaking Welsh to their housekeeper, Jack and Rebecca Pollecoff of Pwllheli spoke English to each other and to their son, Bernard, while Michael Howard of Llanelli was never taught Welsh by his mother.[10] In Bangor, Russian-born Joseph Bolloten is listed in the 1911 census as speaking both Welsh and English, but his wife and eldest son are noted as speaking only English. Many factors account for this. As English was the language of the majority in Wales and a *lingua franca* in most parts of south Wales, Jewish immigrants were convinced that only by learning English could their children have any hopes of succeeding in their new environment. This was consistent with attitudes toward education more generally in Wales during the late nineteenth and early twentieth centuries, where virtually all formal education was conducted in English, as Welsh was considered an inferior language and an obstacle to progress.[11] Despite using the odd Welsh word or phrase when speaking to his mother, the late Leo Abse once noted that in interwar Cardiff:

> Welsh was regarded as a second class language, it was given as an option in the schools, as to whether you could if you wish, speak Welsh if you wanted to, or French, and the overwhelming majority of us, in accordance with the wishes of our parents, in accordance with the pressures, cultural pressures of the time, chose French, Welsh was really not part of our way of thinking.[12]

As English replaced Yiddish as the *lingua franca* of Welsh Jewry, it was never deemed appropriate to incorporate the Welsh language officially into synagogue services in Wales. As we have seen from the example of the Cardiff Old Hebrew Congregation (see Chapter 2), although Hebrew remained the liturgical language of service for Orthodox congregations, from the mid-nineteenth century onwards Welsh synagogues, like synagogues elsewhere in Britain, adopted innovations, including English sermons and an English prayer for the royal family to create a form of Judaism that was better suited to an English-speaking milieu.[13] In 1948, the newly established Reform congregation in Cardiff, the Cardiff New Synagogue, took these innovations to a new level by conducting religious services in both Hebrew and English, in recognition of the fact that English was the vernacular language of its congregants. Although a Welsh-language prayer for Wales was introduced into Sabbath services in 1982 by the congregation's American-born rabbi, Kenneth Cohen, a man who showed a 'great love for Wales, its language, culture and traditions', it proved short-lived, since congregants were unable to pronounce or understand the text.[14]

All this having been said, however, it remains true that a small minority of Jews in Wales speak Welsh as their first language and have incorporated their mother tongue into established religious ceremonies. Between 2001 and 2007, for example, Rita, Nia and Ffion Bevan of Carmarthen celebrated their *b'not mitzvah* (plural of *bat mitzvah*, a Jewish girl's coming-of-age ceremony) at the Cardiff Reform synagogue, where in addition to reading and reciting in English and Hebrew they read a Welsh-language poem written especially for the occasion by the poet, Mererid Hopwood.[15]

Arts and Culture

As well as engaging with the Welsh language, many Jews who lived and live in Wales have displayed an interest in Welsh arts and culture, and have produced creative work reflective of their experiences in the country. Considering the small size of Welsh Jewry, which numbered no more than about five thousand at its peak in 1920, Jewish Wales has contributed much to the field of Welsh- and English-language literature with a number of works set in Wales and exploring the relationship between Welshness and Jewishness.[16] Although Wales features in only a minority of her books, *Brothers* (1983) by Cardiff-born Jewish novelist, Bernice Rubens (1923–2004), explores the Jewish migrant experience in south Wales in the late nineteenth and early twentieth centuries, where parallels with her own ancestry are drawn. Despite Michael Woolf's suggestion that the novel's setting could be in 'Rubens' native Wales or any other small town' in Britain, the significance of the Welsh context is evident throughout the novel, as Donahaye has pointed out.[17] In one scene, for instance, Rubens draws on what she perceives to be the affinities between Welsh Nonconformism and the Jewish religion, while a section on the 1913 Senghennydd mining disaster draws parallels between the suffering and resilience of Welsh miners and the Jews of Eastern Europe.[18]

Perhaps one of the most influential Welsh-Jewish writers of the twentieth century was Cardiff-born Dannie Abse (1923–2015). Although he lived most of his adult life in London, where he worked as a physician, Wales became the subject of a great deal of his literary work, particularly the relationship between his Welshness and Jewishness.[19] Describing himself as a 'five feet eight and a half Welsh-Jew' with 'two roots, that of Dafydd as well as David', he found that to be both Welsh and Jewish was to belong to a double minority.[20] In his autobiographical narrative, 'Survivors', for example, Abse recalled a visit to a London cafe frequented by German-Jewish refugees, where he discovered that very few Jews were aware of their Welsh coreligionists:

> 'So, you're Velsh', he said. I felt constrained to say that I was a Welsh Jew. He did not seem to know, until that moment, Welsh Jews existed. This information, of course, did not embarrass him. On the contrary, I became, suddenly, an exotic. I was introduced all round: 'He's a Velsh Jew.'[21]

Jews born beyond Wales's borders have also contributed to the Welsh literary scene. Judith Maro (1919–2011), for instance, will best be remembered as an Israeli novelist who immersed herself in Welsh-language culture.[22] Raised in British Mandate Palestine, Maro married the sculptor Jonah Jones in 1946 and settled in the Llŷn Peninsula in north Wales in the late 1940s. The Biblical toponymy of Wales was often referenced in her work and she found many similarities between the rugged landscape of north Wales and that of Palestine.[23] Equally important to Maro was the Welsh language, and despite not speaking it fluently she insisted that all her books be translated into Welsh before appearing in English. Her fluency in Hebrew, a language revived as a modern instrument of communication between the late nineteenth and early twentieth centuries, meant she felt a strong affinity with minority languages such as Welsh. As she explained in a translated article for *Y Faner* in 1988:

> the Welsh language is a living, healthy language. My mother-tongue, Hebrew, was restored because people practised and used it, taught

through it in schools and universities, and write the language. Although the situation is so different in Wales, without the mandatory conditions that prompted the Israelis, I see a similarity in the way the problems are faced. And so, despite all the difficulties, I publish in Welsh, because I came to love Wales, and something monstrous for me would be to see the old language disappear to the modern age's bowels of uniformity.[24]

Kate Bosse-Griffiths (1910–98) is another non-Welsh-born Jewish writer of Wales. As mentioned in Chapter 3, she was born into a German-Lutheran family with an assimilated Jewish mother and fled Germany in the late 1930s after being subjected to the same restrictions as German Jews. After meeting her husband John Gwyn Griffiths, a Welsh scholar from the Rhondda, in Oxford, Kate moved to Pentre, south Wales, in 1939, where she 'learnt Welsh as people [there preferred] speaking Welsh to speaking English' and published her first Welsh-language novel, *Anesmwyth Hoen* (Uneasy Joy), in 1941.[25] Because she incorporated German and modern European themes into her work, Bosse-Griffiths's contribution to Welsh-language literature was truly unique.[26] Although references to Jewishness are largely absent from her work, possibly due to the trauma of losing relatives in the Holocaust, her Jewishness was something she nevertheless embraced.[27] As her husband once explained: 'Although Kate does not deal with these things in her work, she certainly had a deep sense about them . . . one thing is certain: she did not want to deny this part of her personality . . . she was a German and a Jew'.[28]

As well as Jewish writers, Jewish refugee artists from Nazi-occupied Europe, who settled in the country from the 1940s onwards and took their Welsh environs as artistic inspiration, have enriched the cultural landscape of Wales. Perhaps the most prominent example is the Berlin-born artist Heinz Koppel (1919–80), who lived in Dowlais, south Wales, between 1944 and 1956 and produced expressionist paintings of the local landscape, transforming the 'grim industrial scene into a world of colour and fantasy'.[29] Some of Wales' Jewish émigré artists took Welsh themes as their subject matter in gratitude to a nation that had offered them refuge during their time of need. Reflecting on his paintings of Welsh miners during his time living in Ystradgynlais between 1944 and 1955, Warsaw-born artist, Josef Herman (1911–2000), described them as 'emotional treasures from . . . a mining community which made [his] new world', while Czech-born artist Ernest Neuschul painted portraits of various

Swansea government officials and local Jewish communal leaders during the Second World War, 'in recognition of the work [they had] been doing for refugees'.[30] Similarly, the main inspiration for artist Karel Lek (b. 1929), a Belgian-Jewish refugee who settled in north Wales in 1940, are the local people and landscape of north-west Wales. With works such as 'Sunday in Bontnewydd' and 'Mr Evan Roberts y diwygiwr', he wanted 'to give something back to Wales', the country where he 'found freedom'.[31]

The Eisteddfod

Alongside artwork and writing, perhaps the ultimate manifestation of Jewish engagement with Welsh culture was the involvement of many Welsh Jews in the eisteddfod, a celebratory festival of Welsh literature, music and performance, which, as Carol Trossett once noted, is 'one of Wales' best known institutions', and 'is consciously associated with notions of Welshness'.[32] Held annually throughout Wales and ranging from small village events to larger festivals such as the National Eisteddfod and the Urdd Eisteddod (Youth Eisteddfod), the eisteddfod is an ancient Welsh custom with a tradition believed to date back to 1176, when a meeting of poetry and music was held at the court of Rhys ap Gruffydd of Deheubarth in Cardigan.[33]

When Jews first became involved in the eisteddfod is unclear, but it was most likely during the nineteenth century, as Jews did not migrate to Wales in considerable numbers until that period. Many Jewish immigrants were involved in the the jewellery trade and some were occasionally engaged in supplying eisteddfod prize medals. During the mid-nineteenth century, for instance, Prussian-born John Aronson, an established jeweller in Bangor, produced medals and supplied ornaments such as a silver harp for local eisteddfods, including those held at Caerfallwch in 1851 and Rhyl in 1863, while H. Freedman of Tonypandy presented the gold medal to the winning conductor at the Porth Cottage Hospital Eisteddfod in 1919.[34]

As well as supplying medals, some Jews in Wales participated in eisteddfod competitions. Indeed, so proud were Welsh-Jewish communities of the achievements of their coreligionists in eisteddfods that their names were regularly published in the *JC*, sometimes appearing as the main piece, or the only piece, of news from the congregation that week.[35] Naturally, as English was, and continues to be, the language spoken by the majority of Welsh Jewry, most competed in competitions where proficiency in Welsh was not required. Ada Cohen of Tredegar, for instance, who is listed as an English speaker in the 1911 census, won a prize for a pianoforte solo at a local eisteddfod in 1913, while Hyam Freedman of Pontycymmer 'was awarded first prize ... for violin' at the 1906 National Eisteddfod in Caernarfon.[36]

Examples do exist of Jews participating in Welsh-language competitions, however. Eleven-year-old Sarah Janner 'obtained the first prize for the Welsh recitation' at the annual eisteddfod of the Barry branch of the Cymmrodorion in 1911;[37] Fannie Stein of Amlwch was 'appointed one of the conductors of the Annual Llangefni County School Eisteddfod' in 1936 due to 'her proficiency in the Welsh language'; the already mentioned Kate Bosse-Griffiths won the short story competition at the 1942 National Eisteddfod with '*Y Bennod Olaf*' ('The Last Chapter'); and Jack Pollecoff of Pwllheli, a Welsh learner, became the first Welsh Jew to be honoured by the Gorsedd of the Bards at the 1968 National Eisteddfod.[38]

Jews in Wales have also sought to incorporate the eisteddfod tradition into their own culture and have been proud to adopt elements of it as their own. During the 1910s, for example, Simon Joseph of Waunlwyd organised annual youth eisteddfods at the Ebbw Vale synagogue, where members participated in competitions such as 'speaking, singing and drama.'[39] Similarly, the Cardiff branch of the Zionist youth group, Young Judeans, held eisteddfods at the Cathedral Road synagogue in the 1930s, while in 1977 a *Purim* (a Jewish festival commemorating Queen Esther's salvation of the Jewish people) eisteddfod was held at Cardiff's Penylan synagogue, where the *cheder* children participated in written, spoken, artistic and musical competitions on Jewish themes.[40]

Surviving records suggest that Jews were generally tolerated and welcomed at eisteddfods. On retiring as a doctor in Nantymoel, south Wales in 1991, Scottish-born Louis Saville said that 'his appointment as adjudicator for the local eisteddfod was evidence of his acceptance by locals'.[41] Nevertheless, there was controversy at the 1962 National Eisteddfod in Llanelli when the award of a medal to the already mentioned Polish-born Jewish artist, Josef Herman, was criticised, as some felt that a medal for 'Services to Welsh Art' should have gone to a Welshman.[42] Although the incident was not regarded as a cause for grave concern – the *JC* reported that the complaint was driven by disparagement of the artist's national identity rather than by anti-Semitism – it has an important

bearing on the question of identity, particularly the Welsh identity of
Wales's Jewish population. It also highlights issues concerning acceptance
and a sense of belonging. As we have seen from Chapter 4, Jews have
generally been tolerated and accepted in Welsh society, but are they
accepted as Welsh? The two things are not the same.

A Sense of Belonging

In 1975, the editor of the *JYB*, Michael Wallach, asked 'do the Jews think
of themselves as Jewish Welshmen or Welsh Jews?' To date, there has been
no sufficient answer to this question, but Welsh identity, like any other, is
constructed by both self and society and in the early twenty-first century
there are Jews in Wales who take pride in being Welsh. However, the
establishing of a Welsh-Jewish identity has been a gradual and complex
process, for Jews and for the wider Welsh society. As Stuart Hall once
noted, 'identity is not as transparent and unproblematic as we think'.[43] He
argues that identity is a production, 'a matter of "becoming" as well as of
"being"', and is fluid, shaped by 'place, time, history and culture' and
remade from one generation to the next.[44] These social and historical
processes through which identities are formed and changed are particularly marked in the history of Welsh Jewry.

As previously noted, the first Jews to settle in Wales during the late
eighteenth and early nineteenth centuries were Ashkenazi Jews from
Central Europe. However, the majority of the present day Welsh-Jewish
population are descendants of Ashkenazi Jews from Eastern Europe who,
as we have seen, arrived in Wales in large numbers during the late nineteenth and early twentieth centuries. They left their native countries to
either flee persecution or to seek economic opportunities, and when they
arrived in Wales they were classified as 'aliens' by the authorities and
regarded as foreigners by the native Welsh. Dora Lipsett, for instance,
settled in Merthyr Tydfil with her Russian family in 1903 and recalled that
when they arrived, 'We were aliens . . . naturally, and we aliens had to
report to the police station.'[45] Even contemporary press reports appear to
have classified Jews as foreigners. In any story involving Jews, their nationality and country of origin were likely to be included. In 1870, for instance,
the *Western Mail* described Charles Huff of Cardiff as 'the foreigner' and 'a
Russian Jew', while in 1900 the *Wrexham Advertiser* described a hawker,
Eli Chenker, as 'a Russian Jew'.[46]

The Yiddish language spoken by the first Jewish settlers, and their limited knowledge of English and Welsh on arrival, must have been a prominent marker of difference. Nay Joseph, for example, recalled that his parents 'could only speak Yiddish, nothing else . . . hardly a word of English' when they first arrived in Brynmawr at the turn of the twentieth century, while Harry Cohen noted that 'not one' of the early Jewish settlers of Pontypridd 'could speak English . . . they communicated in either Yiddish or Russian'.[47] Reflecting on his childhood in early twentieth-century Cardiff, W. C. Elvet Thomas noted that his neighbours were:

> a young Jewish couple, the husband from Poland (and one look at him was enough to proclaim his race), and his beautiful wife from Bessarabia in Southern Russia. The wife's English was very broken . . . They were newcomers from the continent. They knew nothing about Wales.[48]

Besides language, the early settlers found themselves distinguished by their accents. Dannie Abse, for example, recalls that his Polish-born grandparents, Tobias and Annabella Shepherd, who lived in Ystalyfera at the turn of the twentieth century, learnt to speak 'Welsh with a Yiddish accent', which made them stand out. He recalls:

> My grandmother . . . used to speak Welsh with such an accent that they thought she was a Patagonian. Because in those days there was an emigration from Wales and eventually they spoke a rather strange Welsh. So my grandmother . . . spoke Welsh in such a way . . . They were the only Jews in the village and they said to her, 'C'mon tell the truth Annabella fach . . . you're a Patagonian.[49]

If they could afford to pay the fee, naturalisation was a means for Jewish immigrants and their children (under 21 and resident in the United Kingdom, according to the Naturalisation Act 1870) to settle permanently in Wales and acquire the status of 'British subject', as was true for immigrants in other parts of the United Kingdom. The situation of immigrant men was different from that of women since the latter were unable to apply for naturalisation in their own right until 1965, their citizenship status being dependent on the status of their spouses. As part of the naturalisation process, all applicants were required to renounce their previous allegiance to their country of birth, to swear allegiance to the British Crown and to have been resident in the British Isles for at least five years.[50] Following the Aliens Act of 1905, the requirements were altered to exclude any applicants who were unable to read and write in English.[51] The motivation for naturalisation varied, but it was primarily driven by the desire for political, economic and social freedom. David Priceman, a draper from Rhyl, was a 25-year-old Russian subject who sought naturalisation in 1904 'to obtain the rights and capacities of a natural born British Subject from a desire to continue to carry on his business', while Hyman Silverstone, a draper living in Llanelli, was a 35-year-old Russian Jew who applied for naturalisation in 1909 'from the desire to exercise his vote in Parliamentary Elections as well as to obtain exercise and enjoy all the other rights and capacities of a British born subject'.[52]

A certificate of naturalisation was issued to successful applicants, whereby their national identity was reconstructed. A Jew born in Eastern Europe but resident and naturalised in Britain subsequently became officially recognised as being of Jewish ethnic or racial origin; of Polish-Russian birth; a British subject and a British citizen. To take one example: Isaac Pruss of New Tredegar is first listed in the 1901 census as a Russian-born foreign subject. He was naturalised in 1904 and in the 1911 census is listed as a naturalised British subject born in Russia. Thus in considering the development of a consciousness of Welsh identity in Jews, one might argue that for the first generations, the focus was largely, if not wholly, on securing a greater sense of a British, rather than a Welsh identity. However, despite being officially recognised as 'British subjects', many naturalised Jews did not feel British, let alone Welsh. Their ancestral roots lay in their country of origin and they were content to continue with their own language and customs. This was true of Annie Levi and her parents who lived in Gilfach Fargoed in the 1920s. Annie's daughter, Rebecca Fine, observed that:

> [my mother's] lifestyle didn't actually change, my grandfather's lifestyle didn't actually change when they came here ... I think somehow, it was a good thing in a way because it preserved their own culture. I was brought up, my mother always spoke Yiddish to me.[53]

There are, however, examples of first generation Jewish settlers, particularly those who migrated at a young age, who reveal a strong attachment to Wales. They developed a Welsh identity through their upbringing in Welsh society and their country of origin became a foreign land. Morris Silvergleit was born in Warsaw in 1892 and migrated to Aberfan as a teenager. In 1978 he recalled: 'I wasn't born in this country, I was born in . . . Poland, but I've been here long enough to be Welsh actually . . . I'm assimilated. I'm more Welsh than a Welshman.'[54] The same can be said for Isidore Wartski, who was born in Prussia in 1876. His son, John, believes that Isidore would have described himself as 'more Welsh' than his naturalised Polish-born grandfather, Morris, because he lived in Bangor from the age of five.[55] During Isidore's campaign for re-election as Bangor's Mayor in 1940, Alderman John Williams stated that he 'had been a resident of the borough almost long enough to claim himself a native. He had breathed the healthy atmosphere of the town and surrounding Welsh hills from boyhood.'[56] This statement is revealing, indicating that an outsider may, by virtue of the length of time spent in the host community, achieve some sense of belonging.

In addition to Eastern European immigrants, the present Welsh-Jewish community derives from continental refugees who arrived during the 1930s and 1940s to escape Nazism. Consisting mainly of Czech, German and Austrian Jews, many, as we have seen, were classified as enemy aliens by the British government during the Second World War. Narratives of displacement predominate amongst these wartime refugees. Nuremberg-born Lore Gang, for instance, settled in Cardiff in 1939 and despite being naturalised later she 'never wanted to be British. She wanted to be herself, as it were, a continental Jew'.[57] Another wartime refugee, the already mentioned Karel Lek of Beaumaris, regards his arrival in north Wales as something of an accident: 'The misfortunes of the last War brought me, as a boy of eleven, from Antwerp to North Wales, where I have lived for over 70 years. I sometimes wonder whether this qualifies me to call myself a Welshman!'[58]

In some cases, Jewish refugees from Nazi-occupied Europe desired to abandon their links with their country of origin and welcomed a new identity in their country of refuge. This is because the murderous actions of the Nazi regime and its collaborators effectively destroyed the possibility of their re-adoption of a German or Austrian identity.[59] Bill Pollock, for instance, fled Vienna with his family in 1938, eventually settling in south Wales. Having been naturalised as a British subject, he considered himself British rather than Welsh but never described himself as Austrian 'not by any stretch of the imagination. In fact, I haven't been back to Austria since I left in 1938 and I have no wish to go back.'[60] Another example is Leipzig-born Werner K. E. Bernfeld. A refugee from Nazism, he settled in Cardiff during the Second World War and was eager to rebuild his life in Wales, put 'out new roots and become a part of his adopted country'.[61] He soon became 'an enthusiastic supporter of the Welsh way of life', competing in eisteddfods and learning Welsh.[62]

With the second generation, the children of the first settlers, the situation was different. Alan Llwyd's comment on the position of second-generation black people in Wales is just as appropriate for second-generation Jews; some of them had 'an ambiguous identity'.[63] They were born in Wales but felt that they did not belong to the country of their birth. Despite being born in Cardiff in 1928, Bernice Rubens felt no sense of belonging to Wales because her birth in the country was purely a matter of chance. Only later in life did she accept a Welsh identity, but was uncertain whether others would accept her as Welsh. As she explained:

> For any Jew of my generation, wherever they're born is accidental. I was born in Wales simply because my father came from Latvia ... to Cardiff. He could equally have [gone] ... to Liverpool or to Glasgow or indeed, like his brothers, to New York. More important in so far as it influenced my home life, my father mightn't have left Germany at all ... Having been born in Wales, I grew up there, went to University there ... For most people that would probably make me Jewish ... I don't know whether Welsh people think I'm Welsh. I like to think I'm Jewish and also Welsh.[64]

Many second-generation Jewish children experienced the dilemma of being caught between two worlds and cultures: those of their immigrant parents and those of the country they were living in.[65] Ruth Joseph, for instance, was born in Cardiff in 1946, and as a Welsh-born Jewish child of German-Jewish refugees, she recalls having an identity outside Wales:

> I lived a life infused with references – strange names from other worlds – other outside existences ... I came from another place; my parents Holocaust refugees arriving in Cardiff, desperately seeking a place to settle, needing, wanting a new life.[66]

However, without memories of the old country, many second-generation Jews dissociated themselves from the Eastern European or other Continental European cultures that characterised their parents's national identities and sense of belonging. They felt they were Welsh because they were born and raised in Wales, because they were educated in Wales, and because they were a part of the country's day-to-day life. Channah Hirsch, for instance, was of Russian parentage and born in Llanelli in 1913. Despite not having any ancestral roots in Wales, she felt a sense of belonging:

> I was born in Llanelli . . . Llanelli and everything Welsh is in my bones. I loved the clear, crisp air, the skies, the hills and valleys, the murmuring streams, the peace and tranquillity. I belong to Wales and Wales belongs to me.[67]

In a similar vein, Jack Pollecoff of Pwllheli was born in Holyhead in 1903 and was of Russian and English parentage. According to his daughter-in-law, Eve Pollecoff, there was no doubt that Jack felt that he was Welsh. He 'loved that part of the world, and felt rooted there'.[68] Yet the second generation's sense of belonging to Wales did not go unchallenged. The Ystalyfera-born novelist, Lily Tobias, for instance, drew deeply from her own experiences as a second-generation Jewish child living in early twentieth-century south Wales in her short story, 'The Nationalists'. Set in the fictionalised mining town of Trwyntwll, the Jewish protagonist, Leah Klein, was 'born in the village' to Russian-immigrant parents. Despite being Welsh-born, she was regarded as a 'dirty little foreigner' and told 'to go back to Russia, to [her] own country' by some of her contemporaries.[69]

The great change in attitude came with the third and fourth generations, the grandchildren and great-grandchildren of the first arrivals. Although of Eastern or Central European ancestry, having been born in Wales to Welsh- or British-born parents, they had acculturated to both Welsh and wider British society, and thus gradually, over time, became both detached from and unassociated with their ancestor's country of origin. As Cardiff-born Harold Cairns puts it:

> I'm Welsh but I'm certainly British ethnically. My grandparents . . . they're northern Eastern European, and of course, they all came away, they all came [to Britain] in the nineteenth century . . . whilst [my]

grandparents might have been required to be naturalised, my parents didn't. My parents were all naturally British because they were born here ... I'm a Welsh Jew because I was born in Wales and I've lived in Wales for the greater part of my life.[70]

In the process of assimilation, Ashkenazi distinctiveness began to decline and as time passed the old ways were bound to experience the flux of memory. The linguistic competence of the second and third generations, for instance, became greater in English than in Yiddish or German, with the linguistic gap widening markedly between the first and third generation. To quote Leo Abse:

My grandmother ... couldn't speak anything except Yiddish ... My grandfather spoke a fair English, with an accent. He spoke Yiddish to his wife, so if I went to my maternal grandfather's house ... they were in a house where Yiddish was spoken. In my own house there was of course English, predominantly, bits of Welsh, and my mother and father speaking Yiddish when they didn't want the children to know.[71]

Similarly, Adam Buswell of Cardiff (b.1984) experienced this language shift between the generations. His grandmother, a Holocaust survivor, left Continental Europe for Britain after the Second World War, eventually settling in Wales. He recalls that:

I didn't really have conversations as such with my gran. As I say, I only learnt 'Grandma German'. My parents were completely fluent in German and my brother and sister lived with it for a little bit longer than I had ... We didn't really have conversations because, as I say ... she couldn't speak English and there was only so much German I knew.[72]

Although many of the traditions and customs of the first Jewish settlers began to fade as the younger generations integrated into wider Welsh and British society, a Jewish identity, whether cultural or religious, was retained. Like their parents and grandparents, the majority of children were raised in Jewish homes, many keeping kosher and observing various religious rituals such as lighting Sabbath candles and celebrating Jewish holidays. They were also formally immersed in Jewish life through *cheder* lessons, synagogue services and *b'nai* and *b'not mitzvah* ceremonies. The third generation grew up in communities that had adopted Welsh and British secular culture and an appropriate acculturated Judaism. They resisted full assimilation and in the process constructed a hybrid Jewish–Welsh/British identity, enabling them to combine their Jewishness and heritage with a strong commitment to both Wales and Britain. As Cardiff-born Ben Soffa stated in 2012:

> There's definitely a strong Jewish component to [my identity], definitely a Welsh component to it ... even if I know my family's only been in Wales a hundred years it feels like it's something of me.[73]

Welshness

But what is Welshness? Early work on Welsh identity has been criticised for its treatment of the Welsh as one culturally unified group, for its neglect of the variety of ways of expressing a Welsh identity and for its fluidity.[74] Later studies, influenced by Benedict Anderson's representation of national identity as both imagined and socially constructed, have presented a much more complex and multiple image of Welshness.[75] 'How many ways of being Welsh?' asked Graham Day and Richard Suggett.[76] To illustrate the polychromatic nature of Welsh identity in the Welsh-Jewish context, one must consider the differing ways in which Jews in Wales have constructed and imagined their Welsh identities and sense of belonging to the nation.

Reflecting the wider Welsh population, the most important factors associated with Welsh identity for many Jews in Wales are country of birth and residence. Although born to Polish parents, Isaac Samuel described himself in a letter to the *Western Mail* in 1911 'as a Jew, by race and religion, and as a Welshman by birth' since he 'was born and [had] lived in Cardiff all [his] days'.[77] Similarly, the late Rebecca Fine of Gilfach Fargoed described herself a 'Welsh-Jew' because she was 'a Jewess born in Wales'.[78] Conversely, as we have seen, some Jews born in Wales do not consider themselves Welsh and actively resent being so categorised. Leo Abse, for instance, was 'a little sceptical' when he was referred to as a 'Welsh Jew', often quoting the old Yiddish saying that 'because you're born in a stable, it doesn't make you a horse'.[79] Despite being born in Cardiff in 1917, Abse insisted that:

> I was not born in Wales. My mother was born in Ystalyfera and so she was born in Wales, but I was born in Cardiff. The Welsh influences that

would have been pressing upon me if I had been born where my
mother was born, and where my grandfather had lived, mean I would
have been succoured in a very different environment than I was ...
although I have always been called a Welsh Jew, I regard it as ridiculous.[80]

Given Labour's dominance over the Welsh political landscape for most of
the twentieth century, Abse believed that the 'real Wales' existed in the
south Wales coalfield, Labour's electoral heartland where 'the socialist and
anarchist or anarchosyndicalist leaders ... created a world which maintained hope in a socialist Utopia in the face of ... unemployment and
poverty'. Conservatism dominated Abse's Cardiff, however, a minority
political tradition in Wales made up of 'people who ... rejected their
Welsh identity fundamentally' and 'wanted to be snobby-nosed
Englishmen'.[81] With a cosmopolitan character quite different from the
rest of the nation, Abse also thought of Cardiff as a 'mongrel city' that 'had
no real connection to Wales'.[82]

For some Jews born in Welsh-speaking areas of Wales, there is a more
problematic vision of Welshness. Despite being born in Wales they feel
that they are denied a Welsh identity because they do not speak Welsh or
have not engaged themselves in Welsh-language culture. Michael Lee,
born in Llandudno in 1941, describes himself as a Jew born in Wales but
not as a 'Welsh Jew', because he was not raised in a Welsh-speaking household or exposed to 'Welsh [language] culture'.[83] On the flip-side, Alwyn
Pierce-Lloyd was born in Shrewsbury in 1955 but grew up in villages in
mid and north Wales where he learnt to speak Welsh as a child. He
describes himself as a 'Welsh Jew' because practising his religion and
speaking Welsh are 'equally as important' to him.[84]

Nevertheless, when only a minority of Jews in Wales – and of the
Welsh population as a whole – speak Welsh and live in the Welsh-speaking
heartland of north-west and west-central Wales, most cannot relate to a
Welshness that is defined by the Welsh language, even if they identify with
it and sincerely regret their exclusion. Harry Poloway, for instance, was
born in Newport in 1915 and had lived in south-east Wales all his life.
Despite not speaking Welsh he considered himself a Welsh Jew: 'I'm Welsh
through and through ... I've never sat down and cried because I can't
speak Welsh. Oh no. I said look I'd like to, but I can't. End of Story.'[85]
Having been denied the opportunity to learn Welsh as children, some
Jews in Wales, like some non-Jews, have sent their children to

Welsh-medium schools as a way of strengthening their own sense of Welshness. Alan and Laura Liss, for instance, sent their three children to Welsh-medium schools in Cardiff between 1990 and 2005 for precisely this reason, while Devra Applebaum sent her three daughters to Welsh-medium schools in Carmarthen during the same period because she married 'a passionate Welshman' who saw an opportunity to restore to their children a Welsh linguistic heritage of which he felt deprived.[86]

For some older Jews living in Wales there is also a fixed correlation between Welshness and Nonconformity. Bernice Rubens once stated, 'I think I'm Jewish and also Welsh, but you know, I'm not Methodist, I don't have those Nonconformist trappings that make you more Welsh than being born in Wales.'[87] Similarly, an unnamed Welsh Jew suggested in 1975 that 'To be a real Welshman, you must be Chapel.'[88] Indeed, although there is nothing specifically Welsh about Protestant Nonconformism, the fact that it became the majority religious tradition in Wales between the mid nineteenth and early twentieth centuries meant it became central to ideas of Welshness.[89] But as Paul Chambers reminds us, 'Mass participation in Welsh Nonconformity was a fairly short-lived experience', and throughout the twentieth century its influence on Welsh national identity weakened as a result of several factors, including urbanisation, secularisation, emigration and the decline of the Welsh language.[90] Reflecting on religious life in Wales in the last quarter of the twentieth century, John Davies commented that 'with only thirteen per cent of the inhabitants of Wales regularly attending a place of worship, it was difficult to claim that the Welsh were a Christian nation'.[91] Indeed, the notion that Wales is a Nonconformist nation appears increasingly contestable, particularly following the establishment of the National Assembly for Wales in 1999.

With the birth of devolution, a new chapter in Welsh religious identity has emerged. Recent studies have variously highlighted how one of the principal issues for devolution on its inception was to increase citizen involvement, inclusiveness and participation, or what Dai Smith has termed 'the language of citizenship.'[92] In the case of religion, recognition of a religiously pluralistic Wales emerged and non-Christian faiths in Wales were officially recognised as Welsh.[93] The changing nature of Wales's religious landscape was affirmed in 2002 when an Interfaith Council for Wales was established under the auspices and sponsorship of the Welsh National Assembly. It was replaced in 2004 by Faith Communities Forum, a non-Assembly body that is designed to promote dialogue between the

Welsh government and Wales's major faith communities. Since its inception, two representatives from the Cardiff Orthodox and Reform communities have served on the forum, chaired by the first minister, where specific issues relating to the Jewish community, such as *shechita* and burial requirements, have been discussed.[94]

As well as formally identifying Wales as a multi-faith society, devolution has witnessed a concerted effort to raise awareness of Welsh multiculturalism, a recognition that the Welsh people are made up of various cultures and ethnicities. Although Wales has been a multicultural and multi-ethnic society since the nineteenth-century, this, as Neil Evans, Paul O'Leary and Charlotte Williams have pointed out, 'has not always been recognised in official narratives of the nation'.[95] The reasons for this are multifaceted and include the idea that Welsh cultural identity has long been defined by its relation with both 'English' and 'British' notions of multiculturalism. That is, the notion that England, home to 84 percent of the United Kingdom's population and the vast majority of the United Kingdom's ethnic minorities, is the multicultural heart of Britain, with the Welsh forming a homogenous cultural group within this multicultural British framework.[96] This myth of cultural homogeneity has never presented an accurate picture of the Welsh situation, but although the achievement of a truly multicultural society in Wales, one that is recognised, celebrated and embraced by all, is still what Charlotte Williams calls a 'project in the making', some progress has been made since devolution.[97] In the early twenty-first century, there has been a more visible celebration of cultural difference in Wales, a recent example from a Welsh-Jewish perspective being 'The Jewish Way of Life', the touring exhibition of the Board of Deputies of British Jews, which visited the Senedd in 2014. Of course, the idea of a culturally and ethnically inclusive nation is not without its challenges, but the fact that multiculturalism has found a place on the Welsh political agenda demonstrates that efforts are being made to reconstitute our understanding of Welsh cultural identity in the twenty-first century.

Furthermore, national identity is often informed by the everyday representations of the nation, or what Michael Billig terms 'banal nationalism'.[98] Support for the Welsh rugby team is one of the principal ways in which 'banal nationalism' is manifested in Wales. Although the Welshness of rugby is an invention, it has become the archetypal symbol of an inclusive Welsh identity in its capacity to unite people of differing linguistic and ethical backgrounds with a common sense of nationhood.[99] Thus it is through supporting the national rugby team that many Jews across Wales, like the wider Welsh population, express their sense of belonging to the nation. For instance, Ron Silver of Cardiff (b.1942), feels Welsh when he supports Wales at Rugby, while Llanelli-born Michael Howard (b.1941) embraces his Welshness 'whenever Wales play. Mostly it comes out when I'm watching sport. I always try and watch Welsh Rugby matches . . . I'm always rooting for Wales'.[100] Even going back to the 1930s, Jews cheered Wales against England in rugby matches at Cardiff Arms Park. As Dannie Abse revealed:

> These big rugby matches were great fun . . . Three spectators near us wore red shirts and banged silver saucepans, urging the players to victory with screams of Llanelly encouragement and scathing criticisms. And we shouted too, oh how we shouted . . . When the noise was loudest we swore and nobody could hear us.[101]

Jewish support for Welsh rugby has not, however, been accompanied by an extensive affiliation to Welsh nationalism, or support for the Welsh nationalist party, Plaid Cymru. The exact figure of Jewish voters is unknown, but in 1974 it was revealed that a mere three or four Welsh Jews were party members.[102] Two years later, the party leader, Gwynfor Evans, stated in an interview with the *JC* that, 'We have never found any sympathy and support for the national aspirations of the Welsh people among the Jewish community.'[103] Although Jews in Wales have a good historical record in their participation in Welsh civic life, to date there have been no Jewish MPs, councillors or AMs representing Plaid Cymru.[104]

There are several possible reasons for the disjuncture. One is that the Welsh language has been a central, even an inherent component of Welsh nationalism. But as we have seen, most Jews in Wales are unable to speak Welsh, with the majority having settled in the predominantly English-speaking south-east of the country. It may also be because of the intellectual anti-Semitism that appeared in the work of Plaid Cymru's founder, Saunders Lewis. Although Lewis's anti-Jewish writings were not a product of Welsh nationalism, his association with Plaid Cymru may have made the party unappealing to Jews. The thought of Plaid Cymru rounding up Welsh Jews would seem inconceivable, but the actions of nationalist movements in recent history, particularly during the Second World War, has made some Jews cautious of any form of nationalism. As Leo Abse once stated:

I lived through a period where in fact I had seen the Welsh nationalist leaders ... as people I regarded as neo-fascists ... And so given my views, prejudices, you can understand that after the war, after seeing the consequences of the Holocaust ... Having seen what virulent nationalism had done, any sign of nationalism was, for me, tainted.[105]

Kate Bosse-Griffiths, the German refugee who fled the Third Reich in the 1930s after being persecuted for having a Jewish mother, provides a different perspective. Together with her Welsh-speaking husband, J. Gwyn Griffiths, she became a fervent supporter of Welsh nationalism, writing many articles for Plaid Cymru's Welsh- and English-language periodicals and joining *Cymdeithas yr Iaith* (The Welsh Language Society) in 1962.[106] Her actions came as a surprise to her German relatives, but according to her husband, Kate could distinguish between the nonviolent, pacifistic, Welsh nationalism she adopted and the 'perverted nationalism' she fled.[107]

Indeed, a small number of Jews in Wales have been supportive of the Welsh nationalist cause. They include a combination of those who have engaged themselves in Welsh-language culture and those who are Zionists. When Plaid Cymru was established in 1925, its main aims were the promotion of the Welsh language and its culture and gaining full self-government for Wales. These are not unfamiliar ideas for Zionist Jews. Wales, like Israel, is a small nation with a long history of oppression, and both have maintained their ancient languages, Welsh and Hebrew, against all the odds. In view of these similarities, it is unsurprising that some Jews have supported Plaid Cymru. Bridgend-born Alan Liss was involved with Plaid Cymru in the 1960s because he

was a Zionist, and there was a certain generation of Welsh Nationalists who were very pro-Zionist ... because of the revival of the [Hebrew] language ... they were very pro-Jewish, very pro-Israel. It was probably romantic nationalism more than anything. And of course, all the Welsh nationalists were very pro the re-establishment of the state of Israel after two thousand years. They thought, 'If they could do it, then goodness knows ...'.[108]

Nevertheless, as we have seen, when Israel began to lose some of its moral stature in the eyes of the world from the late 1960s onwards, Plaid's positive attitude towards the Jewish homeland began to change. This shift may account for a decline in Jewish support for the party. Kenneth Cohen, the aforementioned rabbi of the Cardiff Reform Synagogue, was an enthusiastic supporter of Welsh nationalism, but became disenchanted with Plaid Cymru because of its criticism of the Israeli government, believing most Jews to feel this way, while Llandudno-born Rona Hart (b.1943), has 'never thought of supporting Plaid Cymru because of their policies on Israel.'[109] But for Jasmine Donahaye, a Jewish member of Plaid Cymru, the party's views on Israel are 'not a problem ... because I'm quite critical of Israel too, and I don't have this unreconstructed Zionist view of things that I used to have'.[110]

Zionism and Israel

Welsh-Jewish identity, like any other in the Jewish diaspora (Jewish presence outside the Land of Israel, the Jewish ancestral home), has increasingly incorporated a sense of being a Zionist. As a sign of this, Zionist societies have been in existence in most, if not all, Welsh-Jewish communities from the early twentieth century onwards, including branches of WIZO, the Jewish National Fund and youth groups such as Hanoar Hatzioni.[111] Nevertheless, for all the work that Welsh Jews have accomplished in fundraising under the banner of Zionism, the formation and support of these societies should not be seen solely through the lens of *aliyah* (emigration to Israel). Rather, these organisations, like other Jewish societies, fulfilled a very important social role in Wales's Jewish communities and played a part in fostering a Welsh-based sense of diasporic Jewish identity.[112] In the process of planning benefits for Israel, for instance, members of Cardiff's branch of WIZO were able to meet other Jewish women and share their experience of being Jewish in Wales. As Stella Schiller Levey of Cardiff recalled in 2002:

> after forty-one years ... I find that membership of 'Ziona' has been an integral part of my ... social life, whereby, by dint of hard work, we have raised thousands upon thousands of pounds for underprivileged Israeli and Arab women and children ... We have had marvellous times raising money and ... I cannot see my social life without it now, whatever else I do.[113]

Although Welsh Jewry has traditionally had strong ties with Israel, the community has not translated its Zionist inclinations into mass emigration. The number of Welsh Jews that have left for Israel since 1948 is difficult to ascertain, but *aliyah* has never been on a large scale (discussed further in Chapter 6). Some Welsh Jews visit Israel on holiday, while others have never visited because they are either critical of Israeli government policies and/or are happy and comfortable being Jewish in Wales. As the late Paul Sugarman of Rhyl stated in 2012, he 'wouldn't want to be anywhere else . . . I've . . . been to Israel, very nice, but I wouldn't want to live there. It's not my home. This [Wales] is my home.'[114] For many Jews, living in Wales, and Britain more generally, was all, but for others there has long been a dilemma where Israel is concerned, which is shared by many Jews of the diaspora: can a diaspora Jew live and lead a truly observant and satisfactory Jewish way of life outside of the Jewish ancestral homeland?[115]

For some, this dilemma has been mediated by the advances in technology and mass communication. Alan Schwartz of Cardiff wrote in 1999 that 'through the internet, video link, Jewish radio and TV programmes . . . as well as affordable flights to Israel, it's possible to be fully integrated into the worldwide web of Jewish life yet maintain a strong Jewish presence in the capital city of Wales.'[116] Yet, for others, living in Wales was Jewishness at one remove. They can offer their financial support to Israel and visit it, but it was no substitute for living there. Cardiff-born Brenda Landes made *aliyah* in 1962 and notes:

> Coming to Israel allows the newcomer to practise Judaism and express Jewish culture in freedom, maybe for the first time. In my case, changing locations was a positive experience. Although I was able to practise Judaism freely in Wales, it was not the Judaism I wanted. In its widest sense, Judaism was far richer to me on kibbutz. Here in Israel, living close to the land, the festival became meaningful and the kibbutz was an expression of basic Jewish values.[117]

For some Jews, emigrating to Israel is about self-asserting their Jewish identity, but despite living away from Wales, many Welsh-Jewish expats also maintain a strong Welsh identity in the promised land. While this led to a good deal of reflective soul-searching when Wales played football against Israel in the 1958 World Cup and 2016 European Championship qualifiers, at the time of writing Netanya's St David's Day dinner, held annually since the last quarter of the twentieth century, continues to attract up to eighty or ninety guests at a time.[118] Indeed, living in Israel has arguably made some Welsh Jews more conscious of their Welshness. As Cardiff-born Malka Liss, who made *aliyah* in 2007, puts it, 'When I'm outside of Wales, I'm proud to be Welsh ... Being in Israel, the Jewish identity is just run of the mill. Everyone's Jewish ... I'm Welsh, and that does differentiate me.'[119]

Attachment to place and a strong sense of local belonging are said to be among the distinctive characteristics of the Welsh, and many Jews, who were either born or lived in Wales but have left, remember their lives in the country with great warmth. Several express the Welsh notion of *hiraeth*, a word that has no direct translation but conveys a range of emotions, including a feeling of longing, yearning, homesickness, nostalgia and grief for Wales. In a piece written for *CAJEX* in 1967, Cardiff-born Joseph Danovitch reveals the *hiraeth* he felt for his native land after making *aliyah* in 1965:

> I still, one day, want to make a sentimental journey and retrace my steps in the Welsh valleys and see again the Welsh people I love and respect. There is too, a hallowed piece of ground forever dear to me, near Roath Park in Cardiff, where lie my dear mother and father.[120]

Yet Danovitch gives no indication that he would one day return to live in Wales, since for him 'the transition from the Land of my Fathers to the Land of my Father's Fathers [was] not difficult'.[121] Indeed, this quote reveals that there are *hiraethau* more complex for some Welsh Jews than simply a longing for Wales. Danovitch emigrated to Israel, but what about the *hiraeth* felt by the Zionist who stayed in Wales? As Grahame Davies once noted 'we're used to a Welsh feeling of *hiraeth* in a foreign land. We're less used to people feeling *hiraeth* within Wales itself.'[122] In fact, some Welsh Jews consider Wales, or the diaspora more generally, as a place of exile and express *hiraeth* for the Jewish homeland in Israel. John Wartski of Bangor, for instance, served with the Israeli army between 1962 and 1967 before settling in Bournemouth. A former Jewish son of north Wales, now living in England, he feels *hiraeth* not for Wales, but for Israel.[123] Although Wartski chose to remain a Diaspora Jew, living in what may be described as 'self-imposed exile', his religious longings for the Holy Land are so intense that he organises annual visits to Israel.[124]

By examining how cultural, linguistic and political traditions particular to the Welsh context have impacted on the lives and identities of Jews in Wales, it is hoped that British-Jewish historians will begin to appreciate the distinctive qualities of the Welsh-Jewish experience and avoid previously misguided suggestions of 'folding' the histories of British Jewries into an 'Anglo-Jewish' framework. Indeed, only by exploring how Jewish life in Britain's four nations reflected and diverged from each other can we begin fully to appreciate the complexity of the British-Jewish experience.

6

Decline and Endurance

THE population of Wales's Jewish communities reached its peak around 1919, when the country was home to nineteen congregations that catered for the religious and social needs of approximately 5,000 Jewish individuals. However, from the 1920s onwards Wales's Jewish communities witnessed a steep decline. In the 1950s, there were eleven Jewish centres serving roughly 4,000 to 4,500 Jews in Wales, but by the 1990s this number had dropped to five centres serving a recorded Jewish population of approximately 2,000 to 2,500 individuals.[1] Such a drop in numbers was not unique to Wales's Jewish centres, however, with Jewish communities elsewhere in the United Kingdom, those other than London and Manchester in particular, having similar demographic trajectories throughout the twentieth century.[2] As we shall see, the reasons behind the decline of Wales's Jewish communities were varied and complex, stretching from the changing career aspirations of the second and third generations to a desire to move to a place with a more extensive Jewish infrastructure. Yet despite the disappearance of most of its synagogues, it is important to stress that an organised Jewish presence, albeit significantly smaller than in the past, continues to exist in Wales in the early twenty-first century.

Decline

During the 1910s the recorded Jewish population of the south Wales coalfield numbered around one thousand and the region was home to some twelve Jewish communities.[3] From the end of that decade onwards, however, the valleys' Jewish communities witnessed a gradual decline and in the early 1980s the last functioning synagogue in the region closed its doors to worshippers for the final time. The smaller communities were the first to disappear and as early as 1918 the handful of Jewish families that made up the Newbridge Hebrew Congregation decided to disband, as they found that they were 'too small in numbers to carry out the essential requirements of religious duties', that is to form a *minyan*.[4] The collapse of Jewish communal life in Newbridge was repeated elsewhere in the south Wales coalfield during the first half of the twentieth century. In 1917, for instance, the population of Ebbw Vale's Jewish community was recorded as one hundred persons, but by the mid-1930s it had decreased to such an extent (about nine individuals) that the town's congregation disbanded in 1936.[5] Similarly, the Jewish communities of Abertillery, Bargoed, New Tredegar and Tonypandy disappeared from the pages of the *JYB* from the mid-1930s onwards, while the synagogues in Tredegar, Aberdare, Brynmawr and Pontypridd closed in 1953, 1957, 1963 and 1978 respectively because of the lack of members to make up a *minyan*.[6] With a fall in membership from 400 to 20 between 1919 and 1979, Merthyr Tydfil Jewry eventually sold its synagogue in 1982 owing to the insufficient financial support the remaining members brought into the community through subscriptions.[7]

The demise of Jewish communal life in the south Wales Valleys was repeated elsewhere in south Wales. Aberavon's Jewish community, for instance, dropped from 99 to 18 people between 1916 and the 1960s, eventually leading to the sale of the synagogue in 1976, while the lack of activity in Bridgend from the early 1930s is evidenced by the absence of articles relating to the community in the *JC* from 1932 onwards.[8] Similarly, Llanelli's Jewish population of 300 individuals in 1924 had slumped to 20 in 1980.[9] With small numbers making it extremely difficult to maintain religious services, both numerically and financially, the synagogue closed in 1982.[10] Even for those communities in south Wales that did not completely disappear, the general pattern throughout the twentieth century was one of decline. In Newport, for example, the reported Jewish population dropped from 250 to 50 between 1917 and 1986, and that of Swansea fell from 1,000 to 180 during the same period.[11] Newport Jewry continued to decline in the 1990s, and with a population of no more than twenty people in 1997 the community sold its Queen's Hill synagogue as it was no longer financially viable to keep the building open for services.[12] Since then, Newport's remaining congregants have been meeting for worship at the community's *Bet*

Tohorah (cleansing house for corpses prior to burial) building on the edge of the city's Jewish cemetery.[13]

Like south Wales, most of north Wales's Jewish communities, centres that had flourished during the late nineteenth and early twentieth centuries, collapsed during the latter half of the twentieth century, with all but one of its five Jewish communities having been disbanded by the 1980s. Although Wrexham's Jewish community is last listed in the *JYB* in 1950, the lack of articles relating to the community in the *JC* from 1929 onwards suggests that there was little activity there in the late 1920s.[14] Bangor's Jewish community fell from 75 to 12 individuals between 1905 and 1963, with the synagogue relocating to a small porch in the Tabernacle Chapel in Garth Road in 1964, as the congregation was unable to afford the upkeep of their house of worship in the Arvonia Buildings.[15] Despite only numbering approximately 12 members, Bangor's Jewish community continued to function until the mid 1980s because the presence of Jewish students and academics at the University College of North Wales, among them Eric Mendoza (professor of Physics) and Kate Loewenthal (lecturer in Psychology), helped to increase the small numbers of those able to attend religious services during term time.[16]

With declining numbers, cooperation between communities and the eventual merger of previously distinct congregations was seen as the only way to ensure the survival of organised Jewish life in north Wales. Thus, in 1968, the communities of Colwyn Bay and Llandudno, then numbering 23 and 45 individuals respectively, began alternating Friday evening services so they could get enough men for a *minyan*. The two communities eventually merged in 1985 to form the Llandudno and Colwyn Bay Hebrew Congregation, meeting at Llandudno's synagogue in Church Walks for worship.[17]

Growth and Decline of Cardiff Jewry

The only Jewish community in Wales that succeeded in stemming the tide of decline, and in fact, witnessed a gradual increase in its population for most of the twentieth century, was Cardiff. According to the *JYB*, the city's recorded Jewish population increased from 1,250 to approximately 3,500 individuals between 1904 and 1968. This increase in population was largely the result of an influx of Jewish families to the city from the declining coalfield communities of the south Wales valleys from the 1930s onwards and the settlement of Jewish refugees from Nazi-occupied Europe, who, as we have seen, arrived in the city in the 1930s and 1940s.[18]

Indeed, in the immediately post-war decades, there was a sense of optimism in Cardiff's Jewish community, and nothing better symbolised this than the construction and opening of a new synagogue for the Cardiff United Synagogue in Ty-Gwyn Road, Penylan, in 1955. The desire to build a new synagogue in Cardiff was sparked by both the ageing and the approaching expiry of the lease of the Windsor Place synagogue.[19] It also reflected the shift that was taking place in Cardiff's Jewish population during this period. By the late 1930s and 1940s a number of Windsor Place's upwardly mobile and prosperous Jews were moving away from inner-city areas such as Canton and Riverside and settling in the new and salubrious suburb of Cyncoed. Since some members of the Cardiff United Synagogue adhered to the Orthodox principle of walking to the synagogue on the Sabbath, Windsor Place (situated approximately two miles away from Cyncoed) 'had outgrown its geographical usefulness' and was deemed too far to travel.[20]

As well as the erection of a new Orthodox synagogue, Cardiff Jewry witnessed the formation of a new congregation in the post-war era. In 1948 a Reform congregation named the Cardiff New Synagogue (henceforth CNS; later renamed the Cardiff Reform Synagogue) was organised by certain members of the Cardiff United Synagogue (henceforth CUS), in reaction to the fact that the congregation becoming increasingly more conservative and Orthodox following the appointment of Rabbi Ber Rogosnitzky as the CUS's *Rav* in 1945.[21] As the adherents of the CNS were originally too few in number to support a full-fledged synagogue, services were held at the Temple of Peace in Cathays Park until an old Methodist Chapel in Moira Terrace was acquired in 1952 and consecrated as a house of worship.[22] In 1949, the congregation secured for their use a section of the public Western Cemetery in Ely for burial purposes, as the existing Jewish cemetery in Highfield Road was restricted to the use of CUS members, and appointed their first full-time minister, Rabbi L. Gerhard Graf of Berlin, who served the CNS until his retirement in 1980.[23]

During the first two decades of its existence, the CNS's membership increased apace. Between 1953 and 1962, for instance, the number of children attending its *cheder* grew from about 36 to over 90, while its affiliated membership increased from 220 to 319 persons between 1949 and 1970.[24] There were a number of reasons for this increase. Firstly, about a third of the original members were Jewish refugees from Nazi-occupied Europe, and since Reform Judaism had long prevailed in Germany, many found the CNS far more suited to their needs than the strict Orthodoxy of the CUS.[25] Secondly, the CNS were accepting of Jews who married non-Jewish spouses, in contrast to the CUS, whose constitution notes that 'Any member of either sex who shall marry a person who is not of the Jewish religion as accepted by the Beth Din shall forfeit all rights of membership and all privileges'.[26] Finally, other Jews became dissatisfied with traditional Orthodox services and practices, and found the more progressive services and attitudes of the CNS more modern and appealing. Michael and Sally Rosen, for instance, were both raised in the Orthodox tradition, but joined the CNS in 1957 as they liked the idea of men and women sitting and worshipping together, rather than being segregated as occurred in Orthodox congregations.[27] One former congregant of the CUS joined the CNS because he wished to be cremated when he died, a practice strongly deplored by the Orthodox community, while Jews living in outlying parts of the city were attracted to the CNS as, unlike Orthodox Judaism, the reform movement permitted driving to synagogue on the Sabbath.[28]

Despite the self-confidence of the immediate post-war decades, from the 1970s onwards Cardiff's recorded Jewish population gradually began to diminish. The number of Jews affiliated with the city's two congregations fell from 2,500 to 2,000 between 1975 and 1980, and by 1995 it was down to 1,200.[29] With a decline in population came the demise of certain Jewish communal facilities and institutions in Cardiff. Cathedral Road's membership, for instance, fell from 402 to 160 between 1959 and 1988, leading to the synagogue's closure in January 1989 as the CUS could no longer afford its upkeep.[30] Moreover, with over 60 per cent of CUS congregants attending the Penylan synagogue for services in the late 1970s, it became clear that the future of Cardiff Orthodoxy lay there.[31]

The closure in 1992 of Wales's last kosher butcher, Krotosky's in City Road, was another sign that Cardiff's Jewish community was shrinking. Although the store closed because of the owner's retirement rather than declining trade, kosher butchers from across the United Kingdom were reluctant to take over the premise, as it was felt a dwindling community of around 1,500 Jews did not provide a sufficiently large clientele to make the venture financially worthwhile.[32] From then onwards, Jews wishing to observe the laws of *kashrut* in Cardiff, and south Wales more generally, in particular the consumption of kosher meat, have relied on both weekly and bimonthly food deliveries from delicatessens and butchers in Birmingham and London to meet their dietary needs.[33]

Why did the communities decline?

The shrinking of Jewish communities throughout the twentieth century, particularly after the Second World War, was not a phenomenon unique to Wales, but reflected a similar trend in most, if not all, Jewish centres in the United Kingdom and the United States.[34] However, such a steep fall from the 1920s onwards in a land virtually free from overt anti-Semitism gives rise to questions; why did Jewish communities in Wales decline so drastically?

In trying to account for the decline, the starting point must be the downturn in the industrial economy of the south Wales valleys and the consequent rise in unemployment in the region during the interwar period. As we have seen, coal mining was the main industry of the south Wales valleys, but during the 1920s the region's mining economy had been hard-hit by the decline in foreign demand for Welsh coal and the decreasing importance of coal as industrial fuel.[35] As coal output declined, unemployment in the industry rose with the number of employed miners falling from 271,161 to 126, 233 between 1920 and 1936.[36] The fate of the coal industry mirrored that of the steel industry, which declined from the 1920s onwards after finding itself unable to compete in an increasingly global steel market.[37] The shut-down of the Ebbw Vale works in 1929 resulted in 54 per cent rate of male unemployment in the town in the early 1930s, while in Dowlais male unemployment was at 80 per cent in the mid 1930s following the closure of its steelworks between 1930 and 1936.[38] As levels of unemployment soared, a total of nearly half a million people emigrated from south Wales in the 1920s and 1930s to find employment elsewhere in the United Kingdom.[39] In just one decade, south Wales's vibrant coalfield society was turned on its head and one of the most dynamic industrial regions in Europe was transformed into one of the most economically deprived.

The Jewish population of the south Wales valleys had grown with the region's industrial growth and there is no doubt that the downward turn of the local economy in the first half of the twentieth century played a fundamental role in the decline of the region's Jewish communities. As noted in Chapter 1, most Jews in the south Wales valleys worked in the service and retail sectors and their economic success relied heavily on the prosperity of the indigenous Welsh working class, their customers. Thus, while Jews were not directly affected by industrial decline in terms of employment, high levels of unemployment in the south Wales Valleys in the 1920s and 1930s dried up the local consumer market on which so many Jewish retailers depended for their livelihoods. Isaac and Ellen Barnett of Bargoed, for instance, 'ran a successful [auctioneering] business in South Wales until hit by the effects of the 1926 General Strike', while Mordecai Boone notes how his father, who 'had a little shop' in Rhymney, 'went broke more or less' after 'the General Strike of 1926' when 'all the miners were out on strike'.[40] Although Jewish pawnbrokers in the region probably profited for a period as valuables were increasingly pledged, poor economic conditions eventually forced Jewish business owners to relocate elsewhere.[41] As Gustave Abrahams of Ebbw Vale revealed in a letter to the Board of Deputies of British Jews in 1929:

> the adverse economic conditions prevailing here [Ebbw Vale] for the last ten years have had the effect of denuding this town of its Jewish inhabitants, until there are now only six Jewish families left.[42]

As was the case for the general population, many of the Jewish residents of the valleys relocated to larger nearby towns and cities, such as Cardiff or other parts of the United Kingdom, where greater economic opportunities existed. Reflecting on her childhood in Tredegar, Minnie Harris (b. 1897) wrote that 'after the First War, many [Jews] left [Tredegar] for the larger towns because of the depression of the '20s'.[43] Although the synagogues of Merthyr Tydfil and Pontypridd functioned until the last quarter of the twentieth century, both communities lost a significant number of congregants during the interwar period, which was undoubtedly linked to economic depression in the region. Merthyr Tydfil's recorded Jewish population fell from 400 to 175 between 1919 and 1937, for example, while the population of Pontypridd's Jewish community decreased from 150 to 40 individuals between 1922 and the 1950s.[44] The demise of approximately sixteen Jewish communities over a period of sixty years was unique to the south Wales valleys, with no other region in the United Kingdom witnessing such a dramatic decrease in Jewish communal life over such a short period of time.

But while the pattern of economic decline and emigration was an important factor in the collapse of most, if not all, of the Jewish communities in the south Wales valleys, it does not explain the decline in the rest of Wales. The causes of that decline are complex and are similar to those that affected other Jewish communities in the United Kingdom outside of London and Manchester: an ageing population; emigration, as the younger generations moved away to university, in search of employment and/or to find a Jewish partner; families relocating to a community with a larger Jewish infrastructure; intermarriage; a lower birth rate; and secularisation.

A significant problem was the fact that the first generations of Jewish settlers in late nineteenth- and early twentieth-century Wales had few successors. Whereas they had continued to work in the trades and occupations that they had brought with them from Eastern Europe, their children and grandchildren were educated in local primary and secondary schools in Wales and had different expectations. Although it was certainly not unheard of for children or grandchildren to take over the family business once they had finished school, a significant number went to university, entered the professions upon graduation, and did not return afterwards.[45] The motivations that drew Welsh-Jewish graduates away from their small communities in Wales varied. Having experienced new opportunities and ideas, many graduates developed a taste for the wider world and decided against returning to their childhood communities to take over their parents' or grandparents' businesses. After studying in London, for instance, Bennett Arron (b.1963) wanted to become an actor and showed little interest in returning to Port Talbot to take over the family glazing business.[46] Similarly, Oxford graduate Bernard Pollecoff (1931–84) chose not to return to his native Pwllheli to run his father's drapery business because he wanted to pursue a career in the chemical industry.[47]

However, the most frequent cause of departure was a sense that the economic climate was better elsewhere. While the Welsh economy in the period 1880–1914 was well-suited to the needs of Jewish immigrant traders and artisans, the same cannot be said for their university-educated and professionally trained children and grandchildren. Dominated by heavy industry and manufacturing, for most of the twentieth century the Welsh economy offered few opportunities for aspiring Jewish professionals to find employment that would utilise their skills,[48] and while the latter half of the twentieth century saw a growth in the service sector in Wales, it was largely confined to roles in public administration, education, health and consumer services.[49] As a result, many Welsh-Jewish graduates, like non-Jewish Welsh graduates, had to leave Wales if they wanted to find work in their chosen fields.[50] Many relocated to the south-east of England, a region that offered greater employment opportunities in a wide-range of comparatively high-growth and high-profit industries, such as financial and legal services.[51]

Indeed, as the career profiles and obituary columns of the *JC* show, many Welsh-Jewish graduates did leave their hometowns, and Wales, to take up employment elsewhere in Britain, particularly in London. One case in point was Derek Prag of Merthyr Tydfil (1923–2010), a Cambridge graduate who worked for an international news agency in London before becoming a director of the European Committee Press and Information Office.[52] Other examples include Aron Owen of Tredegar (1919–2009), who trained as a barrister and became a judge in London; Edward Conway of Llanelli (1911–2000), who was appointed head teacher of the Liverpool Hebrew School in 1944, before serving as head teacher of the Jews' Free School in London from 1958 until his retirement in 1976; and Ronald Bernstein of Swansea (1918–2004), who attended the University of Oxford before training as a barrister in London.[53] In a sense, a large number of second- and third-generation Jews in Wales simply followed the example of their immigrant parents and/or grandparents, since all three generations left their birthplaces to seek 'new worlds' and new economic opportunities elsewhere.[54]

Of course, some Welsh-Jewish professionals were able to carve out successful careers in Wales. They included Ben Hamilton of Dowlais (1896–1979), a solicitor and coroner in Merthyr Tydfil; Eli Reuben of Bangor (1897–1954), a dentist; and David Factor (b.1940), an accountant in Port Talbot.[55] Some Jewish professionals also migrated from elsewhere in the United Kingdom and settled in Wales. They included Gerald Brinks of Hemel Hempstead (1933–91), who worked as a quantity surveyor in Cardiff, and Glaswegian-born Louis Saville (1914–92), a general practitioner in the former mining village of Nantymoel between 1940 and 1991.[56] However, given the substantially fewer opportunities of private sector employment in Wales as compared to England, there has certainly been a net loss of Jewish professionals from Wales.

The Welsh-Jewish communities also produced an array of prominent rabbis who made their mark not in Wales, but in larger Jewish communities in the United Kingdom and across the globe. These included Llanelli-born Isaac Cohen, Chief Rabbi of Ireland from 1959 to 1979; Yisroel Fine of Swansea (b. 1948) who was rabbi to the United Hebrew Congregation of Newcastle and the Wembley Synagogue before being appointed rabbi of Cockfosters and North Southgate Synagogue in 1987; and Tredegar-born Solomon Goldman, rabbi of St John's Wood Synagogue between 1950 and 1976.[57] In fact, despite numbering no more than three hundred individuals at its peak, Llanelli's Jewish community 'produced almost a dozen rabbis and ministers'.[58] Although such appointments were certainly proud occasions for Wales's smaller Jewish communities, they served to drain them of congregants.

Throughout the twentieth century, the number of Jews proceeding to higher education in Wales or elsewhere in Britain was disproportionately high for the size of the population.[59] Although no records are available, it is possible to gain an idea of the extent of Welsh-Jewish university attendance in other ways. For example, according to Nay Joseph, despite numbering only ten families in the 1910s and 1920s, New Tredegar Jewry produced twelve medical doctors, four chemists and three teachers in one generation, while in his 1926 sociological study of 'foreign nationalities' in Merthyr Tydfil, J. Ronald Williams commented that the town's Jewish community was 'imbued with high ideals ... proved by the number of Jewish children who go to our secondary schools and proceed to the Universities'.[60] There are various reasons why a large number of the children and grandchildren of the first Jewish settlers gravitated towards higher education. Firstly, Jewish immigrants in Wales and in the rest of Britain perceived higher education and a professional career as the necessary prerequisites of upward economic mobility. This was stressed by the late Channah Hirsch of Llanelli, who remarked in her memoir that:

> You must remember that our parents were first-generation immigrants, who came to this country penniless, unable to speak the language, and who got married and had to start from scratch completely on their own ... Yet they wanted their children to have an education because ... schooling was considered very important as the route out of poverty ... Parents' concern in those days – and I'm talking about Jewish parents – was to see that their children got an education that would get them to university, and then on to good English professions. They wanted their children to be accountants, solicitors, doctors, pharmacists.[61]

Secondly, as we have seen, in many parts of Eastern Europe, Jews were discriminated against by laws that restricted their access to higher education and a long list of trades and professions. Having been denied such opportunities themselves, most Jewish immigrants were eager for their offspring to take advantage of the expanding higher educational and employment opportunities that were open to them in the United Kingdom. As one former Jewish resident of Pontypridd recalled in 1978, the immigrant Jewish parents wanted their children to reach 'positions in life' that had previously 'been denied to them' in Russia.[62]

Thirdly, Jewish cultural tradition has always incorporated a respect for literacy and learning. Indeed, in the East European *shtetl* no one had more prestige than the Talmudic scholar, who devoted himself with religious intensity to sacred texts. [63] When Eastern European Jewish immigrants came to Britain in vast numbers in the late nineteenth and early twentieth century they brought these values and traditions with them. Some encouraged their sons to become rabbis, and sent them to train in British y*eshivot* (plural of *yeshiva*) in towns and cities such as Manchester and Gateshead, while others transferred the traditional respect for learning and religious scholarship to secular education so that their children could advance socially and economically in Britain. As Leonard Minkes remarked in his memoir of Jewish life in 1920s and 1930s Cardiff:

Jews attach very great importance to education ... In my family, at least, it was so: when at the age of 4½, I entered Splott School, my mother informed me that when I grew up I would go to Oxford, a heroic statement given the family finances ... In the old days, in Eastern Europe, education had meant religious study but already, in the nineteenth century, there was growing pressure for secular education, too, and that was certainly so in Britain.[64]

Another factor that led to the decline of Welsh-Jewish communities was the desire for endogamous marriage. Although there are numerous examples of marriages taking place between two Jews belonging to the same community in Wales, in most of the country's smaller Jewish communities the pool of eligible Jewish singles was often not large enough for hometown matches to be made. The result was that many young Jews from Wales's smaller Jewish centres had to go, or be sent, to larger Jewish centres in the United Kingdom to find their marriage partners (London and

Manchester especially). Reflecting on his teenage years in Merthyr Tydfil, Lionel Bernstein (b.1946) recalled that 'there was nothing' when it came to Jewish dating in the town and how his sister 'was shipped off to a relation in London' at the age of sixteen to find a Jewish partner.[65] Moreover, in her study of courtship and weddings in south Wales, anthropologist Diana Leonard noted that in the post-war decades most of Llanelli's Jewish young 'met their spouse outside the town and ... held their weddings in, for example, London'.[66]

Indeed, it was not uncommon to find announcements in the *JC* of engagements and marriages between small-town Welsh Jews and those from larger Jewish centres in Britain. More often than not, one would read of marriages such as that between of Jessie Goldfoot of Brynmawr and Sydney Taylor of Leeds in 1926 or of Ida Albiston of Wrexham to Alfred Martin of Liverpool in 1930.[67] Although such marriages were happy occasions for the families involved, they drained Wales's smaller Jewish communities of congregants, as the newlyweds rarely settled there. There are many reasons for this, ranging from a desire to live in a more sizeable Jewish community with immediate access to Jewish facilities to the fact that the husband's business activities lay elsewhere. The above mentioned Lionel Bernstein of Merthyr Tydfil, for instance, moved to his wife's native Cardiff in 1967, as she found Merthyr's small Jewish community, then numbering forty individuals, too confining in terms of a Jewish lifestyle, while Llanelli-born Renee Landy settled in Cardiff following her marriage to David Woolf in 1965 because he owned an optometry business in the city and wanted to raise their children in a fully functioning Jewish community.[68] While these two examples did not contribute to the overall decline of Welsh Jewry, their movement from smaller to larger Jewish centres in Wales certainly contributed to the decline of the former.

Jews in Wales generally observed the traditional rabbinic laws and regulations with regard to endogamous marriage, but this is not to imply that Welsh Jewry has been immune to exogamy, that is intermarriage between a Jew and a non-Jew. While Jews in Wales's smaller Jewish communities typically married Jews from elsewhere, the relative scarcity of potential Jewish marriage partners at home occasionally led to courtship with non-Jews. Reflecting on his childhood in Pontypridd's Jewish community in the 1910s and 1920s, a community then numbering around 150 individuals, one former Jewish resident noted that:

> There was a good deal of mixing, in my time, with the general commu-
> nity, and a lot of my friends were non-Jewish, as was many other Jewish
> boys. There was some intermarrying taking place then because of this
> mixing with the population in general.[69]

Although impossible to quantify with any precision, intermarriage
certainly contributed to the numerical decline of Wales's Orthodox Jewish
communities. This was because intermarried couples often disassociated
themselves or, as we have seen from the example of the CUS's constitution,
were excluded, from Wales's Orthodox congregations and reared their
offspring outside of the Jewish faith as a result. In 1928, for instance, Marcus
Gubay of Llandudno, an Iraqi-born Jew, converted to Catholicism after
marrying an Irish woman named Margaret Clarke and raised his three
children as Catholics.[70] Similarly, Cardiff-born Leo Abse married a
non-Jewish Welsh woman named Marjorie Davies in 1955 and although
he retained his Jewish identity, none of his children were raised as Jewish.[71]

Nevertheless, as Amy Shevitz reminds us, 'assimilation can go both
ways'.[72] Far from being linked to the demise of a Jewish community,
intermarriage can also be a factor in a community's survival and growth.
This has been particularly true in the case of Cardiff's Reform community, which, in keeping with other Reform congregations in the United
Kingdom, accepts patrilineal descent as a basis for claiming a Jewish identity. For Orthodox Judaism, intermarriage is an anathema, directly
contravening *halacha*; but for Reform Judaism it is a reality affecting an
increasing number of Jews, and the best way of rectifying an undesirable
situation is to reach out to intermarried couples, fully supporting those
who wished to affiliate with a Jewish community and raise their children
as Jewish.[73] One such example in Cardiff was that of Myer Cohen (1905–
97), who was driven away from the Cathedral Road congregation
(Orthodox) when he married a 'devout Catholic' named Betty Heath in
1934.[74] He was brought back into the fold in 1948, following the establishment of the CNS. Despite not having a Jewish mother, Cohen's son,
Jeffrey, was the first boy to be *bar mitzvah* at the CNS and was an active
member of Cardiff's Reform community until his death in 1987.[75]

As we have seen previously, many of Wales's small Jewish communities
lacked the Jewish infrastructure, such as a resident kosher butcher or a
purpose-built synagogue, that was to be found in larger Jewish centres in
Britain. While many Jews lived with these limitations and made

compromises, others found such an environment unconducive to the intensive Jewish lifestyle they wanted for themselves and their families. Thus the decline of Wales's Jewish communities was also attributable to the desire of some Jews to relocate to somewhere with a more developed Jewish infrastructure. Despite a fondness for her hometown, Swansea-born Deborah Giladi (née Glass) (b.1965) moved in the 1980s to the larger and more developed Jewish community in Manchester because she 'wanted [her] children to have ... the opportunities associated with a Jewish lifestyle that [she] didn't have when [she] was growing up' in south Wales, such as a Jewish day school.[76] Similarly, Kate Loewenthal, a psychology lecturer at the University College of North Wales, relocated with her family from Bangor to Stamford Hill, London, in the late 1960s because she and her husband wanted their daughter to attend a Jewish day school and be reared in a community with extensive Jewish facilities.[77]

Moreover, a sense of exile has been part of the psyche of many Welsh Jews, resulting in the emigration of some to the Promised Land – Israel. A small number of Jews from Wales, including Lily Tobias of Ystalyfera (1897–1984) and Max Seligman of Cardiff (1902–87), relocated to Palestine in the 1920s and 1930s and others have followed since the establishment of the Israeli state in 1948.[78] Although Vivian Lipman speculated in 1954 that 'emigration to Israel ... may have a significant quantitative effect' on the population of British Jewry 'in the future', the number of British Jews who have made *aliyah* since 1948 has not been extensive, with approximately 32,594 individuals emigrating to Israel between 1948 and 2011 (approximately 1–2 per cent of Britain's Jewish population).[79]

A lack of extant figures specific to Wales means that it is impossible to know with any precision the number of Welsh Jews who have made *aliyah*. Despite this, scholars such as Grahame Davies have made unfounded claims that emigration to Israel was one of the main factors in explaining the decline of Welsh-Jewish communities during the latter half of the twentieth century.[80] Although *aliyah* certainly contributed to their decline, existing evidence suggests that it was not a significant factor. For instance, only fourteen announcements of Jews leaving for Israel were made in Cardiff Jewry's quarterly periodical *CAJEX* between 1951 and 1993.[81] Furthermore, an article in the *JC* in 1975 made no mention of *aliyah* when trying to account for the demographic decline of Wales's Jewish communities.[82]

More significant in explaining the decline of Wales's Jewish communities, and British-Jewish communities more generally, has been the 'demographic transition' in the size of Jewish families throughout the twentieth century.[83] Whereas predominantly poor Eastern European Jewish immigrants brought with them a more traditional Jewish pattern of early marriage and large families, their children and grandchildren developed a tendency to marry later and have fewer children or not to marry at all.[84] The reasons behind this shift are many, but the adoption of British middle-class behaviour and values by the second and third generations was arguably one of the main triggers.[85] Indeed, as more and more Jews, both male and female, entered higher education and became more career-minded, the decision to marry and have children was often postponed until later in life.[86] Socially mobile Jews also favoured smaller families, because fewer offspring allowed them to invest more in their children's education and ensure a higher level of material comfort for their families.[87] Moreover, the development of contraceptives throughout the course of the twentieth century meant that Jewish couples, like non-Jewish couples, could control the number of children they wished to have.[88]

Thus, while many immigrant Jewish families in late nineteenth- and early twentieth-century Wales had as many as five to ten children, by the mid twentieth century having two or three children had become the norm for Welsh-Jewish families.[89] The average number of children per Jewish family in Aberavon fell from roughly 3 to 1 between 1901 and 1951, for example, while Bangor's Jewish families decreased from an average of 4.6 to 1.5 children between 1901 and 1951. Similarly, the average number of children in each Jewish family in Pontypridd and Tredegar decreased from 3.2 and 5.6 respectively to 2 between 1901 and 1951.[90] Since the long-term survival of any ethnic/religious group lies ultimately in the hands of their offspring and their ability to reproduce their numbers, the fall in Jewish birth rates has been a significant factor in the decline of Wales's Jewish communities.

One of the clearest trends in the latter half of the twentieth century, particularly for traditional Orthodox congregations, has been the increasing secularisation of both Welsh and British Jewry, with a growing number of Jews disaffiliating themselves from traditional congregational life, especially regular synagogue attendance and religious worship. The reasons for this are varied and complex and include the abandonment by some Jews of their faith and belief in God in response to the Holocaust, as well as the acculturation into wider Welsh and British society of second- and third-generation Jews, who over time became estranged from the traditional religious observances, rituals and way of life of the immigrant generation, the founders of Wales's Jewish communities. While this led some to join non-Orthodox communities such as the Liberal and the Reform, others responded by prioritising a secular Jewish identity, one based on ethnicity and heritage, over a religious one. How many Welsh Jews disassociated themselves from religious observance throughout the twentieth century is impossible to ascertain, but the fact that survey research conducted in the mid-1990s found that 25 per cent of British Jews raised in Orthodox communities were unaffiliated to synagogues shows that traditional religious observance was becoming a marginal activity for many Jews towards the end of the twentieth-century, as it was for non-Jews, particularly Christians.[91]

Endurance

By the turn of the twenty-first century only Jewish cemeteries, visited on occasion by the children or grandchildren of those buried there, provide evidence of once thriving Jewish communities in Wales. In other places, synagogue buildings empty of Jews serve as poignant reminders of Jewish communities that have since faded away. Although the last member of the long-defunct Merthyr Tydfil Hebrew Congregation passed away in 1999, the town's synagogue in Church Street still stands and has planning permission for conversion into apartments.[92] Pontypridd's synagogue has already become apartments, in both Llanelli and Port Talbot the synagogues have become churches and in Tredegar and Brynmawr they have been converted into houses. No longer serving their original purpose, Jewish cemeteries and synagogues in Wales have, to borrow the words of Lee Shai Weissbach, become powerful 'places of memory'.[93] This is because 'they are not only sites where actual events transpired, but also places that have been suffused with a larger meaning because they have come to be reminders of an entire historical experience that has reached its end'.[94]

All this is not to say that Welsh Jewry has completely disappeared, however. Although smaller than in the past, congregations are still viable and a Jewish presence persists in many parts of Wales. The 2011 census returns recorded that 2,064 people in Wales gave 'Jewish' as their religion, but, of course, as mentioned previously, these figures do not necessarily represent the true number of religious Jews accurately, nor do they account for Jews who do not define their Jewishness in religious terms or by membership of a congregation.[95] Thus, while the 2011 census recorded 159 people in Swansea as being religiously Jewish, the active membership of the Swansea Hebrew Congregation numbered no more than twenty individuals.[96] Similarly, ninety-nine people in Newport were recorded in 2011 as Jews by religion, but the number of Jews who paid the membership fee of the Newport Hebrew Congregation was only thirty.[97]

The Newport Hebrew Congregation downsized their synagogue in 1997, and despite the lack of a sufficient number of Jewish men in the city to form a regular *minyan* for religious services, at the time of writing a handful of dedicated and ageing congregants continue to hold weekly *Shabbat* (Sabbath) services in their small synagogue in Risca Road.[98] In 2009 Swansea Jewry sold its 1950s synagogue building in Ffynone Road to the LifePoint Church group and began renting the building's former Lewis Palto Hall, once the centre of Swansea Jewry's social activities and celebrations, for religious worship.[99] Despite insufficient numbers to form a regular *minyan*, at the time of writing congregants meet weekly at the synagogue for Friday evening and *Shabbat* morning services.[100]

With most active members now over the age of seventy, many congregants believe that Swansea Jewry is a dying community and will wither away in the not so distant future.[101] Other members are more optimistic, however, believing that the community's ability in recent years to attract a constantly changing stream of Jewish visitors, as well as Jewish students and staff recruited to higher education in the city, will allow the Swansea Hebrew Congregation to survive for many years to come.[102] Since the early years of this century, the numbers attending summer services at Swansea's synagogue have been swelled by holidaying Jews from London who stay at Swansea University's campus on an almost annual basis, while in 2009 the congregation welcomed the arrival of Israeli-born Itshak Golan following his appointment as a researcher in immunology at Swansea University.[103] In 2013 Golan's son celebrated his *bar mitzvah* at Swansea's synagogue, the first such ceremony to be held by the community for twenty years.[104]

Although the combined population of Cardiff's two Jewish communities, the Orthodox and the Reform, declined from around 3,500 to 802 persons between 1968 and 2011, the city continues to be home to two congregations – the CUS and the Cardiff Reform Synagogue.[105] Nevertheless, the decline in numbers did bring some changes to the infrastructure of both congregations. In 2003, for instance, the CUS sold its synagogue in Penylan as it was 'too large' for its 300 members, replacing it with a new and smaller house of worship in nearby Cyncoed Gardens, where weekly Friday night and *Shabbat* morning services, as well as morning *minyanim* (plural of *minyan*), continue to be held.[106]

The congregation is also numerous enough to afford the services of a full-time rabbi but, like other Welsh-Jewish communities in the past, Cardiff's declining Orthodox community has experienced great difficulty in securing the lasting services of a spiritual leader. Between 1992 and 2012, for instance, the congregation had five rabbis.[107] The reasons for this are many, and are similar to those discussed in Chapter 2. Some rabbis treated Cardiff as a stepping stone in their career and had their sights set on moving to a more prestigious and larger Jewish community in Britain, while others wished to settle in a community with a more substantial Jewish infrastructure. Thus, after five years at Penylan, Rabbi Daniel Levy left for Leeds in 1999 because he and his wife, Naomi, wanted their children to attend a Jewish day school, while Rabbi Yossi Ives left Cardiff in 2003, after three years of service, to take up a pulpit at Richmond Synagogue in London.[108]

Cardiff's Reform community employed a full-time rabbi up until the departure of Rabbi Rachel Montagu for London in 1988.[109] From then onwards the dwindling congregation found it could no longer afford the services of a full-time spiritual leader and between 1990 and 2014 it relied on the services of two part-time rabbis, Elaina Rothman and Charles Middleburgh.[110] Since Middleburgh's departure in 2014 the congregation has relied on congregants to lead services 'as an interim measure', as well as visiting ministers such as Rabbi Monique Mayer of the Bristol and West Progressive Congregation, who, at the time of writing, leads one service a month.[111] An important source of continuity for the community is its synagogue in Moira Terrace, which continues to be used for religious worship and social gatherings, serving approximately 230 adult congregants.[112]

Casual reading of the available literature on Welsh Jewry would lead one to believe that in the early twenty-first century Wales is home to only three Jewish centres – Cardiff, Newport, and Swansea. Grahame Davies, for instance, noted in 2002 that 'there [were] around 1,000 Jews in

Cardiff ... and small communities in Swansea and Newport', while Paul Chambers suggested that the Jewish experience in early twenty-first-century Wales was limited to Cardiff and Swansea.[113] Nevertheless, other Jewish centres continue to function in other parts of Wales than the country's three largest cities. Despite numbering only 15 congregants in 2003, the collapse of the Llandudno and Colwyn Bay Hebrew Congregation was avoided following the community's decision to transfer ownership of their synagogue to the Manchester Lubavitch in 2004.[114] Run primarily as a retreat centre for Jewish families and schools, local Jewry continues to use the synagogue as and when it is needed. Rather than regarding religious observance as an all-or-nothing proposition, congregants do what is feasible. As was revealed by congregant Michael Lee in an interview in 2007:

> the Llandudno Hebrew Congregation still have use of the synagogue as when we need it, and can join in services on Friday evenings or Saturdays when one is being held. We always try to arrange services for special festivals such as Hanukkah and the Jewish New Year and Day of Atonement.[115]

As we have seen from the example of the Rhyl Jewish community, in the right circumstances defunct Jewish communities can be revived. This also appears true of Bangor's Jewish community, which officially dissolved in 1985, but was described in 2009 as undergoing 'a mini-revival'.[116] The origins of this 'mini-revival' can be traced back to 2006, following the appointment of Londoner Nathan Abrams as a lecturer at the University of Wales, Bangor. Having been raised in north London's extensive Jewish community, Abrams was eager to find other Jews living in north-west Wales.[117] After discovering that 361 people in north Wales gave Jewish as their religion in the 2001 census, he set about contacting Jews in the region and bringing them together. With the aid of a £10,000 grant from the Clore Jewish Development Fund in London, Abrams established the 'North Wales Jewish Network' in 2007.[118] Centred in Bangor, the network is not a 'congregation' as such, since it has no dedicated place of worship, but it seeks 'to provide a focal point ... for communal meeting' and 'to raise awareness of the Jewish experience of North Wales ... for the Jews of Gwynedd, Anglesey and surrounding areas'.[119] The network currently has between fifty and sixty members who celebrate Passover together, participate in *Shabbat* services and receive kosher meat and other food-stuffs from Manchester.[120] In 2010 they arranged with Conwy County Council to secure a Jewish burial plot in Llanrhos cemetery, the first to be established in north Wales.[121] Many members have little or no formal Jewish background, and it is because of this openness that the network continues to grow, creating a community 'which is largely virtual', with members remaining 'in contact with each other through an email list', as well as meeting in person from time to time.[122]

A similar Jewish community sprang up in Welshpool in 1996. In a move to help outlying members of the Birmingham Progressive Synagogue sustain religious observance, a Friday night service was held at the home of Anthony Solomons in Welshpool in July 1996. Twenty or so Jews from across mid Wales and the England–Wales border attended, and having found the gathering 'worthy in the religious sense and satisfying socially', they decided to form mid Wales's first Jewish community.[123] Named the Welshpool Jewish Group, the community was listed in the *JYB* for the first time in 1999 and currently has between fifteen and twenty members.[124] Voluntarism appears to be the backbone of community life, with members circulating around each other's homes once every six weeks for Friday night services in the Liberal tradition conducted by the owner of the house.[125]

In less than a hundred years, Wales's organised Jewish presence has declined substantially. Home to approximately nineteen Jewish centres in 1919, only five synagogues remained in the country in 2011. Nonetheless, while most of Wales's Jewish communities have disappeared, others are on-going or are being re-established/established in the early twenty-first century. Although the future of these communities remains uncertain, the prospects for some centres, particularly in north Wales, are brighter than they have been for many years. Welsh Jewry may have declined in numbers but it is still evolving.

Conclusion

To return to a theme raised in the introduction, the term 'Anglo Jewry' has shaped the study of British-Jewish communities either by incorporating the histories of the non-Anglo communities into the larger English ones, or by excluding studies of them altogether. As we have seen, this approach to British-Jewish studies has been adopted by a number of scholars, including Todd Endelman, who considered that 'since the number of Jews who lived in Wales ... was never large, folding them into "Anglo-Jewry" does not distort the overall picture'.[1] This proposition, however, contradicts an earlier statement made by Endelman, who, in defence of the study of British Jewry, argued that small 'numbers do not ... justify the marginalization of Britain in modern Jewish historiography'.[2] If this holds good for Britain in the context of international-Jewish history, then why should the case for Wales be different in the context of British-Jewish historiography? After all, as Endelman reminds us, Welsh Jews 'were not, in a strict sense, "English" Jews'.[3]

Although Welsh Jews have undoubtedly shared and continue to share commonalities with their English, Scottish and Irish counterparts, they did and do exhibit features that are unique. As well as learning English to fit into wider British society, Jewish immigrants living and working in Wales's Welsh-speaking heartlands faced an additional integration hurdle in the form of the Welsh language. They also had to strike a balance between the country's Welsh-language and anglicised cultures, in some instances adopting elements such as the eisteddfod tradition into their own cultural framework. Having explored the particularity of the Welsh cultural context, it is hoped that future historians will ignore Endelman's statement, and also that of Ursula Henriques, who once described the 'cultural' activities of south Wales Jewry as 'typical of provincial Jewries all over Great Britain'.[4]

The Welsh-Jewish experience was also unique in other ways. For instance, Wales was the only country in mainland Britain where Jews arrived indirectly.[5] As mentioned in Chapter 1, established shipping routes during this period meant that the vast majority of Eastern European Jewish migrants entering Great Britain from Continental Europe did so via the eastern English ports of Hull and Grimsby. Smaller numbers also arrived via London and the port of Leith in eastern Scotland. Thus, in order to get to Wales, Jewish immigrants had to travel first via England.[6] As we have seen, chain migration brought large numbers straight to Wales from English ports, while others migrated in steps, living first in one of England's larger Jewish centres.

Moreover, exploring the history of Jewish communities in Wales provides a new perspective on the way geography has helped condition the British-Jewish experience. As noted in Chapter 1, the Jewish communities in the south Wales valleys were unique to British Jewry because in no other part of the United Kingdom were so many of them established in such a small geographical area. As we have seen, in an area stretching approximately thirteen miles across and in length, an estimated sixteen Jewish communities were founded in the late nineteenth and early twentieth centuries. The number of congregations established did not reflect a high population of Jews, since there were only some 1,260 Jewish individuals in the region at its peak in the early 1920s.[7] But the mountainous landscape of the south Wales coalfield essentially divided and scattered the region's Jewish population into numerous small communities. If the region had been flat, it would have been easier for Jews to reach each other and it is likely that fewer Jewish communities would have been established, as happened in the Durham coalfield, which was home to only two synagogues, Bishop Auckland and Durham.[8]

Situated on the western side of Britain, Wales's geographical position had a significant impact on the make-up of British Jewry between 1939 and 1945. As discussed in Chapter 3, during the Second World War the greater part of Wales was designated an area safe from enemy bombing, a factor that resulted in an influx of over 200,000 evacuees from England, both Jewish and non-Jewish. Wales was not entirely unique in this instance, however, as during this period 'safe areas' in England and Scotland also saw the arrival of evacuated Anglo-Jews and the establishment of wartime

Jewish communities, such as the Amersham United Synagogue Membership Group in Buckinghamshire.[9] Nonetheless, unlike Scotland and England, most of Wales was designated a reception area and thus arguably received the largest number of evacuated Jews in Britain during this period. The exact figures are not known, but the presence of the evacuees certainly led to a dramatic increase in the population of Welsh Jewry for a brief period, a phenomenon that was not experienced by other Jewries in the United Kingdom.

The sharp decline of the south Wales coalfield's recorded Jewish population during the interwar period, from approximately 1,260 in the early 1920s to 496 in 1939, was also unique to Welsh Jewry, since no other region in the United Kingdom witnessed such a dramatic decrease in its Jewish population at this time.[10] As we have seen from Chapter 6, the economic depression that hit the south Wales coalfield during the 1920s and 1930s was the main instigator of this decline and the exodus of Jews simply reflected a wider pattern of emigration from the region when nearly half a million people left the valleys to seek employment and economic opportunities elsewhere in the United Kingdom.

The relations of north Wales's Jewish communities with the larger Jewish centres of north-west England are an interesting dimension to this study. As mentioned in Chapter 1, north Wales's Jewish communities, with the exception of Colwyn Bay, emerged in the late nineteenth and the early twentieth centuries as a result of internal migration within Britain, with Jewish pedlars looking for locations where trade would face less competition than would be found in Liverpool and Manchester. Furthermore, in Chapter 2 we have seen how, with the aid of Jewish organisations and individuals from Liverpool and Manchester, Jews in north Wales were able to maintain their Jewish identities and were encouraged to do so. Indeed, so reliant was north Wales Jewry on north-west England's larger Jewish centres that the former would have been unlikely to have prospered had the latter not existed. The history of north Wales Jewry is therefore a part and parcel of the histories of Liverpool and Manchester Jewries, and historians writing on the Jewish metropolises of north-west England can learn a great deal from Welsh-Jewish historiography, however marginal events in north Wales may appear to them.

Additionally, exploring the history of all Wales's Jewish communities, both large and small, as well as those Jews who lived away from organised centres, has permitted us to appreciate the complex character of Welsh

CONCLUSION

Jewry, and British Jewry as a whole. Evidently, the histories of Wales's smaller Jewish settlements are in some ways similar to that of its larger Jewish centres. In both small and large communities, for instance, migration was the key to growth and development, Jewish communal social activities were organised and maintained and religious concerns were central. But Wales's smaller Jewish communities were also different in many respects. Their Jewish infrastructure was not as extensive as that in Wales's larger Jewish centres, for instance, and while the situation varied from community to community, smaller Jewish communities typically lacked the necessary population base and financial resources to build their own synagogues, to attract long-serving ministers and to maintain Jewish facilities such as a resident kosher butcher. Yet despite the challenges they faced, each of Wales's smaller Jewish communities was able to maintain an observant Jewish lifestyle.

Moreover, the conspicuous absence of multiple or dissident congregations, which often occurred in other, typically larger, Jewish centres in Britain such as Cardiff, Glasgow, Manchester and Swansea, was a feature of Wales's smaller Jewish settlements. This was primarily because of a lack of numbers, but it was also significant that, unlike most British-Jewish communities, they were not subject to successive waves of immigration from different parts of Europe throughout the nineteenth century. As we have seen, most of Wales's small Jewish communities were founded in the latter half of the nineteenth century and composed entirely, or almost entirely, of East European immigrants. As a result, there was usually no need to form a breakaway congregation that did not share the liturgical traditions of an already established community. Although Llanelli, Wrexham and Port Talbot were exceptions, the rival congregations established in these three towns were short-lived, lasting no more than a few years, because the communities lacked the resources to sustain more than one synagogue. Compromises were therefore made in all three places and the differing religious needs of members were accommodated in a single congregation, as happened in other small Jewish centres in the United Kingdom, such as Dundee in Scotland.[11]

While historians of British Jewry can learn much from Welsh-Jewish history, the same can be said for Welsh historians. In the context of religion, Welsh historians have tended to ignore Jews or marginalised their histories in favour of the Nonconformist experience. Of course, this scholarly focus is to a great extent justified, for Nonconformity comprised

161

the largest group of religious bodies in Wales between the nineteenth and mid twentieth centuries. Nevertheless, in all the scholarly attention paid to Christian institutions something essential has been missed, for Judaism, the oldest non-Christian faith in Wales, has been a fundamental feature of the Welsh religious landscape since the mid eighteenth century. Indeed, in post-devolutionary Wales where, as D. Densil Morgan points out, 'pluralism has become an undoubted characteristic of the [country's] religious life', it would be a mistake to think that the full story of the Welsh religious experience can be told without considering the histories of Jews and other religious minorities in Wales.[12]

For some historians, Welsh-Jewish history is nothing more than a tale of persecution and suffering, part of what the historian Salo Wittmayer Baron called the 'lachrymose conception of Jewish history'.[13] The focus of this narrative has long been the Tredegar riots of 1911 and the Esther Lyons case, which, rather frustratingly, have been used by historians such as Geoffrey Alderman to prop up arguments for a long tradition of Welsh anti-Semitism, as well as to generalise non-Jewish attitudes towards Jews in Wales. Yet, as Paul O'Leary reminds us, these incidents 'have been scrutinized so assiduously [by historians] . . . because they were not a common occurrence' in Welsh-Jewish history.[14] Indeed, in comparison to the histories of Jews in other European countries, the Welsh-Jewish experience, like the British-Jewish experience, was remarkable by virtue of its freedom from overt persecution. As noted in Chapter 4, Jews have generally faced little, if any violence, in Wales and social and occupational discrimination, while certainly not absent, was neither systematic nor pervasive.

The record of social and political integration was also remarkable. Jews in Wales mixed to an unprecedented degree with non-Jews, in informal and formal settings, and faced no obstacles in accessing positions of honour and influence in Welsh society. For example, Masonic lodges in Wales, bastions of male-establishment privilege, admitted Jews in sufficient numbers in the nineteenth and twentieth centuries to obviate the need for Jews to establish their own lodges, as happened in the United States. Nor did Jews in Wales feel the need to form their own societies because they were excluded from sports and social clubs, as happened in other places in Britain, such as London and Manchester. Another measure of their successful integration is their involvement in the civic life of the towns and cities in Wales in which they settled; Jews met little or no problem in being elected to, and taking up public positions as, councillors, mayors, justices of the peace and members of parliament for Welsh constituencies.

Toleration, however, is never absolute, and while the Welsh record of tolerance toward its Jewish population has generally been good, the country's acceptance of Jews has never been unconditional. As Jasmine Donahaye points out with reference to non-Jewish Welsh attitudes to Jews in Welsh literature, 'tolerance . . . denotes a conditional acceptance' that can be revoked if the culturally or ethnically different "other" . . . wields perceived power within the framework of the dominant culture'.[15] Indeed, toleration depends on external circumstances and, as Neil Evans reminds us, in the context of Wales it is important to ask 'in which circumstances were Welsh people likely to be tolerant and in which intolerant?'[16] Thus, Jewish immigrants were generally tolerated in nineteenth and twentieth century Wales because the majority of them worked as merchants and traders and avoided competing directly with the native Welsh and others in the labour market. Nevertheless, as we have seen from the events in Dowlais in 1903, when Jews did compete for employment in Wales, they faced the same workplace intimidation suffered by other immigrant workers, such as the Irish. Furthermore, periods of great social unrest and uncertainty, like an economic depression or a war, often ignited feelings of resentment and hostility towards the culturally or ethnically different 'other', especially if that other appeared to be performing well or was perceived to be benefiting from the existing circumstances. It can be argued that this is precisely what happened in the Monmouthshire valleys in August 1911, when the business premises of immigrant Jewish shopkeepers were attacked because they were seen to be succeeding in making a profit at a time when native Welsh workers were suffering from economic hardship.

In his examination of Jewish and non-Jewish relations in nineteenth- and twentieth-century Wales, William Rubinstein concluded that the relationship was generally harmonious since 'philo-semitism' – defined as 'admiration and support for Jews by gentiles'– was 'a recognizable and distinctive part of Welsh culture'.[17] This, according to Rubinstein, was a consequence of both 'the rise of Nonconformity' and the diffusion of liberal religious values in Wales during the eighteenth and nineteenth centuries. While Rubinstein is correct in noting that Welsh Nonconformists, having been oppressed themselves for their religious beliefs, both empathised with Jewish religious persecution and shared an affiliation with the Hebrew Bible, it is too simplistic and rigid to conclude that this identification equated to a 'love of Jews'.[18] This is because the toleration of religious difference is not the same as the toleration of ethnic and cultural difference. In this instance, we are reminded of Lloyd George, whose admiration and respect for the Jewish religion and the 'People of the Book' did not prevent him from occasionally subscribing to age-old racial stereotypes concerning Jews, particularly when he felt threatened and undermined by the ethnic 'other'.

In sum, the history of the Jews in Wales is not a sombre tale of failure and enervation, as Alderman has claimed.[19] Nor, however, is it the opposite – a successful and peaceful story – as Rubinstein would like to suggest.[20] Stark, one-sided characterisations of the Welsh-Jewish past like these are not illuminating. This is because historians who focus solely on the good fortune of Welsh Jewry, as well as those who only dwell on its difficulties, fail to confront the ambiguity of its past. They draw an image that is at once too neat and too one-dimensional, largely because they bring their own agendas and commitments to the task. By forswearing the urge to pronounce Welsh-Jewish history as a success or a failure, this book has restored balance and complexity to the Welsh-Jewish experience. In doing so, some historians may argue that it work has taken a 'safe' route, but both sides of the coin have to be taken into consideration if we are to develop our historical understanding of Welsh-Jewish life.

Although the population of Wales's Jewish communities has severely declined since the 1930s, it is to be hoped that the overwhelming pessimism with which this aspect of Welsh-Jewish history has been treated with in the past can be replaced with a sense of optimism. In 1999, David Morris concluded at the turn of the new millennium that 'the future of Welsh Jewry must surely be in doubt' and 'seems sealed'.[21] However, given the right conditions, not only can dwindling Jewish communities continue to function, but extinct centres can also revive and even thrive. The revival of the Rhyl Hebrew Congregation in the mid twentieth century and of Bangor Jewry in the early twenty-first century are living proof of this. While Wales has not received a significant influx of Jews since the arrival of refugees from Nazi-occupied Europe, the country, particularly the north Wales coastline, continues to attract Jewish holidaymakers from Liverpool and Manchester and is a place to which some of them go to retire, drawn by the region's tranquillity, beautiful scenery, affordable housing and relative proximity to north-west England's Jewish centres.[22] The coastal position of some of Wales's university towns and cities, such as Aberystwyth and Swansea, and the relatively low cost and ease of converting self-catering university accommodation to their religious needs, have made them popular summer holiday destinations for Hasidic families from London and Manchester since the last quarter of the twentieth century.[23] Yet, at the time of writing, the numbers visiting Aberystwyth have declined dramatically following a healthy and safety dispute in 2013 over the lighting of Sabbath candles in university-owned accommodation.[24]

Welsh universities continue to attract Jewish students and academics and, as the capital city of Wales, Cardiff has long attracted a sprinkling of Jewish hospital workers, civil servants, university staff and students, and young professionals. As one of the 'fastest growing economies in Europe' in the early twenty-first century, there is hope that employment opportunities will continue to attract Jewish workers to the city in years to come.[25] Whether they will identify with their local Jewish community it is impossible to predict, but a continuing in-migration of Jews could be a valuable boost to the continuance of congregational life in Wales. The future of Welsh Jewry has yet to be written, and only time will tell what will become of Wales's Jewish centres. What remains clear, however, is that the fate of Wales's Jewish communities is not sealed.

The population of Wales's Jewish communities in selected years drawn from the Jewish Year Book, 1896–2010

	1896	1906	1917	1928	1939	1947	1959	1968	1976	1986	1999	2010
Aberavon and Port Talbot			99	99	46	46	19	18	18			
Aberdare		20a	90	90	63	63	24	8	8			
Abertillery		60	100	100	14							
Bangor	30	75	65	40	20	30	34	20	16	30		
Barry Dock			38	36								
Brynmawr	12a	135	135	135	49	49	26	16	6			
Cardiff		1250	2025	2225	2300	2300	3000	3500	2500	1770	1500	940
Colwyn Bay							24	23	23			
Ebbw Vale			100	80	9							
Llandudno							50	45	45	30b	45b	15b
Llanelli		70	70	300	100	120	100	38	38	20		
Merthyr Tydfil		300	300	400	175	175	100	40	20			
Neath					15							
Newport		130	250	250	250	180	180	100	100	50	10	39
Pontypridd	150	100	100	100	147	147	37	22	22			
Porthcawl							105					
Rhyl		55	55	55				60	40			
Swansea	300	400	1000	1000	565	565	520	418	240	180	245	170
Tredegar	102	100	175	175	39	39						
Wrexham	40	30	69	69	69	69						

a Families   b Combined figures for the Llandudno, Colwyn Bay and Rhyl Hebrew Congregation

Glossary

Aliyah: lit. 'to ascend' in Hebrew. The emigration of Jews to Israel or being called up for a *mitzvah* in the synagogue.

Ashkenazi: Jews originating in Central, Western and Eastern Europe whose common vernacular language was Yiddish.

Bar/Bat mitzvah: ceremonies marking the thirteenth birthday of a Jewish male and twelfth birthday of a Jewish female, the age at which he/she achieves religious responsibility.

Bet Tohorah: lit. 'house of purification' in Hebrew. A covered room in a Jewish cemetery where the corpse is cleansed before burial.

Beth Din: Jewish court of law.

Beth Hamedrash: lit. 'house of instruction' in Hebrew. A place of study where the *Talmud* and other aspects of Jewish learning are taught.

B'nai/B'not mitzvah: plural of *bar/bat mitzvah*.

Chazzan: lit. 'Cantor' in Hebrew. The name applied to the Reader at public services.

Cheder: lit. 'room' in Hebrew. The Jewish school in which children are taught the elements of Hebrew and religion.

Hachshara: an agricultural training centre for Jewish youth in preparation for *Aliyah*.

Hachsharot: plural of *hachshara*

Halacha: Jewish law.

High Holy Days: the festivals of *Rosh Hashanah* and *Yom Kippur* and the period of repentance in the first ten days of the Jewish New Year.

Kashrut: Jewish dietary laws.

Kehillah: lit. 'Community'. Applies to the administrative body of Jewish communities and originates from the word *kahal* (assembly).

Kibbutz: a community settlement in Israel, usually agricultural, organised under collectivist principles.

Kol Nidre: lit. 'all vows' in Aramaic. Opening prayer of the *Yom Kippur* services.

Kosher: the term applied to food properly prepared according to Jewish law and custom.

Maftir: lit. 'one who concludes' in Hebrew. As well as the regular number called up to read sections of the *Torah* each *Shabbat,* an additional person is summoned to read the *Haftorah* (a portion from the works of the prophets).

Meshummad: lit. 'destroyed one' in Hebrew. One who has abandoned his or her faith.

Mikvah: a special bath used primarily by married Orthodox Jewish women to keep the laws of family purity.

Mikvaot: plural of *mikvah.*

Minyan: the quorum of ten male Jews over the age of thirteen required for an Orthodox communal religious service.

Minyanim: plural of *minyan.*

Mizrahi: lit. 'Eastern Jews' in Hebrew. The general name for Jews of Middle-Eastern origin. Most Mizrahi Jews observe customs similar to those of Sephardi Jews, due to the dispersion of the latter throughout the Muslim World following their expulsion from Spain in 1492. This has led to the terms Sephardi and Mizrahi being used interchangeably by many.

Mohel: trained official who performs the rite of circumcision.

Purim: a Jewish festival held in spring (on the fourteenth or fifteenth day of Adar) to commemorate the defeat of Haman's plot to massacre the Jews, as recorded in the Biblical book of Esther.

Rav: lit. 'master' in Hebrew. The title *Rav* is used to designate Orthodox rabbis, especially to distinguish them from those who bear the title Rabbi but have not yet received rabbinical ordination.

Rosh Hashanah: lit. 'head of the year' in Hebrew. Festival of the Jewish New Year.

Sephardi: lit. 'Spanish Jews' in Hebrew; Jews originating from the Iberian Peninsula. They possess their own ritual, vernacular language (Ladino) and distinctive pronunciation of Hebrew.

Shabbat: the Jewish day of rest, observed from sunset on Friday evenings until sunset on Saturday evenings.

Shammas: a person who assists in the synagogue and maintains the building.

Shechita: Jewish method of ritual slaughter, in which the animal is killed by one stroke of a very sharp knife across the throat, completely severing the trachea, carotid arteries and jugular veins.

Shochet: lit. 'butcher' in Hebrew. Someone who has been specially trained and licensed to slaughter animals in accordance with the laws of *shechita*.

Shtetl: a small Jewish town or village in eastern Europe.

Shul/Shool: lit. 'school'. Yiddish for synagogue.

Talmud: lit. 'learning' in Hebrew. The collection of ancient Rabbinic writings constituting the basis of religious authority in Orthodox Judaism.

Talmud Torah: lit. 'learning of the Law' in Hebrew. Institute for Jewish religious instruction, usually larger and more formally organised than the *cheder* and preparatory to the *Beth Hamedrash*.

Torah: consists of the five books of the Hebrew Bible (known to non-Jews as the Old Testament) that were given by God to Moses on Mount Sinai and include within them all of the biblical laws of Judaism.

Treiber: Yiddish for porging— the process of removing the sciatic nerve, certain fats, and blood vessels from a slaughtered animal.

Tzedakah: lit. 'righteousness' in Hebrew. Charitable giving; philanthropy. *Tzedakah* is more than simply charity; it embraces a larger principle of doing good to ensure that the needs of others are met.

Yeshiva: Rabbinic colleges in which the *Talmud* is studied and taught.

Yeshivot: plural of *yeshiva*.

Yom Kippur: lit. 'Day of Atonement' in Hebrew. The holiest day of the year for Jews, who traditionally observe it with a 25-hour period of fasting and intensive prayer.

Notes

Notes to Introduction

1 See, for example, Glanmor Williams, *The Welsh and their Religion: Historical Essays* (Cardiff, 1991); Gareth E. Jones, *Modern Wales: A Concise History* (Cambridge, 1994).

2 Ieuan Gwynedd Jones and David Williams (eds), *The Religious Census of 1851: A Calendar of the Returns Relating to Wales, Vol. 1: South Wales* (Cardiff, 1976). See, for instance, Matthew Cragoe, *Culture, Politics, and National Identity in Wales, 1832–1886* (Oxford, 2004), p. 64; Gwyn A. Williams, *When was Wales?* (London, 1979), p. 15.

3 Paul Chambers and Andrew Thompson 'Coming to Terms with the Past: Religion and Identity in Wales', *Social Compass*, 52/3 (2005), 340.

4 Richard C. Allen and David Ceri Jones with Trystan O. Hughes (eds), *The Religious History of Wales: Religious Life and Practice in Wales from the Seventeenth Century to the Present Day* (Cardiff, 2014) is a recent example of a study that addresses the history of Wales's diverse religious landscape.

5 Sidney Salomon, *The Jews of Britain* (London, 1938). See also John Cannon, *A Dictionary of British History* (Oxford, 2009), p. 362; Miri J. Freud-Kandel, *Orthodox Judaism in Britain Since 1913: An Ideology Forsaken* (London, 2006).

6 A by no means comprehensive list includes Geoffrey Alderman, *London Jewry and London Politics 1889–1986* (London, 1989); Gerry Black, *Living up West: Jewish Life in London's West End* (London, 1994); Murray Freedman, *Leeds Jewry: The First Hundred Years* (York, 1992); Nikos Kokosalakis, *Ethnic Identity and Religion: Tradition and Change in Liverpool Jewry* (Washington, 1982); Tony Kushner, *Anglo-Jewry since 1066: Place, Locality and Memory* (Manchester, 2009); Rosalyn D. Livshin, *The History of the Harrogate Jewish Community* (Leeds,

1995); Aubrey Newman, *Birmingham Jewry, Vol. 1, 1749–1914* (Leicester, 1980); Lewis Olsover, *The Jewish Communities of North-East England 1755–1980* (Gateshead, 1980); Cecil Roth, *The Rise of Provincial Jewry: The Early History of the Jewish Community in the English Countryside, 1740–1840* (Oxford, 1950); Judith Samuel, *Jews in Bristol: The History of the Jewish Community in Bristol from the Middle Ages to the Present Day* (Bristol, 1997); Bill Williams, *The Making of Manchester Jewry, 1740–1875* (Manchester, 1985).

7 An exception, of course, is the Scottish city of Glasgow, 'the Second City of the British Empire', which was home to a large number of Jews in the twentieth century – approximately 5,000 Jews in 1901 and 10,000 by 1939. For examples of works on Glasgow Jewry, see Ben Braber, *Jews in Glasgow, 1870–1939: Immigration and Integration* (London, 2007); Kenneth E. Collins, *Glasgow Jewry: A Guide to the History and Community of the Jews of Glasgow* (Glasgow, 1993).

8 Although Tony Kushner and Hannah Ewence's recently edited volume *Whatever Happened to British Jewish Studies* refers to the historical examination of Jews in the United Kingdom as 'British Jewish Studies', the monograph continues to slip into the usage of 'Anglo-Jewish' as the all-encompassing term. See Tony Kushner and Hannah Ewence (eds), *Whatever Happened to British Jewish Studies?* (London, 2012).

9 This approach has been adopted by many British historians more generally, including Brian Harrison. See Brian Harrison, *Finding a Role?: The United Kingdom 1970–1990* (Oxford, 2009), pp. xv–xvi.

10 Todd M. Endelman, *The Jews of Britain, 1656–2000* (Berkeley, 2002), p. 12.

11 Nathan Abrams, *Caledonian Jews: A Study of Seven Small Communities in Scotland* (North Carolina, 2009), p. 9; William D. Rubinstein, *A History of the Jews in the English-Speaking World: Great Britain* (London, 1996).

12 The school of 'New British History' emerged in response to John G. A. Pocock's seminal article 'British History: A Plea for a New Subject', which called for an equal treatment of the histories of all four nations of the United Kingdom without jeopardising their separate histories and identities. See John G. A. Pocock, 'British History: A Plea for a New Subject', *Journal of Modern History*, 47 (1975), 601–28.

13 John Campbell, 'The Jewish Community in Britain', in Sheridan Gilley and William J. Sheils (eds), *The History of Religion in Britain: Practice and Belief from Pre-Roman Times to the Present* (Oxford, 1994), pp. 62–85. The absence of Irish Jewry in Campbell's chapter may be in deference to the ideas of the editors, who note in the introduction to their volume that 'This book is the first

one-volume history of religious belief and practice in England, Wales and Scotland.' See, Gilley and Sheils, *History of Religion in Britain*, p. 5.

14 See Raphael Langham, *The Jews in Britain: A Chronology* (Basingstoke, 2005), p. 3; Geoffrey Alderman, *Modern British Jewry* (Oxford, 1998); Pamela Fletcher Jones, *The Jews of Britain: A Thousand Years of History* (Gloucestershire, 1990).

15 Harold Pollins, *The Economic History of the Jews in England* (London, 1982), p. 9.

16 Pollins, *Economic History of the Jews*, p. 9.

17 Endelman, *The Jews of Britain*, p. 130.

18 See, for instance, Geoffrey Alderman, 'The Jew as Scapegoat? The Settlement and Reception of Jews in South Wales before 1914', *Transactions of the Jewish Historical Society of England*, XXVI (1974–8), 62–70; Ursula Henriques (ed.), *The Jews of South Wales, 2nd edn* (Cardiff, 2013); Harold Pollins, 'The Jewish Community of Brynmawr, Wales', *Jewish Journal of Sociology*, L, 1–2 (2008), 5–32.

19 Despite its all-encompassing title, David Morris's doctoral thesis is predominantly a history of south Wales Jewry. See David Morris, 'The history of the Welsh Jewish communities, 1750 to the present' (unpublished PhD thesis, University of Wales, 1999). This focus on south Wales is in keeping with other areas of Welsh history, especially industrial history, which some argue 'has been "valley centric"'. See, for instance, Keith Gildart, 'Men of Coal: Miners' Leaders in North-East Wales 1890–1961', *Llafur*, 8, 1 (2000), 111.

20 See, for instance, Bernard Goldblum, 'Swansea', in Aubrey Newman, *Provincial Jewry in Victorian Britain: Papers for a Conference at University College, London Convened by the Jewish Historical Society of England* (London, 1975), p. 55; Neville H. Saunders, *Swansea Hebrew Congregation, 1730–1980* (Swansea, 1980); Leonard Mars, 'Immigration and Anglicization: Religious Education as an Issue in the Swansea Hebrew Congregation, 1894–1910', *Jewish Journal of Sociology*, 39, 1–2 (1997), 76–86; Janet M. Neilson, 'The History and Influence of Swansea's Jewish Community, 1730–2006', *Minerva*, 14 (2006), 23–36; Henriques (ed.), *The Jews of South Wales*; Glenn Jordan, Colin Heyman, Eve Lavine, Cai Parry-Jones, Diana Soffa, and Chris Weedon (eds), *Hineni: Life Portraits from a Jewish Community* (Cardiff, 2012); Pollins, 'The Jewish Community of Brynmawr', 5–32; Wendy Bellany, 'A Vanished Community', *Merthyr Historian*, 16 (2001), 38–47.

21 Geoffrey Alderman, 'The Jew as Scapegoat?', 62–70; Geoffrey Alderman, 'The Anti-Jewish Riots of August 1911 in South Wales', *Welsh History Review*, 6 (1972), 190–200.

22 Colin Holmes, 'The Tredegar Riots of 1911: Anti-Jewish Disturbances in South Wales', *Welsh History Review*, 11 (1982), 214–25; Anthony Glaser, 'The

Tredegar Riots of August 1911', in Henriques (ed.), *The Jews of South Wales*, pp. 151–176.

23 Abraham Wiener, 'An Episode in South Wales: How Dr Moses Hyamson Lost the British Chief Rabbinate', *Menorah Journal* (Autumn, 1951), 134–50; W. D. Rubinstein, 'The Anti-Jewish Riots of 1911 in South Wales', *Welsh History Review*, (1997), 669. Rubinstein's argument is part of a broader argument that he and his wife have constructed in which the English-speaking world is characterised as 'philo-Semitic'. See William D. Rubinstein and Hilary L. Rubinstein, *Philosemitism: Admiration and Support in the English-Speaking World for Jews, 1840–1939* (New York, 1999).

24 Geoffrey Alderman, 'The Anti-Jewish Riots of August 1911 in South Wales: a Response', *Welsh History Review*, 20 (2001), 564–71.

25 Paul O'Leary, 'Conflict and Co-operation: The Jews of South Wales and the Study of Welsh Jewry', in Henriques (ed.), *The Jews of South Wales*, pp. xiv–xv.

26 Rubinstein, 'The Anti-Jewish Riots of 1911', 670.

27 Neil Evans 'Comparing Immigrant Histories: The Irish and Others in Modern Wales', in Paul O'Leary (ed.), *Irish Migrants in Modern Wales* (Liverpool, 2004), pp.158–78; Neil Evans, 'Immigrants and Minorities in Wales, 1840–1990: a Comparative Perspective', in Charlotte Williams, Neil Evans and Paul O'Leary (eds), *A Tolerant Nation?: Revisiting Ethnic Diversity in a Devolved Wales* (Cardiff, 2015), pp. 22–50.

28 Leo Abse, 'A Tale of Collaboration not Conflict with the "People of the Book"', *New Welsh Review* 22 (Autumn 1993), 19.

29 Jasmine Donahaye, *Whose People? Wales, Israel, Palestine* (Cardiff, 2012), p. 7.

30 Dai Smith, *Wales: A Question for History* (Bridgend, 1999), p. 98; Kenneth O. Morgan, *Rebirth of a Nation: Wales 1880–1980* (Oxford, 1982), p. 148. The riots have also attracted the attention of Anglo-Jewish film director, Paul Morrison, who directed the Oscar-nominated film *Solomon and Gaenor* (1999). For an in-depth discussion of the film, see Paul O'Leary, 'Film, History and Anti-Semitism: *Solomon and Gaenor* (1999) and the Representations of the Past', *North American Journal of Welsh Studies*, 7 (2012), 38–52.

31 Historians such as Geoffrey Alderman and Todd Endelman have argued that the earlier works of British-Jewish history such as that written by Cecil Roth and Vivian Lipman were 'whiggish' and 'apologetic' in tone, focusing primarily on the progression and successes of Jews in Britain; see, for instance, Roth, *A History of the Jews* (1961); Vivian D. Lipman, *A Century of Social Service: The Jewish Board of Guardians, 1859–1959* (London, 1959). For discussions on

the 'whiggish' approach to British-Jewish history, see Alderman, 'The Jew as Scapegoat?', 63–4; Endelman, *The Jews of Britain*, pp. 4–6.

32 Alderman, 'The Jew as Scapegoat?', 64.

33 Grahame Davies, *The Chosen People: Wales and the Jews* (Bridgend, 2002); Donahaye, *Whose People?*; Neil Evans 'Comparing Immigrant Histories', in O'Leary (ed.), *Irish Migrants*, pp. 158–78; Neil Evans, 'Immigrants and Minorities in Wales', in Williams, Evans and O'Leary (eds), *A Tolerant Nation?*, pp. 22–50; Colin Hughes, *Lime, Lemon, and Sarsaparilla: The Italian Community in South Wales, 1881–1945* (Bridgend, 1991), pp. 121–2; Paul O'Leary, *Immigration and Integration: The Irish in Wales, 1798–1922* (Cardiff, 2002), p. 157.

34 Sharman Kadish, *Jewish Heritage in Britain and Ireland: An Architectural Guide* (Swindon, 2015), pp. 248–57; Sharman Kadish, 'The Jewish Presence in Wales: Image and Material Reality', in Martin O'Kane and John Morgan-Guy (eds), *Biblical Art from Wales* (Sheffield, 2010), pp. 272–91.

35 William A. Williams, *Encyclopaedia* of Wrexham (Wrexham, 2001), p. 183. Despite mentioning the existence of Jewish communities in north Wales, Lavinia Cohn-Sherbok's chapter on Judaism in Wales focuses on south Wales. The same can be said for Campbell's section on Welsh Jews in his chapter on Jews in Britain. See Lavinia Cohn-Sherbok, 'Judaism,', in Allen and Jones with Hughes (eds), *The Religious History of Wales*, pp. 238–53; Campbell, 'The Jewish Community in Britain,', pp. 427–48.

36 Abrams, *Caledonian Jews*, p. 10.

37 See, for instance, Morris, 'The History of the Welsh Jewish Communities'; Neville H. Saunders, *Swansea Hebrew Congregation, 1730–1980* (Swansea, 1980); Neilson, 'The History and Influence of Swansea's Jewish Community', pp. 23–36; Ursula Henriques, 'Epilogue', in Henriques (ed.), *The Jews of South Wales*, pp. 207–17.

38 *North Wales Express*, 15 January 1909.

39 Bill Williams, 'Heritage and Community: The Rescue of Manchester's Jewish Past', in Tony Kushner (ed.), *The Jewish Heritage in British History: Englishness and Jewishness* (Abingdon, 1992), p. 128.

40 Bill Williams, 'Heritage and Community', in Kushner, *The Jewish Heritage*, p. 141.

41 Ursula Henriques, 'Preface', in Henriques (ed.), *The Jews of South Wales*, p. vii.

42 Tony Kushner, 'Reviewed work(s): The Jews of South Wales: Historical Studies by Ursula R. Q. Henriques', *Albion: a Quarterly Journal Concerned with British Studies* 25/4 (1993), 747.

43 The Hineni exhibition project features fifty-nine edited life stories and photographic portraits from the Cardiff Reform Jewish community. The collection has since been deposited in the sound archive at St Fagans National History Museum (henceforth SFNHM). See Jordan, Heyman, Lavine, Parry-Jones, Soffa and Weedon (eds), *Hineni.*

44 Paul Thompson, *Voice of the Past: Oral History* (New York, 2000), p. 25.

45 Shaul Esh and Geoffrey Wigoder, 'Oral History and its Potential Application', in Julius Gould and Shaul Esh (eds), *Jewish Life in Modern Britain* (London, 1964), pp. 140–55; Jerry White, *Rothschild Buildings: Life in an East End Tenement Block, 1887–1920* (Abingdon, 1980); Rosalyn Livshin, 'Acculturation of the Children of Immigrant Jews in Manchester, 1890–1930', in David Cesarani (ed.), *The Making of Modern Anglo-Jewry* (Oxford, 1990), pp. 79–96.

46 Arthur Marwick, *The New Nature of History: Knowledge, Evidence, Language* (Chicago, 2001), p. 136.

47 Lynn Abrams, *Oral History Theory* (London, 2016), p. 86.

48 For more on this, see Mark Roseman, *A Past in Hiding: Memory and Survival in Nazi Germany* (New York, 2002).

49 See Brian Harrison, 'Oral History and Recent Political History', *Oral History*, 1, 3 (1972), 46; Patrick O' Farrell, 'Oral History: Facts and Fiction', *Oral History Association of Australia Journal*, 5 (1982–3), 3–9 (reprinted from *Quadrant*, November 1979); Thompson, *Voice of the Past*, pp. 25–82; Alistair Thomson, 'Making the Most of Memories: The Empirical and Subjective Value of Oral History', *Transactions of the Royal Historical Society* 9 (1999), 291–301.

50 Alessandro Portelli, 'What Makes Oral History Different', in Robert Perks and Alistair Thomson (eds), *The Oral History Reader* (Abingdon, 2015), p. 52. Of course, subjectivity is not unique to oral history since written sources such as letters, diaries and memoirs also contain information regarding personal historical experiences.

51 The controversy over the Jews' Free School (JFS) case in London between 2006 and 2009 is a good example of this. For further information, see *Guardian*, 16 December 2009.

52 György Konrád, 'Aphorisms on the Durability of Jews', *Partisan Review*, 65/4 (1998), 548.

53 Geoffrey Alderman, *The Jewish Community in British Politics* (Oxford, 1983), p. vii.

54 Nathan Abrams points out that such sources need to be treated with caution since names of non-Jews can also appear in official Jewish records. See Nathan Abrams, *Caledonian Jews*, p. 177.

55 Recovering information on female occupation in available census material is difficult for a number of reasons. In keeping with the Victorian and Edwardian ideology of 'separate spheres', the census between 1841 and 1911 typically classified men as workers and wage-earners and women as dependants, meaning that the space for female occupation was left blank in most cases. Unmarried women's occupations were occasionally recorded, while the occupations of married women, if recorded at all, often appeared in relation to their husband's work. For more on this, see Robert B. Shoemaker, *Gender in English Society 1650–1850: The Emergence of Separate Spheres?* (Abingdon, 2013), p.149.

56 Nationality and Naturalisation: Schmeres, Morris Henry (known as Morris Henry Smith), 20 October 1911, HO 144/1149/210501, The National Archives, Kew (henceforth TNA).

57 *Jewish Chronicle* (henceforth *JC*), 31 January 1936.

58 Letter from the joint editors of the *JC* to Henry Samuels, 1936, D/D JR 1/1/6 36/34, Glamorgan Archives (henceforth GA).

59 *JYB*, 1945–46, 19; *JYB*, 1935, 635.

60 It also provides invaluable information on British Jewry's religious leaders and various communal institutions.

61 Although a census on religion was conducted by the government in England, Wales and Scotland in 1851, it was separate from the 1851 United Kingdom Census. Popularly called the '1851 Religious Census', this was a census of 'Accommodation and Attendance at Worship' rather than of worshippers themselves. For more on this, see Jones and Williams (eds), *The Religious Census of 1851: A Calendar of the Returns Relating to Wales, Vol. 1: South Wales* (Cardiff, 1976).

62 David Graham, Marlena Schmool and Stanley Waterman, *Jews in Britain: A Snapshot from the 2001 Census* (London, 2007), p. 5.

63 Kenneth Collins, 'Maintaining a Jewish Identity in Scotland', in John Beech, Owen Hand, Mark A. Mulhern, and Jeremy Weston (eds), *Scottish Life and Society: A Compendium of Scottish Ethnology, Vol. 9, The Individual and Community Life* (Edinburgh, 2005), p. 490.

64 Graham, Schmool and Waterman, *Jews in Britain*, p. 15.

65 This is a common feature of many Jewish diasporas. See, for instance, Nathan Abrams, *Caledonian Jews*, p. 11; Maurice Freedman and James. W. Parkes (eds), *A Minority in Britain: Social Studies of the Anglo-Jewish Community* (London, 1955), p. 64.

66 Lee S. Weissbach, *Jewish Life in Small-Town America: A History* (New Haven, 2005), p. 28.

67 Weissbach, *Jewish Life*, p. 28.
68 Weissbach, *Jewish Life*, p. 29.
69 *JYB*, 1896–1939.

Notes to Chapter 1

1 Patricia Skinner (ed.), *The Jews in Medieval Britain* (Woodbridge, 2003), p. 1. No decisive evidence has been adduced to show the presence of Jewish settlers in Britain before the eleventh century, but there is some varied evidence worthy of consideration indicative of the presence of Jews in Roman Britain. See Shimon Applebaum, 'Were there Jews in Roman Britain?', *Transactions of the Jewish Historical Society of England*, 17 (1951–2), 189–205.

2 John Gillingham, 'Conquering the Barbarians: War and Chivalry in Twelfth-Century Britain', *Haskins Society Journal*, 4 (1992), 83.

3 Skinner (ed.), *The Jews in Medieval Britain*, p. 2. After the Norman conquest of 1066, Jews were permitted to settle in England to work as royal tax collectors and moneylenders, activities forbidden to Christians. As they were taxed heavily, the wealth they earned in this trade proved to be extremely beneficial to the Crown. The position of Jews in medieval English society was extremely volatile, however, and depended heavily on the policies of the then reigning monarch. When Edward I ascended the throne in 1272, for instance, he imposed new restrictions on moneylending and imposed harsh taxes on Jews, which led to a sharp rise in Jewish poverty and the subsequent decline of their fiscal utility in the late thirteenth century. This, along with growing religious hostility and sheer rapacity on behalf of the English Crown, led to their expulsion in 1290. On the expulsion, see Robin R. Mundill, *England's Jewish Solution. Experiment and Expulsion, 1262–1290* (Cambridge, 1998).

4 Joe Hillaby, 'Jewish Colonisation in the Twelfth Century', in Skinner (ed.), *The Jews in Medieval Britain*, p. 39.

5 David Stephenson, 'Jewish Presence in, and Absence from, Wales in the Twelfth and Thirteenth Centuries', *Jewish Historical Studies*, 43 (2011), 11; *Close Rolls of the Reign of Henry III, 1247–51* (London, 1922), p. 557. Stephenson also notes the presence of a rabbi in mid-Wales during the mid-thirteenth century named 'Master Samuel of Radnor'. This is a mistranscription, however, since the original record refers to 'Master Simon of Radnor', a canon who was closely associated with Hereford Cathedral during the thirteenth century.

6   Roll of Debts given by Jews to the king, E 101/249/10, TNA.

7   The same is true for Cok of Chepstow, who also appears only in records relating to the Bristol Jewish community. Roll of Debts given by Jews to the King, E 101/249/10, TNA; Zefira Entin Rokéah, 'An Anglo-Jewish Assembly or 'Mini Parliament' in 1287', in Michael Prestwich, Richard Britnell and Robin Frame (eds), *Thirteenth Century England, VIII : Proceedings of the Durham Conference, 1999* (Woodbridge, 2001), 85.

8   Joe Hillaby and Caroline Hillaby, *The Palgrave Dictionary of Medieval Anglo-Jewish History* (Basingstoke, 2013), p. 64; see also Michael Adler, *Jews of Medieval England* (London, 1939), p. 219.

9   Adler, *Jews of Medieval England*, p. 219; Joe Hillaby and Caroline Hillaby, *Palgrave Dictionary*, p. 64.

10   E. A. Lewis, 'The Development of Industry and Commerce in Wales during the Middle Ages', *Transactions of the Royal Historical Society*, 17 (1903), 103.

11   Extract from Edward I's charter to the town of Caernarfon (1284), XM/5564/63, Caernarfon Record Office (henceforth CRO); see also Adolphus Ballard and James Tait (eds), *British Borough Charters 1216–1307* (Cambridge, 1923), p. 142. The exclusionary element of the charters is also pointed out by Hillaby and others. See Joe Hillaby, 'Jewish Colonisation in the Twelfth Century', in Skinner, *The Jews*, p. 39; Hillaby and Hillaby, *Palgrave Dictionary*, p. 143; Stephenson, 'Jewish Presence', 8; John Campbell, 'The Jewish Community in Britain', in Sheridan Gilley and William J. Sheils (eds), *The History of Religion in Britain: Practice and Belief from Pre-Roman Times to the Present* (Oxford, 1994), p. 72.

12   For more on the expulsion, see Robin R. Mundill, *England's Jewish Solution. Experiment and Expulsion, 1262–1290* (Cambridge, 1998).

13   Ballard and Tait (eds), *British Borough Charters*, p. 142.

14   William Rees, *South Wales and the March, 1284–1415: A Social and Agrarian Study* (Oxford, 1924), p. 222; Hillaby, 'Jewish Colonisation in the Twelfth Century', in Skinner (ed.), *The Jews in Medieval Britain*, p. 40.

15   Israel Abrahams, 'Joachim Gaunse: A Mining Incident in the Reign of Queen Elizabeth', *Transactions of the Jewish Historical Society of England*, 4 (1899–1901), 83–101; William D. Rubinstein, Michael A. Jolles, and Hilary L. Rubinstein (eds), *The Palgrave Dictionary of Anglo-Jewish History* (Basingstoke, 2011), p. 315.

16   William J. Davies, *Hanes Plwyf Llandyssul* (Llandysul, 1896), p. 154; 'Priododd â boneddiges o Iuddewes gyfoethog.' I am grateful to Meic Birtwistle for pointing this source out to me. The subject became the focus of a Welsh-language television documentary called *Gwreiddiau: Yr Iddewes* in 2012.

17 Will of Edward Jones, Llandysul, 1744, National Library of Wales Wills Online (henceforth NLW):viewer.library.wales/474440#?c=0&m=0&s=0&cv=0

18 Neville H. Saunders, *Swansea Hebrew Congregation, 1730–1980* (Swansea, 1980), p. 29.

19 *Sundays in Wales: Visits to the Places of Worship of the Quakers, the Unitarians, the Roman Catholics and the Jews by a Week-day Preacher* (Swansea, 1859), p.29; Transcription of the 1768 Counterpart Lease relating to the acquisition of a plot of land on Town Hill from the Burgesses of Swansea to David Michael, D/D SHC 26/1, West Glamorgan Archives (henceforth WGA).

20 *Herald of Wales*, 12 August 1933.

21 *Cambrian*, 23 May 1818. Sharman Kadish incorrectly states that Goat Street's synagogue was erected in 1818; see Kadish, *Jewish Heritage in Britain and Ireland*, p. 256.

22 *JC*, 7 October 1859.

23 *Cardiff and Merthyr Guardian*, 3 October 1846; James H. Clark, *Cardiff and its Neighbourhood* (Cardiff, 1853), p. 46; *Ewen's Guide and Directory for the Town of Cardiff and its Environs* (1855).

24 *JC*, 15 April 1859.

25 Ieuan Gwynedd Jones and David Williams (eds), *The Religious Census of 1851: A Calendar of the Returns Relating to Wales,* p. 175; *JC*, 1 March 1867; *Monmouthshire Merlin*, 16 February 1867.

26 *JC*, 26 July 1867; 3 January 1873; 27 June 1873.

27 *Cardiff Times,* 8 June 1867; *JC*, 26 July 1867

28 *JC*, 17 September 1880.

29 Ordnance Plan of the Parish of Neath (Southampton, 1878), O.S., British Library (henceforth BL).

30 Williams, *The Making of Manchester Jewry*, p. 32; The 1841 census lists Joseph Hyman as a 65-year-old hawker, 'from foreign parts' and living in Liverpool with his wife and seven children.

31 *Pigot's Directory of North Wales and South Wales* (1828–9).

32 *North Wales Chronicle* (henceforth *NWC*), 3 July 1828; 17 March 1831.

33 *NWC*, 26 August 1854.

34 Endelman, *The Jews of Britain*, p. 80.

35 Abrams, *Caledonian Jews*, p. 66.

36 For more on the history of Liverpool and Manchester Jewry, see Nikos Kokosalakis, *Ethnic Identity and Religion: Tradition and Change in Liverpool Jewry* (Washington, 1982); Bill Williams, *The Making of Manchester* and *Jewish Manchester: An Illustrated History* (Derby, 2008).

37 Bill Williams, *The Making of Manchester*, p. 32.

38 *NWC*, 10 June 1830.

39 Kenneth E. Collins, *Go and Learn: The International Story of Jews and Medicine in Scotland* (Aberdeen, 1988), p. 75; Cormac Ó Gráda, *Jewish Ireland in the Age of Joyce: a Socioeconomic History* (Princeton, 2006), p. 54.

40 Based on the 1851 census, Vivian Lipman estimated that there were between 250 and 350 Jews living in south Wales in 1850; see Vivian D. Lipman, *A Century of Social Service: The Jewish Board of Guardians, 1859–1959* (London, 1959), p. 187 and 'A Survey of Anglo-Jewry in 1851', *Transactions of the Jewish Historical Society of England*, 17 (1953), 171–88.

41 Vivian D. Lipman, *A History of the Jews in Britain since 1858* (Leicester, 1990), p. 12.

42 Tony Kushner and Katherine Knox (eds), *Refugees in an Age of Genocide: Global, National and Local Perspectives during the Twentieth Century* (London, 1999), p. 19; Geoffrey Alderman, *Modern British Jewry* (Oxford, 1998), p. 112.

43 Alderman, *Modern British Jewry*, p. 112; Kushner and Knox (eds), *Refugees in an Age of Genocide*, p. 19.

44 Endelman, *The Jews of Britain*, p. 129; Kushner and Knox (eds), *Refugees in an Age of Genocide*, p. 20.

45 Lloyd P. Gartner, *American and British Jews in the Age of the Great Migration* (London, 2009), p. 56.

46 Sarah E. Karesh and Mitchell M. Hurvit (eds), *Encyclopedia of Judaism* (New York, 2006), p. 373.

47 Olga Litvak, *Conscription and the Search for Modern Russian Jewry* (Bloomington, 2006), p. 7.

48 Gartner, *American and British Jews*, p. 2.

49 Yohanan Petrovsky-Shtern, *Jews in the Russian Army, 1827–1917: Drafted into Modernity* (Cambridge, 2008), p. 135. For further information on the Cantonist system, see Larry Domnitch, *The Cantonists: the Jewish Children's Army of the Tsar* (New York, 2003).

50 Nationality and Naturalisation: Hyman Factor, Certificate 7,774 issued 4 March 1921, HO 144/1659/262957, TNA.

51 Nationality and Naturalisation: Solomon Krupp, Certificate 19118 issued 3 June 1910, HO 144/1054/187985, TNA.

52 Oleg Budnitskii, *Russian Jews between the Reds and the Whites, 1917–1920* (Philadelphia, 2012), p. 18; Endelman, *The Jews of Britain*, p. 127.

53 See Nicholas J. Evans. 'Indirect Passage from Europe: Transmigration via the UK, 1836–1914', *Journal for Maritime Research* (2001), 70–84.

54 Endelman, *The Jews of Britain*, p. 128.

55 Nicholas J. Evans, 'Indirect Passage from Europe Transmigration via the UK, 1836–1914', *Journal for Maritime Research*, 3/1 (2001), 71.

56 Harold Pollins, *Hopeful Travellers: Jewish Migrants and Settlers in Nineteenth-Century Britain* (London, 1989), p. 25.

57 Peter Braham, '"Swirls and Currents" of Migration: Jewish Emigrants from Eastern Europe, 1881–1914', in W. T. R. Pryce (ed.), *From Family History to Community History* (Cambridge, 1994), p. 79.

58 Hasia Diner, *The Jews of the United States, 1654–2000* (Berkeley, 2006), p. 81.

59 David Cesarani, 'Social Memory, History, and British Jewish Identity', in Glenda Abramson (ed.), *Modern Jewish Mythologies* (Cincinnati, 2000), p. 25.

60 *HaYom*, 24 August 1886, quoted in Gartner, *American and British Jews*, p. 5.

61 'U.S., Boston Arrivals of Jewish Immigrants from HIAS Records, 1882–1929' reveals that the Policovsky family arrived in Boston on 11 January 1913; see *www.ancestry.com* for further details.

62 Kenneth Collins, Second Jewry: *The Jews of Glasgow in the Age of Expansion, 1790–1919* (Glasgow, 1990), p. 71; Susan L. Tananbaum, *Jewish Immigrants in London, 1880–1939* (London, 2015), p. 22.

63 Renee Woolf, interview with Cai Parry-Jones, Cardiff, 27 January 2012, 11822, Sound Archive, SFNHM.

64 Abrams, *Caledonian Jews*, p. 124.

65 See, for example, *First Annual Conference of the Society for the Promotion of Social Service* (Niagara Falls, 1908), p. 42; William Paul Dillingham, *Reports of the Immigration Commission* (Washington, 1911), p. 339.

66 Cesarani, 'Social Memory', in Abramson (ed.), *Modern Jewish Mythologies*, p. 26; Abrams, *Caledonian Jews*, p. 124.

67 *JC*, 5 January 1906.

68 Alderman, *Modern British Jewry*, p. 115.

69 Nationality and Naturalisation: Max Sefstone, Certificate 14264 issued 22 March 1904, HO 144/740/114669, TNA.

70 Dora Lipsett, interview with David Jacobs, 21 May 1978, 6012/1, Sound Archive, SFNHM; Nationality and Naturalisation: Mache Colpstein (known as Morris Colpstein), Certificate 6,663 issued 17 June 1920, HO 144/1609/393321, TNA.

71 See 1911 census.

72 *CAJEX*, 27-1 (1977), p. 74.

73 Nationality and Naturalisation: Benjamin and Jossel Aronovitch, Certificate 6,059 and 6,060 issued 15 April 1920, HO 144/1612/394249; Hyman Factor, Certificate 7,774 issued 4 March 1921, HO 144/1659/262957; Aaron Factor,

Certificate A20430 issued 20 July 1911, HO 144/1133/206693; Raphael Levi, Certificate 21454 issued 18 November 1911, HO 144/1170/214848; Harry Goodman, Certificate 18792 issued 9 February 1910, HO 144/555/186705; Israel Goodman, Certificate 17514 issued 6 August 1908, HO 144/885/168024; Moses Goodman, Certificate 18789 issued 9 February 1910, HO 144/555/186706; Sidney Goodman, Certificate 19631 issued 22 October 1910, HO 144/1095/196794; Joseph Clompus, Certificate 2,483 issued 16 January 1917, HO 144/1378/266267; Samuel Solomon, Certificate 7,102 issued 21 September 1920, HO 144/ 1566/261484, TNA. Thanks to David Morris for pointing this out to me.

74 Jacqueline Magrill, interview with Sue Mansell, 13 September 2011, Hineni, 11742, Sound Archive, SFNHM.

75 Channah Hirsch, *My Llanelli: The Gateshead of Wales* (London, 2009), p. xi.

76 Evans, 'Indirect Passage', 71.

77 Evans, 'Indirect Passage', 71.

78 Nationality and Naturalisation: Davidov, Berko (known as Barnett Davies). Certificate 25468 issued 4 September 1914, HO 144/1320/252943; Peretz Sharff. Certificate A22970 issued 22 January 1913, HO 334/59/22970, TNA.

79 Nationality and Naturalisation: Israel Garlick, Certificate 8,558 issued 6 December 1921, HO 144/1705/420320, TNA.

80 1901 and 1911 census; Nationality and Naturalisation: Louis Snipper, Certificate 13336 issued 31 March 1903, HO 144/696/105168, TNA.

81 *JYB*, 1904–1914.

82 *JYB*, 1904–1912.

83 *JYB*, 1904.

84 John Davies, Nigel Jenkins, Menna Baines, and Peredur Lynch (eds), *The Welsh Academy Encyclopaedia of Wales*, pp. 612 and 841.

85 Nationality and Naturalisation: Joseph Janner, Certificate 23598 issued 10 June 1913, HO 144/1261/236323; Nationality and Naturalisation: Abraham Hauser, Certificate 24047 issued 19 September 1913, HO 144/1281/241028, TNA.

86 *The South Wales Jewish Review*, 10 (October 1904), 147; *JYB*, 1909.

87 Nationality and Naturalisation: Jacob Kahn, Certificate A9893 issued 20 October 1897, HO 144/414/B25059; Nationality and Naturalisation: Raphael Levi, Certificate 21454 issued 18 November 1911, HO 144/1170/214848, TNA.

88 *JC*, 28 September 1923.

89 *JYB*, 1904; Dai Smith, *Wales: A Question for History* (Bridgend, 1999), p. 61.

90 *JC*, 22 August 1902; 21 May 1909.

91 Davies, Jenkins, Baines and Lynch (eds), *Encyclopaedia of Wales*, p. 553.

92 David Egan, *Coal Society: A History of the South Wales Mining Valleys 1840–1980* (Llandysul, 1987), p. 4.

93 *JC*, 4 June 1875.

94 However, they were not the only ethnic group to occupy a particular economic niche. Italian migrants, for example, opened restaurants and coffee shops in the area to cater for miners and their families. See Colin Hughes, *Lime, Lemon & Sarsaparilla: The Italian Community in South Wales, 1881–1945* (Bridgend, 1991); Bruna Chezzi, *Italians in Wales and their Cultural Representations, 1920s–2010s* (Newcastle Upon Tyne, 2015).

95 *JC*, 1 October 2004.

96 An article on Dowlais Jewry in the *JC* from 1877, for instance, deplored the fact that its Jewish traders were neglecting the Sabbath; see *JC*, 14 September 1877.

97 Bill Williams, 'The Jewish Immigrant in Manchester: The Contribution of Oral History', *Oral History*, 7 (1979), 47.

98 Lloyd Gartner, *The Jewish Immigrant in England, 1870–1914*, 3rd edn (London: Vallentine Mitchell, 2001), p. 57.

99 Judy Hornung, interview with Diana Soffa, 20 February 2011, Hineni, 11722, Sound Archive, SFNHM.

100 *Cardiff, Newport & District Trades Directory* (1914).

101 Robert Michael, *A Concise History of American Antisemitism* (Lanham, 2005), p. 27.

102 Dawn Burton, *Credit and Consumer Society* (Oxford, 2012), p. 16.

103 Jewish miners were not unique to Wales, as there were examples of such in Scotland, particularly Dunfermline; see, Abrams, *Caledonian Jews*, p. 98.

104 *JC*, 24 June 1910; Harry Cohen, interview with David Jacobs, 12 January 1978, 6009/1, Sound Archive, SFNHM.

105 Geoffrey Alderman, *Controversy and Crisis: Studies of the History of the Jews in Modern Britain* (Brighton, MA: 2008), p. 62.

106 *JC*, 25 February 1944; 26 March 1976; Walter Sendell, interview with Conrad Wood, 7 August 1992, 12614, Imperial War Museum (henceforth IWM).

107 *JC*, 2 May 1884; *JYB*, 1912.

108 *JYB*, 1904-1920; *Western Mail*, 17 October 1895.

109 The *JC* from 1902 reveals that Jews in Aberdare had been meeting for divine service at the synagogue at 19A Seymour Street for nearly fifteen years; see *JC*, 27 June 1902.

110 *JC*, 5 October 1888; 17 October 1890; 5 October 1894; 15 October 1897; 7 December 1900; 15 January 1904; 16 November 1906; 5 February 1915; 8 October 1915. High Holy Day services were held in Ferndale in 1904, but

there is no record of any formal congregation; see *South Wales Jewish Review*, 10 (October 1904), 147.

111 Alderman, 'The Anti-Jewish Riots of August 1911 in South Wales: a Response, 191.

112 *JC*, 2 February 1894; 31 March 1905; 29 November 1907.

113 John Davies, *A History of Wales* (London, 2007), p. 321.

114 *CAJEX*, 27/1 (1977), p. 78.

115 *JC*, 11 July 1913; 21 January 1927.

116 *JC*, 17 December 1915.

117 Anthony Glaser and Ursula Henriques, 'The Valleys Communities', in Henriques (ed.), *The Jews of South Wales*, p. 55.

118 Swansea Hebrew Congregation Minute Book, 1909–1932, 288; D/D SHC 1/2, WGA.

119 Joseph Shepherd, interview with David Jacobs, 8 November 1976, 6010 and 6011, Sound Archive, SFNHM.

120 *Slater's Directory* (1850).

121 William Pinnock, *The History and Topography of North Wales: With Biographical Sketches, &c. and a Correct Map* (London, 1822), p. 48.

122 *JC*, 23 September 1892; 7 September 1894.

123 *JC*, 4 May 1894.

124 *JC*, 6 April 1945.

125 *JC*, 21 May 1909. The author wishes to note an editorial error in Cai Parry-Jones, 'Bangor's Notable Families – The Wartskis and the Pollecoffs', *Shemot: The Journal of the Jewish Genealogical Society of Great Britain*, 21, 2 (2013), 10, where an image of the former Wartski shop in Llandudno (a Goldsmiths jewellers at the time of writing) has been incorrectly captioned. The year 1778 refers to the establishment of Goldsmiths and not the year Wartski's was founded. For more on the history of the Wartski business, which continues to operate as 'Wartski of Llandudno' in Grafton Street, Mayfair, see Geoffrey C. Munn, *Wartski: The First Hundred and Fifty Years* (Woodbridge, 2015).

126 *JC*, 28 April 1871.

127 *JC*, 28 May 1905; 25 May 1906; 1 July 1910; 12 June 1914; 19 May 1924.

128 For more on the history of Jews in the Ottoman Empire, see Stanford J. Shaw, *The Jews of the Ottoman Empire and the Turkish Republic* (Basingstoke, 1991).

129 *Llandudno Advertiser and District Gazette*, 6 September 1968. Grahame Davies's claim that the Llandudno and Rhyl Jewish communities mainly consisted of Sephardi Jews is incorrect. Like other Jewish communities in Wales,

Llandudno and Rhyl Jewry mainly consisted of Ashkenazi Jews from Eastern Europe; see Davies, *The Chosen People*, p. 211.

130 *JC*, 1 July 1898; *JC*, 15 July 1898.

131 *Rhyl Journal*, 12 September 1896.

132 *JYB*, 1933.

133 *JYB*, 1935.

134 *JC*, 29 November 1907.

135 *JC*, 19 April 1929.

136 *JYB*, 1919. The 1919 edition of the *JYB* estimates that there were 4,884 Jews living in Wales that year, but the actual population of Welsh Jewry was likely to be higher than this owing to the reasons stated in the introduction.

137 *JYB*, 1919.

Notes to Chapter 2

1 Britain is also home to Masorti Judaism (known as Conservative Judaism in North America), which was founded in the United Kingdom by Rabbi Louis Jacobs (1920–2006) and views *halacha* as binding but subject to historical development. No Masorti congregations have been established in Wales to date.

2 *JC*, 4 May 1894; 2 January 1903.

3 *CAJEX*, 11-4 (1961), pp. 65–7; *JC*, 4 October 1889.

4 Weissbach, *Jewish Life*, p. 180.

5 For more on the religious policies of Hermann Adler, see Benjamin J. Elton, *Britain's Chief Rabbis and the Religious Character of Anglo-Jewry, 1880–1970* (Manchester, 2009), pp. 71–163; Israel Finestein, *Anglo-Jewry in Changing Times: Studies in Diversity 1840–1914* (London, 1999), pp. 215–50; Endelman, *The Jews of Britain*, pp. 167–9.

6 *NWC*, 14 May 1898; *JC*, 12 May 1899.

7 Letter from the Office of the Chief Rabbi to C. Solomon, 11 December 1917, ACC/2805/04/02/124, London Metropolitan Archives (henceforth LMA).

8 *JC*, 11 June 1858; *JC*, 7 October 1859.

9 *Western Mail*, 24 March 1871; *JC*, 1 June 1877.

10 *JC*, 9 May 1884; *JC*, 21 June 1901.

11 *Llanelly Mercury*, 20 May 1909; *JC*, 29 March 1912.

12 *JC*, 8 April 1921.

13 *CAJEX*, 11-4 (1961), p. 66; *JC*, 13 July 1900.

14 *Llanelly and County Guardian*, 20 May 1909.

15 *JC*, 12 September 1913.

16 *JC*, 27 February 1914; Anthony Glaser and Ursula Henriques also note that the construction of Merthyr Tydfil's second synagogue burdened the congregation with debt. For more on this, see Glaser and Henriques, 'The Valleys', in Ursula Henriques (ed.), *The Jews of South Wales*, p. 56.

17 *JC*, 13 December 1907; 13 February 1914.

18 *JC*, 25 May 1913; 13 July 1913.

19 *JC*, 9 July 1948.

20 *JC*, 29 October 1897; 26 October 1900; 23 November 1900; 29 November 1907.

21 *JYB*, 1897–1930.

22 *JC*, 27 June 1902.

23 *JC*, 7 May 1915; Letter from Mr Caller to Chief Rabbi, 30 September 1917, ACC/2805/04/02/124, LMA.

24 Copy of letter sent to Tonypandy congregants regarding the erection of a purpose-built synagogue, undated, ACC/2805/04/02/124, LMA; *JYB* 1912-1927; letter from the Chief Rabbi to the secretary of the Board of Deputies, 13 January 1927, ACC/2805/04/02/124, LMA.

25 *JC*, 25 November 1910.

26 Simon Eckley and Don Bearcroft (eds), *Voices of Abertillery, Aberbeeg and Llanhilleth* (Stroud, 1996), p. 102.

27 *JC*, 21 January 1927.

28 *JC*, 8 July 1910; *Western Mail's Cardiff Directory* (1911); Neville H. Saunders, *Swansea Hebrew Congregation, 1730–1980* (Swansea, 1980), p. 53.

29 *JC*, 1 April 1898; 4 February 1927; 21 February 1941.

30 *Aberdare Leader*, 9 December 1905; *CAJEX*, 24-4 (1974) p. 32.

31 *JC*, 25 October 1895; 12 September 1913; Harry Cohen, interview with David Jacobs; Renee Woolf, interview with Cai Parry-Jones.

32 Letter of appeal, Brynmawr Hebrew Congregation, February 1928, ACC/2805/4/2/130, LMA; *Bimah*, 27 (September 2001), p. 22.

33 Swansea's first *mikvah*, the oldest known Jewish ritual bath in Wales, was situated in the back garden of a house in Wellington Street. It served the Jewish community from around 1835 until the close of the nineteenth century; see agreement between W. Lewis and M. Marks regarding lease of premises in Wellington Street, 3 July 1835, D/D SHC 27/3, WGA; letter from H. Goldberg to the Chief Rabbi, 13 April 1902, Swansea Hebrew Congregation

Letter Books, 1901–1904, D/D SHC 2/26, WGA; Swansea Hebrew Congregation Minute Book, 11 September 1911, 16 March and 18 April 1915, D/D SHC 1/2, WGA. An article from the *Cardiff Times* reveals that there were two baths at the Goat Street synagogue; see *Cardiff Times*, 12 December 1908; Saunders, *Swansea Hebrew Congregation*, p. 53; Sharman Kadish, *Jewish Heritage in Britain and Ireland*, p. 257.

34 Sharman Kadish, *The Synagogues of Britain and Ireland: An Architectural and Social History* (New Haven, 2011), p. 134.

35 *Western Mail*, 14 July 1884; *CAJEX*, 9-3 (1959), p. 82; *Surveyor and Municipal and County Engineer*, 25 (17 June, 1904), pp. 749–50. Similar facilities were provided in other British-Jewish communities, such as Birmingham and Nottingham. See Kadish, *The Synagogues of Britain and Ireland*, p. 134.

36 Shirley Goldsmith, interview with Cai Parry-Jones, Menai Bridge, 7 February 2012, 11826, Sound Archive, SFNHM; Michael Lee, interview with Cai Parry-Jones, Llandudno, 5 March 2012, 11825, Sound Archive, SFNHM.

37 *JC*, 12 April 1849; 4 May 1849; conveyance of the Jewish Burial Ground and piece of land adjoining part of the Town Hill site, 30 April 1864, D/D SHC 27/4, WGA.

38 *Evening Express*, 23 April 1901.

39 This practice is acceptable under Jewish law providing that the portion of the cemetery allocated to the Jewish community is given as a permanent possession and is separated from non-Jewish sections by some form of boundary, such as a hedge or a railing; see Ronald L. Eisenberg, *The JPS Guide to Jewish Traditions* (Philadelphia, 2004), p. 89.

40 Sharman Kadish, 'Jewish Funerary Architecture in Britain and Ireland since 1656', *Jewish Historical Studies*, 43 (2011), 75.

41 *JC*, 15 April 1859; *Merthyr Telegraph*, 3 September 1864.

42 *JC*, 27 July 1894.

43 *JC*, 5 December 1919; 13 August 1920.

44 *JC*, 7 February 1913; 2 May 1924; Graves Register 1877– *c.*1959, D/D SHC 8/1, WGA; letter from I. H. Benjamin to unknown, 18 June 1928, ACC/3121/D2/077, LMA.

45 *JC*, 8 May 1896; 19 August 1927; 17 June 1938. Hannah Cammerman of Abertillery, for example, was buried in Brynmawr in 1926, while Moses Freedman of Tonypandy was buried in Pontypridd in 1915 (noted by author during a visit to Glyntaff Cemetery in 2012).

46 *JC*, 23 September 1932; 3 January 1947.

47 This was not unique to Wales, however. Other Jewish congregations in the United Kingdom and the United States split because of internal disputes; see, for example, Abrams, *Caledonian Jews*, pp. 65–94; Weissbach, *Jewish Life*, pp. 156–76.

48 *CAJEX*, 11-4 (1961), p. 65.

49 *CAJEX*, 35-2 (1985), p. 18; Swansea Hebrew Congregation Minute Book, 12 December 1915, D/D SHC 1/2, WGA; spelled 'Jackower', see *JC*, 27 February 1914.

50 *CAJEX*, 35-2 (1985), p. 18; *JC*, 25 February 1916; 10 March 1916.

51 *JYB*, 1899.

52 *JYB*, 1896–8; *JC*, 25 January 1985; *JC*, 9 April 1895; 12 September 1895; 8 May 1896; 14 August 1896.

53 *JC*, 3 December 1915.

54 *JC*, 11 August 1899.

55 *JYB*, 1904–42.

56 *JC,* 30 November 1888.

57 *JC*, 1 November 1889; 7 March 1890; 14 May 1897.

58 *JC*, 28 April 1933; CUS Account Book, 226, DJR/6/76, GA; *Bimah*, 43 (July 2005), p. 12.

59 *Western Mail*, 30 March 1899.

60 *Evening Express*, 23 April 1901; *JC*, 9 January 1891; 28 August 1891. This was in keeping with the reforms of the Chief Rabbi, Nathan Marcus Adler, who refashioned Judaism to accentuate a growing commitment to the Victorian religious milieu. See Eugene C. Black, 'The Anglicization of Orthodoxy: The Adlers, Father and Son', in Frances Malino and David Sorkin (eds), *From East and West: Jews in a Changing Europe, 1750–1870* (Cambridge, 1991), pp. 295–325.

61 *Western Mail*, 30 March 1899; *South Wales Daily News*, 19 April 1900.

62 *CAJEX*, 2-2 (1952), p. 30; *JC*, 17 June 1904.

63 *CAJEX*, 2-2 (1952), p. 30. Merches Place was also used for *cheder* lessons and Talmudic study until the building was sold in the late 1940s; see Cardiff United Synagogue Account Book, pp. 281–385, DJR/6/76, GA (henceforth CUS).

64 *JC*, 2 November 1900; *JYB*, 1906.

65 *JC*, 15 March 1918.

66 *JC*, 28 April 1933.

67 *JC*, 27 April 1934; 2 November 1934; 29 May 1936; 7 January 1938; 23 June 1939; 2 February 1940; 8 March 1940.

68 *JC*, 28 April 1933; 25 July 1941; 22 August 1941; 5 December 1941; CUS Account Book, 226, DJR/6/76, GA; *Bimah*, 43 (July 2005), p. 12.

69 *JC*, 28 November 1941.

70 Swansea Hebrew Congregation Minute Book, 9–11 December 1895, D/D SHC 1/1, WGA. Swansea's case was not unique and similar conflicts arose between 'native' and immigrant Jews in other Jewish communities in Britain during this period; See, for instance, Abrams, *Caledonian Jews*; Endelman, *The Jews of Britain*; Gartner, *The Jewish Immigrant in England*.

71 *JC*, 9 November 1906; 11 October 1907.

72 *JYB*, 1910; Swansea Hebrew Congregation Minute Book, 11 October 1898 and 20 January 1899, D/D SHC 1/1, WGA. Tobias Shepherd relocated to Ystalyfera at the turn of the twentieth century; see Jasmine Donahaye, *The Greatest Need: The Creative Life and Troubled Times of Lily Tobias, a Welsh Jew in Palestine* (Aberystwyth, 2015), p. 10.

73 Letter from I. R. Levi to the Office of the Chief Rabbi, 9 March 1923, ACC/2805/04/02/123, LMA; Swansea Hebrew Congregation Minute Book, 10 July 1909, D/D SHC 1/2, WGA.

74 Beth Hamedrash Minute Book, 26 February 1921, D/D SHC 1/7, WGA.

75 This trend in Swansea was repeated in other cities in Britain such as London and Manchester, that saw many poor and aspiring Jewish immigrants gradually climb the economic ladder in the first half of the twentieth century, eventually moving out of working-class districts and settling in middle-class areas. For more on this, see Hannah Ewence, '"Hands across the Tea": Renegotiating Jewish Identity and Belonging in Post-war Britain', in Maria Diemling and Larry Ray (eds), *Boundaries, Identity and Belonging in Modern Judaism* (London, 2015), pp. 148–61; Endelman, *The Jews of Britain*, p. 230.

76 *JC*, 22 June 1951. Swansea's Goat Street synagogue was destroyed in the Blitz in 1941.

77 Lee Shai Weissbach, 'East European Immigrants and the Image of the Jews in the Small-Town South,' *American Jewish History*, 85, 3 (1997), 243.

78 Brynmawr's Hebrew Congregation, also established by Eastern European immigrants in the late nineteenth century, was not free from internal disagreements, but the congregation never officially split. For more on this, see Harold Pollins, 'The Jewish Community of Brynmawr, Wales', *Jewish Journal of Sociology*, L, 1–2 (2008), 19–23; Brynmawr Hebrew Congregation: correspondence with the Chief Rabbi's Office in London concerning disputes, 1910, ACC/2805/03/02/038, LMA.

79 Julius Carlebach, 'The Impact of German Jews on Anglo-Jewry Orthodoxy,

1850–1950', in Werner E. Mosse and Julius Carlebach (eds), *Second Chance: Two Centuries of German-Speaking Jews in the United Kingdom* (Tübingen, 1991), p. 407.

80 Derek Taylor, *British Chief Rabbis 1664–2006* (London, 2007), p. 323.

81 See the records of the Office of the Chief Rabbi, ACC/2805, LMA. The practice of giving spiritual leaders the title 'Reverend' was abandoned in the latter half of the twentieth century; see William D. Rubinstein, Michael A. Jolles and Hilary L. Rubinstein (eds), *The Palgrave Dictionary of Anglo-Jewish History* (Basingstoke, 2011), p. 154.

82 Geoffrey Alderman, *Modern British Jewry* (Oxford, 1998), p. 92. For more on Jews' College, see Albert M. Hyamson, *Jews' College, London, 1855–1955* (London, 1955).

83 Carlebach, 'The Impact of German Jews on Anglo-Jewry Orthodoxy', in Mosse and Carlebach (eds), *Second Chance*, p. 407.

84 Bernard Susser, *The Jews of South-West England: The Rise and Decline of their Medieval and Modern Communities* (Exeter, 1993), p. 140.

85 *JC*, 14 May 1858; 9 August 1872; *Glasgow Herald*, 31 July 1869.

86 *JC*, 24 March 1893; 17 February 1893; the *JC* incorrectly notes 'J. Hamburg'.

87 *JC*, 7 March 1941.

88 *JYB*, 1918-1920.

89 *CAJEX*, 3-2 (1953), pp. 46–48.

90 *JC*, 23 July 1937.

91 *JC*, 23 June 1939.

92 *JC*, 25 May 1945; 27 September 1946.

93 *JC*, 9 May 1947; *CAJEX*, 34-3 (1984), p. 17.

94 In the 1920s, for instance, the Aberavon and Port Talbot Hebrew Congregation sent an annual donation of £1. 1. 0 to the fund, while the minute books of both the Swansea Beth Hamedrash and the Hebrew Congregation reveal that its members also donated to the fund; See letter from A. Factor, Aberavon, to J. H. Taylor, 14 September 1922, ACC/2805/4/2/1, LMA; Beth Hamedrash Minute Book, 21 January 1912, D/D SHC 1/7, WGA; Swansea Hebrew Congregation Minute Book, 11 June 1979, D/D SHC 1/5, WGA.

95 See, for instance, Nathan Abrams, *Caledonian Jews*; Weissbach, *Jewish Life*.

96 *JYB*, 1914–40; *JC*, 24 May 1996.

97 *JYB*, 1896–40.

98 *JYB*, 1898–1943; *JC*, 12 May 1905; 6 October 1905; 27 January 1911; 12 May 1911; 22 October 1920; 10 March 1922; 14 April 1922; 17 August 1928; 8

August 1930; 8 September 1933; 25 December 1936; 15 October 1937; 23 January 1942; letter from I. Wartski to A. Feldman, 12 August 1918, ACC/2805/4/02/002, LMA.

99   *JC*, 18 January 1901; 23 October 1903;

100 *JC*, 29 April 1904.

101 Harry Cohen, interview with David Jacobs.

102 Letter from M. Isaacs to unknown, 12 December 1927, ACC/2805/1/04/01, LMA.

103 Letter from I. Livingstone to the Chief Rabbi, 1 March 1920, ACC/2805/04/05/032, LMA.

104 Letter from H. Goldman to I. Livingstone, 2 April 1926, ACC/2805/01/04, LMA. For more on the Provincial Minister's Fund, see Isaac Livingstone, *Fifty Years of Service: The Jubilee of the Provincial Jewish Ministers' Fund* (London, 1935).

105 Swansea Hebrew Congregation Minute Book, 5 October 1902, and 5 March 1905, D/D SHC 1/1, WGA; *JC*, 13 July 1906. For more on the ministry of Revd Simon Fyne, see Leonard Mars, 'The Ministry of the Reverend Simon Fyne', in Henriques (ed.), *The Jews of South Wales*, pp. 111–30.

106 Swansea Hebrew Congregation Minute Book, January 1908, D/D SHC 1/1, WGA.; Swansea Hebrew Congregation Minute Book, 9 November 1913, D/D SHC 1/2, WGA.

107 *JC*, 18 January 1918; 7 November 1975.

108 *JC*, 13 June 1930; 25 April 1969.

109 *CAJEX*, 11-4 (1961), p. 67; *JC*, 24 May 1966.

110 *JC*, 11 August 1944.

111 *JC*, 12 June 1914.

112 *JC*, 5 June 1964.

113 *JC*, 20 May 1960.

114 *JC*, 22 October 1920.

115 *JC*, 25 February 1905.

116 *JC*, 21 February 1919; 6 June 1919; 6 August 1920.

117 Bernard Susser, 'Statistical Accounts of all the Congregations in the British Empire 5606/1845', in Aubrey Newman, *Provincial Jewry in Victorian Britain: Papers for a Conference at University College, London Convened by the Jewish Historical Society of England* (London, 1975), pp. 16–24.

118 Salmond S. Levin, 'The Changing Pattern of Jewish Education' in Salmond S. Levin (ed.), *A Century of Anglo-Jewish Life 1870–1970* (London, 1970), pp. 58–9.

119 Susser, *The Jews of South-West England*, p. 248. There was also a hope that by offering English-language lessons, Jewish day schools would play a key role in the acculturation of Jewish immigrant children into British (i.e. English) society. For more on this, see Israel Finestein, *Scenes and Personalities in Anglo-Jewry 1800–2000* (London, 2002), pp. 52–95.

120 *JC*, 21 December 1866.

121 *JC*, 21 December 1866. A Jewish collegiate school offering both Jewish religious instruction and secular education was established in Merthyr Tydfil in 1878 under the direction of Revd Henry P. Levy, but it appears to have dissolved in 1880 following Levy's departure for Cardiff. See *Merthyr Telegraph*, 23 August 1878; 16 January 1880.

122 *JC*, 7 November 1873.

123 *JC*, 13 December 1872; 19 September 1873.

124 *JYB*, 1912 and 1919.

125 *JC*, 9 November 1866.

126 *JC*, 5 August 1870; 9 December 1870.

127 *JC*, 28 July 1871; 11 August 1871; 17 May 1872.

128 *JC*, 18 October 1912; 9 March 191; *Weekly Mail*, 14 August 1880.

129 Geoffrey Alderman, *Modern British Jewry* (Oxford, 1998), p. 91; Finestein, *Scenes and Personalities*, pp. 56–8.

130 *JYB*, 1899; *JC*, 12 July 1895.

131 *JC*, 12 July 1895; Bridgend Jewish Education Report, 1927, ACC/2805/01/04/002, LMA.

132 Cyril Cohen, interview with Trudy Browning and Diana Soffa, 11 March 2010, Hineni, 11706, Sound Archive, SFNHM; Lena and Leslie Burns, interview with David Jacobs.

133 Joyce Arron, interview with Cai Parry-Jones, Swansea, 23 January 2013, 11818, Sound Archive, SFNHM; letter from Revd D. Wolfson to E. Stein, 28 March 1940, WM 1780/28, Anglesey Archives.

134 Letter from Rev. E. Berry to the Chief Rabbi, 8 March 1920, ACC/2805/04/02/075, LMA.

135 Ben Hamilton, interview with David Jacobs.

136 Jacqueline Magrill, interview with Sue Mansell.

137 Cynthia Kahn, *Wild Water Lilies: A Young Girl's War-Time Diary 1940–1945* (Chessington, 2005), pp. 47–61.

138 *JC*, 15 January 1904; 11 July 1913; 20 March 1914; Leonard Minkes, 'A Jewish Boyhood in Cardiff ', *Planet*, 164 (April/May 2004), 55.

139 *JC*, 28 December 1900.

140 *JC*, 22 July 1921.

141 Report of Llanelli Hebrew Classes, 12 July 1938, ACC/2805/01/04/002, LMA.

142 *JC*, 12 May 1899.

143 Report of Llandudno Hebrew Classes, 1 July 1952, MS179 AJ 289/5/7, Hartley Library, University of Southampton (henceforth HLUS).

144 Charles Arron, interview with Cai Parry-Jones, Swansea, 23 January 2013, 11817, Sound Archive, SFNHM.

145 Renee Woolf, interview with Cai Parry-Jones.

146 Harry Cohen, interview with David Jacobs.

147 Leonard Minkes, 'A Jewish Boyhood in Cardiff', *Planet*, 164 (April/May 2004), 55.

148 Channah Hirsch, *My Llanelli: The Gateshead of Wales* (London, 2009), p. 75.

149 John Wartski, interview with Cai Parry-Jones, Bournemouth, 19 March 2012, 11812, Sound Archive, SFNHM.

150 *CAJEX*, 19-1 (1969), p. 27.

151 *Cambrian*, 31 October 1890; *Cardiff Times*, 6 February 1909; Lena and Leslie Burns, interview with David Jacobs, 25 May 1978, 6014/2, Sound Archive, SFNHM.

152 *Johns' Newport Directory* (1907–1913).

153 Swansea Hebrew Congregation Minute Book, Balance Sheet: 1905–06, D/D SHC 1/1. Silver was the first of many kosher butchers to serve Swansea Jewry. Others included Meyer Lipshitz and Bessie Dulin, who also sold kosher meat in Swansea market between the 1910s and the 1930s, and the 1940s and 1970s respectively. See *Wales Trades Directory* (1912); Swansea Hebrew Congregation Minute Book, Balance Sheet: 1931–32, D/D SHC 1/2; Swansea Hebrew Congregation Minute Book, Statement of Account for the year ending 31 October 1954, D/D SHC 1/3.

154 *Kelly's Directory of Monmouthshire and South Wales* (1901); *JC*, 31 January 1992.

155 A. Rivlin, letter to the Chief Rabbi, 13 June 1934, ACC/2805/04/02/029, LMA; *Kelly's Directory of Monmouthshire and South Wales* (1910); *Western Mail's Cardiff Directory* (1922).

156 *CAJEX*, 36-2 (1986), p. 21; *Kelly's Western Mail Directory* (1949). During the same period there were three kosher bakers serving Cardiff Jewry, including 'Adler the baker in Eldon Road' and 'Marcovitch and Zemla's in Wood Street'. There was also Gotlib's in Bridge Street, which opened in the 1940s.

157 *CAJEX*, 25-1 (1975), p. 31.

158 Simon Joseph, *My Formative Years: A Jewish Boy's Childhood in South Wales in the Early 1900s* (London, 1994), pp. 39–40.

159 Harry Cohen, interview with David Jacobs; *JC*, 3 August 1894.

160 Eve Pollecoff, interview with Cai Parry-Jones, London, 10 November 2011, 11804, Sound Archive, SFNHM; Paul Sugarman, interview with Cai Parry-Jones, Rhyl, 19 April 2012, 11813, Sound Archive, SFNHM.

161 'The Only Jews in the Village': youandus.theus.org.uk/womens-view/features/the-only-jews-in-the-village

162 Joyce Arron, interview with Cai Parry-Jones; Renee Woolf, interview with Cai Parry-Jones.

163 *JC*, 17 June 1892; 12 April 1907; *JYB*, 1900.

164 For further works on Jewish philanthropy in Britain, see Mordechai Rozin, *The Rich and the Poor: Jewish Philanthropy and Social Control in Nineteenth-Century London* (Brighton, 1999); Haim Sperber; 'Philanthropy and Social Control in the Anglo-Jewish Community during the Mid-Nineteenth Century (1850–1880)', *Journal of Modern Jewish Studies*, 11, 1 (2012), 85–101.

165 *JYB*, 1900; *JYB*, 1904. Dora Lipsett, interview with David Jacobs.

166 *JC*, 12 November 1897; *JC*, 27 February 1914.

167 *JC*, 24 December 1915.

168 Leslie and Lena Burns, interview with David Jacobs; *JC*, 10 March 1916; 12 September 1919; 26 February 1915; 13 July 1917; 23 January 1920.

169 *JC*, 1 May 1914.

170 *Merthyr Times and Dowlais Times and Aberdare Echo*, 3 October 1895; *Evening Express*, 5 May 1899; *South Wales Daily News*, 19 May 1894; *Western Mail*, 29 April 1874.

Notes to Chapter 3

1 William D. Rubinstein, *A History of the Jews in the English-Speaking World: Great Britain* (London, 1996), p. 280.

2 For more on the history of the German occupation of the Channel Islands and the deportation of its Jewish population, see Frederick E. Cohen, *The Jews in the Channel Islands during the German Occupation: 1940–1945* (London, 2000).

3 Rubinstein, *A History of the Jews*, p. 280.

4 See, for instance, Daniel Snowman, *The Hitler Émigrés: The Cultural Impact on Britain of Refugees from Nazism* (London, 2002); Gerhard Hirschfeld (ed.), *Exile in Great Britain: Refugees from Hitler's Germany* (Atlantic Highlands, 1984); Richard Bolchover, *British Jewry and the Holocaust* (Oxford, 2003); Pamela Shatzkes, *Holocaust and Rescue: Impotent or Indifferent? Anglo-Jewry 1938–1945* (Basingstoke, 2002).

5 Two books contain chapters on the history of Jewish industrialists and medical refugees in south Wales, but the literature is not extensive; see Anthony Glaser, 'Jewish Refugees and Refugee Industries', in Ursula R. Q. Henriques (ed.), *The Jews of South Wales*, 2nd edn (Cardiff, 2013), pp. 177–205; Paul Weindling, 'The Jewish Medical Refugee Crisis', in Pamela F. Michael and Charles Webster (eds), *Health and Society in Twentieth-Century Wales* (Cardiff, 2006), pp. 183–200.

6 William D. Rubinstein, *The Left, the Right and the Jews* (New York, 2015), p. 17.

7 Anthony Grenville, *Jewish Refugees from Germany and Austria in Britain 1933–1970: Their Image in AJR Information* (London, 2010), p. 5.

8 Grenville, *Jewish Refugees*, p. 5. For more on this, see Louise London, 'Immigration Control Procedures and Jewish Refugees, 1933–1939', in Werner E. Mosse and Julius Carlebach (eds), *Second Chance: Two Centuries of German-Speaking Jews in the United Kingdom* (Tübingen, 1991), pp. 485–517.

9 Paul Weindling, 'Medical Refugees in Britain and the Wider World, 1930–1960: Introduction', *Social History of Medicine*, 22/3 (2009), 451.

10 Ari J. Sherman, *Island Refuge: Britain and Refugees from the Third Reich, 1933–1939* (Ilford, 1994), p. 21.

11 Naomi Baumslag, *Murderous Medicine: Nazi Doctors, Human Experimentation, and Typhus* (Westport, 2005), p. 90.

12 Paul Weindling, 'The Contribution of Central European Jews to Medical Science and Practice in Britain, the 1930s–1950s', in Mosse and Carlebach (eds), *Second Chance*, p. 253.

13 Kenneth Collins, 'European Refugee Physicians in Scotland, 1933–1945', *Social History of Medicine*, 22/3 (2009), 513–16.

14 Tony Kushner, 'An Alien Occupation – Jewish Refugees and Domestic Service in Britain, 1933–1948', in Mosse and Carlebach (eds), *Second Chance*, p. 560.

15 Weindling, 'The Contribution of Central European Jews', in Mosse and Carlebach (eds), *Second Chance*, p. 247. The Scottish Triple Qualification Board, however, allowed refugee doctors to take the final examinations after only one year of clinical studies; see Collins, 'European Refugee Physicians in Scotland', 528.

16 Weindling, 'The Jewish Medical Refugee Crisis', in Michael and Webster (eds), *Health and Society in Twentieth-Century Wales*, p. 188.

17 *Bimah*, 68 (May 2012), p. 54; *JC*, 28 January 1977; Weindling 'The Jewish Medical Refugee Crisis', pp. 145–98.

18 *CAJEX*, 3-1 (1953), p. 66; 27/3 (1977), p. 25; Miscellaneous correspondence, including a letter from Dr Bernfeld's brother following Dr Bernfeld's death,

1972-4, DCNS 7/24, GA; Samson Wright, 'Our Colleagues in Austria', *The Lancet* (9 April 1938), 865.

19 Bill Williams, *Jews and Other Foreigners: The Rescue of the Victims of European Fascism, 1939–1940*, (Mancheste, 2011), p. 36; Hirschfeld, '"A High Tradition of Eagerness . . .": British non-Jewish Organisations in Support of Refugees', in Mosse and Carlebach, *Second Chance*, p. 605.

20 Society for the Protection of Science and Learning (hereafter SPSL), Box 51/1, f. 17 and 26, Bodleian Library, Oxford (henceforth BLO).

21 Letter from J. F. Rees to Thomson, 2 December 1938, SPSL, 130/3, f. 189, BLO.

22 Geoffrey Alderman, *Modern British Jewry* (Oxford, 1998) p. 273; Rubinstein, *A History of the Jews*, p. 337.

23 Rudolf Vierhaus, *Deutsche Biographische Enzyklopädie 2., überarbeitete und erweiterte Ausgabe* (München, 2005), p. 107.

24 Martin Swales, 'Heller, Erich (1911–1990)', *Oxford Dictionary of National Biography* (online edn, January 2008): *www.oxforddnb.com/view/article/92861*

25 Herbert Loebl, 'Refugees from the Third Reich and Industry in the Depressed Areas of Britain', in Mosse and Carlebach (eds), *Second Chance*, p. 382.

26 Loebl, 'Refugees from the Third Reich', in Mosse and Carlebach (eds), *Second Chance*, p. 382.

27 Glaser, 'Jewish Refugees', in Henriques (ed.), *The Jews of South Wales*, p. 185.

28 Herbert Loebl, 'Industry in the Depressed Areas', in Mosse and Carlebach (eds), *Second Chance*, p. 385.

29 Bill Pollock, interview with Cai Parry-Jones, London, 10 November 2011, Hineni, 11755, Sound Archive, SFNHM.

30 Billie Holden, interview with Diana Soffa, 20 August 2010, Hineni, 11715, Sound Archive, SFNHM.

31 Peter Longerich, *Holocaust: The Nazi Persecution and Murder of the Jews* (Oxford, 2010), p. 66.

32 Refugee Industries. Analysis of Replies to Questionnaire re Present and Post-War Activities of Refugee Industries in Wales and Monmouthshire, DIDC/68, GA.

33 *JC*, 10 May 1940.

34 *JC*, 30 June 1939.

35 *JC*, 15 December 1939.

36 Norman Bentwich, *Wanderer in War, 1939–45* (London, 1946), p. 30; Refugee Industries. Analysis of Replies to Questionnaire, DIDC/68, GA.

37 Judith T. Baumel-Schwartz, *Never Look Back: The Jewish Refugee Children in Great Britain, 1938–1945* (West Lafayette, 2012), pp. 50–1.

38 Baumel-Schwartz, *Never Look Back*, p. 52.

39 Patricia Heberer, *Children During the Holocaust* (Lanham, 2011), p. 73.

40 Heberer, *Children During the Holocaust*, p. 74.

41 Heberer, *Children During the Holocaust*, p. 357.

42 Ronald Stent, 'Jewish Refugee Organisations', in Mosse and Carlebach (eds), *Second Chance*, p. 591; Martin Gilbert, *Kristallnacht: Prelude to Destruction* (London, 2007), p. 227. Other British organisations and individuals, both Jewish and non-Jewish, also became involved in the rescue and reception of child refugees from Austria, Czechoslovakia and Germany. They included Nicholas Winton, the B'nai B'rith Care Committee for Refugee Children and the Women's Appeal Committee, among others.

43 Baumel-Schwartz, *Never Look Back*, p. 89.

44 Baumel-Schwartz, *Never Look Back*, pp. 113–17.

45 *JC*, 16 December 1938; 3 February 1939.

46 Baumel-Schwartz, *Never Look Back*, p. 119.

47 *First Annual Report of the Movement for the Care of Children from Germany Ltd*, Central British Fund Archives, 27/28/153, Wiener Library (henceforth WL).

48 Letter from Anneliese Barth to Mrs Leverton, 21 November 1988, 1368/2/2/11, WL.

49 Ellen Davis, *Kerry's Children: A Jewish Childhood in Nazi Germany and Growing up in South Wales* (Bridgend, 2004), p. 65.

50 *JC*, 18 August 1939.

51 Jeremy Josephs with Susi Bechhöfer, *Rosa's Child: The True Story of One Woman's Quest for a Lost Mother and a Vanished Past* (London, 1996), p. 26; *JC*, 2 September 1988.

52 Baumel-Schwartz, *Never Look Back*, pp. 117–18.

53 *JC*, 12 May 1939.

54 *CAJEX*, 19-2 (1969), p. 52; *JC*, 12 May 1939; 19 December 1939.

55 Frieda Korobkin, *Throw your Feet over your Shoulders: Beyond the Kindertransport* (Pittsburgh, 2012), pp. 80–7; *JC*, 30 October 1942; Bertha Leverton and Shmuel Lowensohn (eds), *I Came Alone: The Stories of the Kindertransports* (Lewes, 1990), pp. 253–4.

56 Baumel-Schwartz, *Never Look Back*, p. 138.

57 Baumel-Schwartz, *Never Look Back*, p. 150.

58 Baumel-Schwartz, *Never Look Back*, p. 140.

59 *Chayenu: Organ of the Torah Va'Avodah Movement and Brit Chalutzim Datiim of Western Europe*, 1/1 (November–December 1939), 11; *JC*, 15 September 1939; Baumel-Schwartz, *Never Look Back*, p. 145.

60 *JC*, 20 June 1941; Herman Rothman, interview with Peter M. Hart, February 2008, 30627, IWM; Martin Steinberger, interview with Hermione Sacks, date unknown, C410/104, BL.

61 E. Wynne Williams, 'Jewish Refugees at Gwrych Castle', *Abergele Field Club and Historical Society Review*, 1 (1982) 2–5.

62 Martin Steinberger, interview with Hermione Sacks; *JC*, 2 August 1940; 6 February 1942; 3 July 1942; Baumel-Schwartz, *Never Look Back*, p. 139.

63 *JC*, 2 August 1940.

64 Bracha Habas, *Sefer Aliyat ha'noar* (Jerusalem, 1940), pp. 178–9; Perez Leshem, *Strasse zur Rettung: 1933–1939 aus Deutschland Vertrieben-bereitet sich jüdische Jugend auf Palästina vor* (Tel Aviv, 1973), p. 201.

65 Thea Sonnenmark, interview with Toby Blum-Dobkin and Lucia Ruedenberg, 26 March 1990, 1990.V.4, Museum of Jewish Heritage, New York.

66 The results of the Kindertransport Survey carried out by the Association of Jewish Refugees in 2007 can be found online: *www.ajr.org.uk/documents/KinderTransport_Survey_2007_Final_Databases_21Aug2009_-clean_results_deduped_renumbered.xls*.

67 Baumel-Schwartz, *Never Look Back*, p. 148.

68 Herman Rothman, interview with Peter M. Hart; Manfred Alweiss, 'My Exodus from Berlin', *Kindertransport Newsletter* (April 2006): *www.ajr.org.uk/documents/ktapro6.pdf*

69 For more on the Welsh context, see Chezzi, *Italians in Wales*, p. 43.

70 François Lafitte, *The Internment of Aliens* (Harmondsworth, 1940), pp. 37–63.

71 An example from Wales included Austrian-Jewish draper Abraham Hardman of Glynneath, the father of Leslie Hardman, one of the first Jewish chaplains to enter Bergen-Belsen on its liberation in 1945, who was interned as an 'enemy alien' in 1914; see Leslie Hardman, interview with Lyn E. Smith, 22 September 1997, 17636, IWM.

72 Mark Donnelly, *Britain in the Second World War* (London, 1999), p. 47.

73 Baumel-Schwartz, *Never Look Back*, p. 185.

74 Ted Jones, *Both Sides of the Wire: The Fredericton Internment Camp*, vol. 1 (Fredericton, 1988), pp. 17–19.

75 Letter from Eli Dror to unknown, *c*.1988, 1368/2/2/29, WL.

76 Scipio, *100,000,000 Allies – If We Choose* (London, 1940), p. 102.

77 Ronald Stent, *A Bespattered Page? The Internment of His Majesty's 'Most Loyal Enemy Aliens'* (London, 1980), pp. 9–10.

78 Billie Holden, interview with Diana Soffa.

79 George Schoenmann, *Memoirs . . . The Long Road to Retirement* (Cardiff, 2011), pp. 68–9.

80 Bob Gregory, interview with Eve Lavine, 1 June 2011, Hineni, 11737, Sound Archive, SFNHM.

81 Herman Rothman, interview with Peter M. Hart.

82 John Welshman, *Churchill's Children: The Evacuee Experience in Wartime Britain* (Oxford, 2010), pp. 18–21.

83 Davies, *A History of Wales*, p. 583.

84 Stuart Broomfield, *Wales at War: The Experience of the Second World War in Wales* (Stroud, 2009), p. 28.

85 Tony Kushner, 'Horns and Dilemmas: Jewish Evacuees in Britain during the Second World War', *Immigrants and Minorities*, 8 (1988), 276.

86 *JC*, 15 December 1939; 27 February 1953.

87 Maurice I. Hesselberg, Bangor 1939–1942: A Memoir, 5, XM/12325, CRO.

88 Victor Sassoon, interview with Cai Parry-Jones, London, 17 April 2012, 11809/1-8, Sound Archive, SFNHM.

89 Malcolm Eagle's reminiscences: *www.timewitnesses.org/evacuees/~malcolm.html*

90 *JC*, 13 June 1941.

91 *JC*, 13 June 1941; 7 November 1941.

92 *JC*, 20 June 1941; 7 November 1941; 18 October 1968.

93 *JC*, 17 April 1942.

94 *JC*, 3 July 1942.

95 *JYB*, 1945–46.

96 *JC*, 1 November 1940.

97 *JC*, 31 January 1941; 11 April 1941; 5 December 1975; Michael Shafran and Rita Hyman, interview with Cai Parry-Jones, London, 17 August 2011, 11810, Sound Archive, SFNHM; memories of Hazel Frances Snowden (née Brown): *www.bbc.co.uk/history/ww2peopleswar/stories/06/a4294406.shtml*

98 Paul Sugarman, interview with Cai Parry-Jones.

99 Paul Sugarman, interview with Cai Parry-Jones. *JC*, 25 July 1941.

100 *JC*, 25 July 1941; 29 August 1941; 5 September 1941; 26, December 1941; 9 January 1942; 20 March 1942; 1 May 1942; 14 August 1942; 25 June 1943; 5 November 1943; 7 March 1947.

101 *JC*, 7 March 1947. Evacuated Jewish families and individuals in Colwyn Bay were later joined by Jews working for the Ministry of Food in London, which relocated its headquarters to the seaside town in June 1940. Rona Hart, telephone interview with Cai Parry-Jones, 2 July 2012, 11814, Sound Archive, SFNHM.

102 *JC*, 5 September 1941; 15 January 1943.

103 Ray Sopher, interview with Cai Parry-Jones, London, 11 December 2011, 11805, Sound Archive, SFNHM; *JC*, 15 January 1943; 29 January 1943.

104 *JC*, 6 February 1942; 27 March 1942; 9 April 2010; *JYB*, 1949–68.

105 *JC*, 27 October 1939; 2 August 1940.

106 *JC*, 11 October 1940; 17 October 1941; 9 May 1975; 5 November 1943.

107 Frank E. Schwelb, 'Abernant Lake Hotel, Llanwrtyd Wells, Wales': *www.czechsinexile.org/places/abernant-en.shtml*. The Czechoslovak State School was established by the Czech government-in-exile for refugee children in Great Britain and taught around 140 pupils, most of whom were Jewish. A small number were Roman Catholic, Protestant, or without religious affiliation. The school was first located in Camberley, Surrey, and then evacuated to Hinton Hall, near Nantwich, Shropshire. In 1943, Hintol Hall 'was crumbling', and the evacuated school relocated to the Abernant Lake Hotel in Llanwrtyd Wells, in Wales; see, Vera Gissing, *Pearls of Childhood* (London, 1988), pp. 86–98.

108 Hanna Backer, interview with Cai Parry-Jones, Cardiff, 18 September 2012, 11811, Sound Archive, SFNHM; Gissing, *Pearls of Childhood*, pp. 104–5.

109 Bryan S. Johnson (ed.), *The Evacuees* (London: Gollancz, 1968), p. 90.

110 Papers of Revd James Williams Parkes, MS60.07.006.005, HLUS.

111 William J. Gruffydd, 'Editor's Notes', *Y Llenor*, 20 (1941); excerpt in Davies, *The Chosen People*, pp. 168–9.

112 Quoted in D. Hywel Davies, *The Welsh Nationalist Party, 1925–1945: A Call to Nationhood* (Cardiff, 1983), p. 231.

113 Joseph P. Clancy (ed.), *Selected Poems: Saunders Lewis* (Cardiff, 1993), p. 4.

114 Tony Kushner, *The Persistence of Prejudice: Anti-Semitism in British Society during the Second World War* (Manchester, 1989), p. 123. The number of Jews in the armed forces during the First World War amounted to 55,000 or 18 per cent of British Jewry; see William D. Rubinstein, Michael A. Jolles and Hilary L. Rubinstein (eds), *The Palgrave Dictionary of Anglo-Jewish History* (Basingstoke, 2011), p. 36.

115 *South Wales Argus*, 26 September 2012.

116 *JC*, 26 September 2003; 5 May 1944; 24 June 2004; Book of Honour and Order of Service for the Consecration and Unveiling of the 1939–45 War Memorial at Cathedral Road Synagogue, Cardiff, DJR/2/4, GA; *CAJEX*, 18-4 (December 1968), p. 63.

117 Henry Morris, *We Will Remember Them: A Record of the Jews who Died in the Armed Forces of the Crown from 1939* (London, 1989), p. 3.

118 Book of Honour and Order of Service, DJR/2/4, GA; Morris, *We Will Remember Them*, pp. 48–104.

119 *JC*, 31 October 1941; 22 May 1942.

120 Peter Leighton-Langer, *The King's Own Loyal Enemy Aliens: German and Austrian Refugees in Britain's Armed Forces, 1939–1945* (London, 2006), p. 9.

121 Steven Karras, *The Enemy I Knew: German Jews in the Allied Military in World War II* (Minneapolis, 2009), p. 13.

122 Vivian D. Lipman, *A History of the Jews in Britain since 1858* (Leicester, 1990), p. 230.

123 Stephen Dale, interview with Lyn E. Smith, 26 August 1994, 14582, IWM.

124 Morris, *We Will Remember Them*, p. 54; *Pembroke and Pembroke Dock Observer*, 4 May 2012.

125 Grenville, *Jewish Refugees*, p. 40.

126 Helen P. Fry, *German Schoolboy, British Commando: Churchill's Secret Soldier* (Stroud, 2010), p. 73.

127 Letter from Brian Grant to G. R. Jones, Chief Executive of Gwynedd Council, 26 January 1998, Private Papers of B. Grant, 99.59.1, IWM; Karras, *The Enemy I Knew*, p. 85; James Leasor, *The Unknown Warrior* (London, 1980), p. 12; *Daily Mail*, 22 May 2009.

128 *Daily Mail*, 22 May 2009.

129 Ian Dear, *Ten Commando 1942–1945* (London, 1987), pp. 171–200; Martin Sugarman, *Fighting Back: British Jewry's Contribution in the Second World War* (London, 2010), p. 290.

130 Nicholas van der Bijl, *Commandos in Exile: No. 10 (Inter-Allied) Commando 1942–1945* (Barnsley, 2008), p. 32; Martin Sugarman, *Fighting Back*, p. 290.

131 Helen Fry, *The King's Most Loyal Enemy Aliens: Germans Who Fought for Britain in the Second World War* (Stroud, 2007), p. 67.

132 J. Gwyn Griffiths, *Teithiau'r Meddwl: Ysgrifau Llenyddol Kate Bosse-Griffiths* (Talybont, 2004), p. 110.

133 Jasmine Donahaye, '"Gartref – bron": Adversity and Refuge in the Jewish Literature of Wales', in Alyce von Rothkirch and Daniel Williams (eds), *Beyond the Difference: Welsh Literature in Comparative Contexts* (Cardiff, 2004), p.47.

134 Donahaye, *The Greatest Need*, pp. 85–106.

135 *Glamorgan Gazette*, 27 November 1914; Merthyr Tydfil Hebrew Congregation Roll of Honour: http://cemeteryscribes.com/blog/roll-of-honour-merthyr/; Donahaye, *The Greatest Need*, pp.85–106.

136 *JC*, 20 September 1963; Michael Shafran and Rita Hyman, interview with Cai Parry-Jones.

Notes to Chapter 4

1 See Charlotte Williams, Neil Evans and Paul O'Leary (eds), *A Tolerant Nation?: Revisiting Ethnic Diversity in a Devolved Wales* (Cardiff, 2015), pp. 1–23; Trevor Fishlock, *Wales and the Welsh* (London, 1972); Hywel Francis and David Smith, *The Fed: A History of the South Wales Miners in the Twentieth Century* (London, 1980), p. 429. More generally, Colin Holmes points out that there has traditionally been 'an emphasis upon Britain as a centre of liberty and toleration'; see Colin Holmes, *A Tolerant Country?: Immigrants, Refugees and Minorities in Britain* (London, 1991), pp. 98–9.

2 Neil Evans, 'Immigrants and Minorities in Wales', in Williams, Evans and O'Leary (eds), *A Tolerant Nation?: Revisiting*, p. 24; Charlotte Williams, 'Passports to Wales? Race, Nation and Identity', in Ralph Fevre and Andrew Thompson (eds), *Nation, Identity and Social Theory: Perspectives From Wales* (Cardiff, 1999), pp. 77–8.

3 Vaughan Robinson and Hannah Garner, 'Place Matters: Exploring the Distinctiveness of Racism in Rural Wales', in Sarah Neal and Julian Agyeman (eds), *The New Countryside: Ethnicity, Nation and Exclusion in Contemporary Britain* (Bristol, 2006), p. 50; Vaughan Robinson, 'Exploring Myths about Rural Racism: a Welsh Case Study', in Charlotte Williams, Neil Evans and Paul O'Leary (eds), *A Tolerant Nation? Exploring Ethnic Diversity in Wales* (Cardiff, 2003), p. 160.

4 Michael Hechter, *Internal Colonialism: The Celtic Fringe in British National Development, 1536–1966* (London, 1975).

5 Charlotte Williams, 'Passports to Wales?', in Fevre and Thompson (eds), *Nation, Identity and Social Theory*, p. 79.

6 Sandra Betts and Charlotte Williams, 'Gender and "race"', in Hugh Mackay (ed.), *Understanding Contemporary Wales* (Cardiff, 2010), pp. 91–124.

7 Williams, 'Passports to Wales?', in Fevre and Thompson (eds), *Nation, Identity and Social Theory*, p. 84; Neil Evans, 'Internal Colonialism? Colonisation, Economic Development and Political Mobilisation in Wales, Scotland, and Ireland', in Graham Day and Gareth Rees (eds), *Regions, Nations and European Integration: Restructuring the Celtic Periphery* (Cardiff, 1991), pp. 235–64.

8 A by no means comprehensive list of works that deal specifically on this subject includes Alan Llwyd, *Black Wales: A History of Black Welsh People* (Cardiff, 2005); Paul O'Leary, 'Anti-Irish riots in Wales, 1826–1882', *Llafur*, 5/4 (1991), 27–36; Jon Parry, 'The Tredegar anti-Irish riots of 1882',

Llafur, 3/4 (1983), 20–3; Charlotte Williams, '"Race" and Racism: Some Reflections on the Welsh Context', *Contemporary Wales*, 8 (1995), 113–31; Williams, Evans and O'Leary (eds), *A Tolerant Nation?: Exploring*; Williams, Evans and O'Leary (eds), *A Tolerant Nation?: Revisiting*.

9 Jasmine Donahaye, '"By Whom Shall She Arise? For She is Small": The Wales-Israel Tradition in the Edwardian Period', in Nadia Valman and Eitan Bar Yosef (eds), *The Jew in Late-Victorian and Edwardian Culture: Between the East End and East Africa* (London, 2009), p. 162.

10 The one exception is William Rubinstein's reassessment of the Tredegar riots, which overstates that Jewish and non-Jewish relations in Wales were unremittingly positive; see W. D. Rubinstein, 'The Anti-Jewish Riots of 1911 in South Wales', *Welsh History Review*, (1997).

11 For a discussion of non-Jewish and Jewish relations in Welsh literature, see Donahaye, *Whose People?*.

12 Philo- and anti-Semitism are both difficult to define, but the terms are employed here to mean support/opposition towards Jews only, rather than Semitic peoples more generally; Geoffrey Alderman, 'The Jew as Scapegoat? The Settlement and Reception of Jews in South Wales before 1914', *Transactions of the Jewish Historical Society of England*, XXVI (1974–8), 67; Rubinstein, 'The Anti-Jewish Riots', 670.

13 David Cesarani, 'Reporting Antisemitism: The *Jewish Chronicle* 1879–1979', in Siân Jones, Tony Kushner, and Sarah Pearce (eds), *Cultures of Ambivalence and Contempt: Studies in Jewish-non-Jewish Relations* (London, 1998), p. 255; Bryan Cheyette, *Constructions of 'the Jew', in English Literature and Society: Racial Representations, 1875–1945* (Cambridge, 1995), p. 8; Bryan Cheyette, 'Neither Excuse nor Accuse: T. S. Eliot's Semitic Discourse', *Modernism/Modernity*, 10 (2003), 433.

14 Paul O'Leary, 'Conflict and Co-operation', in Henriques (ed.), *The Jews of South Wales*, p. xiv.

15 Davies, *The Chosen People*, p. 12.

16 *JC*, 13 July 1894; *Western Mail*, 15 March 1873.

17 *JC*, 11 October 1889.

18 *JC*, 17 July 1908.

19 *Cardiff and Merthyr Guardian*, 12 April 1856; *North Wales Guardian*, 11 August 1899. For further examples, see 'Fashionable Jewish Wedding at Pontypridd', *Western Mail*, 7 December 1878; 'Jewish Wedding at Newport', *Western Mail*, 6 November 1884.

20 *Carnarvon and Denbigh Herald*, 19 January 1912.

21 *Cardiff Times*, 4 March 1882; *Merthyr Express*, 11 March 1882; *Western Mail*, 26 May 1882; *South Wales Daily Post*, 15 December 1905.

22 *Cambria Daily Leader*, 3 November 1913.

23 *South Wales Evening Post*, 28 April 1933.

24 *JC*, 12 May 1933.

25 *JC*, 9 December 1938; 22 March 1940.

26 For more on the BUF's anti-Jewish activity, see Daniel Tilles, *British Fascist Antisemitism and Jewish Responses, 1932–40* (London, 2015).

27 See, for instance, Stephen M. Cullen, 'Another Nationalism: The British Union of Fascists in Glamorgan, 1932–40', *Welsh History Review*, 17/1 (1994), 101–14; Hywel Francis, *Miners Against Fascism: Wales and the Spanish Civil War* (Abersychan, 2004), p. 40. The BUF targeted south Wales in the 1930s, an area suffering from high levels of unemployment, in an attempt to sway the working-class vote.

28 *JC*, 1 May 1936; Francis, *Miners Against Fascism*, pp. 42–3.

29 Francis, *Miners Against Fascism*, p. 41. Working-class organisations were also the main impetus behind anti-fascist campaigns in Scotland during the 1930s. For more on this, see Henry Maitles, 'Blackshirts Across the Border: The British Union of Fascists in Scotland', *Scottish Historical Review*, 82,/213/1 (2003), pp. 92–100.

30 *JC*, 30 October 1936.

31 *JC*, 27 November 1936; 28 August 1936.

32 *JC*, 18 June 1937.

33 *JC*, 4 September 1936; *Western Mail*, 8 October 1936; 21 October 1936. This reflected wider trends in Britain, with the Board of Deputies of British Jews establishing a defence committee in July 1936. For more on this, see Tilles, *British Fascist Antisemitism*, p. 191.

34 *JC*, 4 June 1937.

35 *JC*, 7 April 1939; 6 April 1945; *NWC*, 10 November 1939.

36 *South Wales Jewish Review*, 6 (June 1904), 91; *JC*, 6 November 1896; 20 September 1895; 21 February 1896; 16 April 1923.

37 Untitled Newspaper Clipping, 21 April 1978, XML 4558/46/129, CRO; *JC*, 23 June 1978.

38 *JC*, 10 June 1949; 12 February 1965; 17 June 1966. Other Jewish cinema owners included Rudolph Abse (father of Dannie and Leo) and Max Corne, both of Cardiff.

39 *JC*, 5 June 1987; 11 August 2006; 24 May 2012; 3 August 2012.

40 Several Welsh Jews have served as MPs for parliamentary constituencies outside Wales, including Barnett Janner (1892–1982) and his son Greville

Janner (1928-2015), Maurice Edelman (1911–75) and Michael Howard (1941–).

41 *JC*, 14 November 1958; 20 May 1994; 5 July 1996; Cameron Hazlehurst, Sally Whitehead, Christine Woodland (eds), *A Guide to the Papers of British Cabinet Ministers, 1900–1964* (Cambridge, 1997), p. 270.

42 *South Wales Daily Post* 5, 6, 7, 8, 14, 20 November 1918.

43 Hector Bolitho, *Alfred Mond: First Lord Melchett* (London, 1933), pp. 201–11.

44 Beth Hamedrash Minute Book, 12 December 1918, D/D SHC 1/7, WGA.

45 For more on this, see Stephen Meredith 'A "Strange Death" Foretold (or the Not So "Strange Death" of Liberal Wales): Liberal Decline, the Labour Ascendancy and Electoral Politics in South Wales, 1922–1924', *North American Journal of Welsh Studies*, 7 (2012), 18–37. Michael Wallach wrote in the *JC* 'that Sir Alfred Mond failed to carry Swansea many years ago because he was a Jew'; see *JC*, 28 November 1975.

46 *JC*, 26 October 1906; 12 November 1920.

47 *JC*, 22 March 1957; 13 February 1970; Charles Arron, interview with Cai Parry-Jones.

48 *JC*, 10 January 1908; 18 October 1918; 22 February 1924; 29 October 1926.

49 Neil Evans and Paul O'Leary, 'Playing the Game: Sport and Ethnic Minorities in Modern Wales', in Williams, Evans and O'Leary (eds), *A Tolerant Nation?: Revisiting*, p. 153.

50 Tony Collins, 'Jews, Antisemitism, and Sports in Britain, 1900–1939', in Michael Brenner and Gideon Reuveni (eds), *Emancipation Through Muscles: Jews and Sports in Europe* (Lincoln, 2006), p. 147; Abrams, *Caledonian Jews*, p. 35. David Dee, *Sport and British Jewry: Integration, Ethnicity and Anti-Semitism, 1890–1970* (Manchester, 2013).

51 *JC*, 4 November 1938; 18 August 1939; 29 May 1964.

52 Untitled newspaper clippings, April 1961 and 21 April 1978, XML 4558/46/129, CRO; *CAJEX*, 11-4 (1961), p. 53.

53 Joyce Arron, interview with Cai Parry-Jones; Norma Glass, interview with Cai Parry-Jones, Swansea, 23 January 2013, 11816, Sound Archive, SFNHM; *JC*, 29 June 1934; 26 October 1934.

54 *JC*, 22 September 1911; 17 August 1923; *CAJEX*, 1/4 (1951), p. 38; Neville Saunders, *Swansea Hebrew Congregation, 1730–1980* (Swansea: Swansea City Council, 1980), p. 25. Neil Evans and Paul O'Leary note the same reasons for the existence of Irish sporting teams in south Wales; see Evans and O'Leary, 'Playing the Game', in Williams, Evans and O'Leary (eds), *A Tolerant Nation?: Revisiting*, p. 155.

55 Leo Abse, 'A Tale of Collaboration not Conflict with the "People of the Book"', *New Welsh Review* 22 (Autumn 1993), 17; Jeffrey S. Gurock, *Judaism's Encounter with American Sports* (Bloomington, 2005), pp. 15–19. Although his sporting career began in London, one of Welsh Jewry's most prominent athletes was the track and field sprinter, David Jacobs (1888–1976), who was born in Cardiff and was the first British Jew to win an Olympic gold medal (at the 1912 Summer Olympics in Stockholm).

56 *JC*, 31 December 1965. Brothers David (1867–1929) and Evan James (1869–1902) were born in Bonymaen, Swansea, to a Jewish mother, but were not raised Jewish as she married a non-Jewish Welshman; see James A. Davies, *A Swansea Anthology* (Bridgend, 1996), p. 55.

57 *JC*, 25 February 2007; 21 January 2011; 22 February 2013.

58 *JC*, 2 March 1951; 4 August 1978.

59 *JC*, 4 August 1978; 13 July 1962.

60 Tony Kushner, 'Clubland, Cricket Tests and Alien Internment', in David Cesarani and Tony Kushner (eds), *The Internment of Aliens in Twentieth Century Britain* London, 1993), p. 91; Gisela Lebzelter, 'Political Anti-Semitism in England 1918-1939', in Herbert A. Strauss (ed.), *Hostages of Modernization: Studies on Modern Antisemitism 1870–1933/39* (Berlin, 1993), p. 400; Dee, *Sport and British Jewry*, pp. 174–75.

61 *South Wales Echo*, 15 August 1934; *JC*, 2 July 1954. There is no verifying evidence to suggest that these incidences were driven by specific enmity towards Jews as Jews.

62 *JYB*, 1901–68.

63 Cormac Ó Gráda, *Jewish Ireland in the Age of Joyce: a Socioeconomic History* (Princeton, 2006), p. 203; Ó Gráda notes that that Jewish immigrants in late nineteenth-century Ireland lived in close proximity to non-Jews, which helped to minimise the tensions and suspicions between natives and newcomers in Ireland.

64 Michael Howard, interview with Cai Parry-Jones, London, 26 April 2012, 11820, Sound Archive, SFNHM.

65 Rona Hart, interview with Cai Parry-Jones.

66 W. C. Elvet Thomas, 'A People Apart', in Meic Stevens (ed.), *A Cardiff Anthology* (Bridgend, 1987), p. 50.

67 Thomas M. Devine, *The Scottish Nation 1700–2007* (London, 2006), p. 520.

68 Michael Shafran and Rita Hyman, interview with Cai Parry-Jones; Vicki Lazar, interview with Cai Parry-Jones, London, 13 December 2011, 11806, Sound Archive, SFNHM.

69 *CAJEX*, 11/3 (1961), p. 9.

70 J. Ronald Williams 'The Influence of Foreign Nationalities on the Life of the People of Merthyr Tydfil', *Sociological Review*, 28 (1926), 150.

71 Donahaye, *Whose People?*, p. 12.

72 *South Wales Jewish Review*, 9 (September, 1904), 130.

73 Donahaye, *Whose People?*, p. 131.

74 *JC*, 20 September 1963.

75 Donahaye, '"By Whom Shall She Arise?', in Valman and Yosef (eds), *The Jew in Late-Victorian and Edwardian Culture*, p. 161.

76 Abrams, *Caledonian Jews*, p. 181; Davies, *The Chosen People*, p. 20; Dorian Llywelyn, *Sacred Place, Chosen People: Land and National Identity in Welsh Spirituality* (Cardiff, 1999), p. 182.

77 Donahaye, '"By Whom Shall She Arise?', p. 165; Donahaye, *Whose People?*, pp. 3–33.

78 David Lloyd George, 'Afterword', in Philip Guedalla, *Napoleon and Palestine* (London, 1925), pp. 45–55.

79 *CAJEX*, 24/4 (1984), p. 26; Ben Hamilton, interview with David Jacobs.

80 Letter from Isidore Wartski to the Chief Rabbi, 22 April 1923, ACC/2805/4/2/2, LMA.

81 Alwyn Pierce-Lloyd, interview with Cai Parry-Jones, Bangor, 3 November 2011, 11802, Sound Archive, Sound Archive, SFNHM.

82 Lily Tobias, *My Mother's House* (London, 1931), p. 31.

83 Geoffrey Alderman, 'The Anti-Jewish Riots of August 1911 in South Wales: A Response, 568; Campbell, 'The Jewish Community in Britain', in Gilley and Sheils (eds), *The History of Religion in Britain*, p. 438; Glaser, 'The Tredegar Riots of August 1911', in Henriques (ed.), *The Jews of South Wales*, p. 159.

84 Alderman, 'The Anti-Jewish Riots of August 1911: A Response', 568.

85 Alderman, 'The Jew as Scapegoat?', 67.

86 *Times*, 7 September 1911.

87 *Times*, 7 September 1911.

88 Rubinstein, 'The Anti-Jewish Riots', 670.

89 Donahaye, *Whose People?*, pp. 12–13.

90 Davies, *The Chosen People*, p. 168.

91 Owen M. Edwards, *O'r Bala i Geneva* (Wrexham, 1922), pp. 43–60.

92 *Carmarthen Weekly Reporter*, 1 December 1899.

93 Henry N. Bunbury (ed.), *Lloyd George's Ambulance Wagon: Being the Memoirs of William J. Braithwaite, 1911–1912* (London, 1957), p. 174

94 Geoffrey Alderman, *Controversy and Crisis: Studies of the History of the Jews in Modern Britain* (Brighton, MA, 2008), p. 77; Donahaye, *Whose People?*, p. 72.

95 Alderman, 'The Jew as Scapegoat?', 67; Glaser, 'The Tredegar Riots', in Henriques (ed.), *The Jews of South Wales*, p. 159.

96 Alderman, 'The Anti-Jewish Riots of August 1911 in South Wales: A Response', 567.

97 *South Wales Daily News*, 23 September 1904. Similar incidents occurred in Bangor in 1914 and Aberdeen in 1893; see *JC*, 22 May 1914; Kenneth Collins, 'A Community on Trial: The Aberdeen Shechita Case, 1893', *Journal of Scottish Historical Studies*, 30 (2010), 75–92.

98 For a detailed discussion on the ambiguous attitudes displayed by Welsh Christian conversionists towards Jews, see Donahaye, *Whose People?*, pp. 39–65.

99 Alderman, 'The Jew as Scapegoat?', 70; *Western Mail*, 30 Jul 1870; *Cardiff and Merthyr Guardian*, 2 July 1870.

100 *Cardiff and Merthyr Guardian*, 22 August 1868; *Cardiff Times*, 31 July 1869.

101 Ursula Henriques, 'Lyons versus Thomas: The Jewess Abduction Case', in Henriques (ed.), *The Jews of South Wales*, p. 142.

102 *South Wales Daily News*, 5 October 1903.

103 *South Wales Daily News*, 5 October 1903; *JC*, 2 October 1903.

104 Harry Cohen, interview with David Jacobs.

105 Anne J. Kershen, 'Immigrants, Sojourners and Refugees', in Chris Wrigley (ed.), *A Companion to Early Twentieth-Century Britain* (Oxford, 2009), p. 142; David Feldman, *Englishmen and Jews* (New Haven, 1994), pp. 166–84.

106 London, *Whitehall and the Jews*, p. 16.

107 This was also the case for other immigrant labourers in nineteenth- and early twentieth-century Wales, such as the Irish; see O'Leary, *Irish Migrants*, pp. 101–18.

108 *Western Mail*, 13 February 1903.

109 *Western Mail*, 3 September 1903; *Merthyr Express*, 12 September 1903; *The Times*, 3 September 1903; *JC*, 4 September 1903.

110 *JC*, 11 September 1903.

111 *JC*, 4 September 1903; 23 October 1903.

112 *Merthyr Express*, 12 September 1903.

113 *South Wales Daily Post*, 13 February 1903.

114 Pollins, *The Economic History*, p. 18.

115 Runnymede Commission on Antisemitism, *A Very Light Sleeper: The Persistence and Dangers of Anti-Semitism* (London, 1994), p. 34.

116 Thomas Parry (ed.), *Gwaith Dafydd ap Gwilym* (Cardiff, 1952), pp. 3, 208.

117 *Western Mail*, 11 January 1879.

118 *Merthyr Express*, 2 May 1903. While a similar complaint was raised eight years later in Tredegar, and has been cited by some historians as one of the main causes of the 1911 riots, there is no existing evidence to suggest that rioters in Tredegar were driven primarily by '"rich Jew" anti-Semitism', as Alderman suggests; Alderman, 'The Anti-Jewish Riots', 196; Glaser, 'The Tredegar Riots', in Henriques (ed.), *The Jews of South Wales*, pp. 163–5; Holmes, 'The Tredegar Riots of 1911', 219–22.

119 Alan Campbell, Nina Fishman and David Howell (eds), *Miners, Unions, and Politics, 1910–47* (Aldershot, 1996), p. 128.

120 Arthur Horner, *Incorrigible Rebel* (London, 1960), p. 152.

121 Horner, *Incorrigible Rebel*, p. 152.

122 For works discussing the anti-Semitic writings of Saunders Lewis, see Grahame Davies, *The Chosen People*, pp. 31–2 and *Sefyll yn y Bwlch: Cymru a'r Mudiad Gwrth-Fodern: Astudiaeth o Waith R. S. Thomas, Saunders Lewis, T. S. Eliot a Simone Weil* (Cardiff, 1999); Donahaye, *Whose People?*, pp. 79–82.

123 The myth of a Jewish conspiracy to dominate the world gained wide currency following the publication of the *Protocols of the Elders of Zion*, which first appeared in Russia at the turn of the twentieth century and soon pervaded much political literature and sentiment throughout Europe. For more on this, see Steven L. Jacobs and Mark Weitzman (eds), *Dismantling the Big Lie: The Protocols of the Elders of Zion* (Jersey City, 2003).

124 *Y Ddraig Goch*, Rhagfyr 1926.

125 *Y Ddraig Goch*, Mehefin 1933; Alun R. Jones and Gwyn Thomas (eds), *Presenting Saunders Lewis* (Cardiff, 1973), p. 178.

126 Richard Wyn Jones, *The Fascist Party in Wales?: Plaid Cymru, Welsh Nationalism and the Accusation of Fascism*, trans. Richard Wyn Jones and Dafydd Jones (Cardiff, 2014), p. 43.

127 Donahaye, *Whose People?*, p. 79.

128 Donahaye, *Whose People?*, p. 80.

129 *Y Ddraig Goch*, Mehefin 1933: 'Bu erlid ar yr Iddewon a dioddefodd y diniwed yn ddiamau gyda'r niweidiol'.

130 *Baner ac Amserau Cymru*, 2 Awst 1939: 'groes i holl egwyddorion cyfiawnder'; 23 Rhagfyr 1942: 'erchyllterau newydd tuag at yr Iddewon'.

131 Davies, *The Chosen People*, p. 32; Donahaye, *Whose People?*, p. 79.

132 *Baner ac Amserau Cymru*, 7 Chwefror 1945. Attitudes of sympathy and empathy

towards Jews were also present in Lewis's post-war literary work, including his play *Esther* (1960). See Davies, *The Chosen People*, p. 32.

133 *JC*, 13 August 1976.

134 *JC*, 27 August 1976; 31 March 1978.

135 *JC*, 22 September 1995.

136 *JC*, 27 September 2005. Dafydd Elis-Thomas, then a Plaid Cymru Assembly Member and Presiding Officer of the National Assembly for Wales, caused an upset in 2008 when he called for assembly members to boycott the visit of Israeli Ambassador Ron Prosor; see *JC*, 13 June 2008.

137 *JC*, 6 May 1977; 13 May 1977; 28 October 1977; 11 November 1977; *Western Mail*, 26 October 1977.

138 *Western Mail*, 26 October 1977; *New Leader*, 16 January 1978.

139 *JC*, 13 May 1977; 28 October 1977; 11 November 1977.

140 *JC*, 28 April 1972; Swansea Hebrew Congregation Minute Book, 9 October 1978, D/D SHC 1/5, WGA; Newport's Jewish cemetery was also vandalised in 1994, but 'the attack was not [believed to be] racially motivated as the Christian cemetery was also attacked'; see *West Quest Magazine* (March 1994), 9, D/D SHC 24/1, WGA.

141 For recent examples, see '"Klan man" harassed Asian shopkeeper', *Western Mail*, 14 February 2002; 'Neo-Nazis are convicted of race hatred charges', *South Wales Echo*, 25 June 2010; 'Bully from Wrexham made Nazi salute to Jewish teenager in Ysbyty Glan Clwyd A&E,' *Daily Post*, 30 September 2011.

142 Paul Sugarman, interview with Cai Parry-Jones; *JC*, 8 August 1947.

143 *Independent*, 13 July 2002; *JC*, 19 July 2002. In 2005, vandals broke into Newport's synagogue, but according to the congregation's then president, Avrahom Davidson, it was not 'an act of anti-Semitism; just people wanting shelter or looking for money'; see *JC*, 22 April 2005.

144 Geoffrey G. Field, 'Anti-Semitism with the Boots Off', in Strauss (ed.), *Hostages of Modernization*, pp. 294–325.

145 Paul O'Leary, 'Foreword to the New Edition', in Henriques (ed.), *The Jews of South Wales*, pp. xiv–xv.

Notes to Chapter 5

1 Endelman, *The Jews of Britain*, p. 12.

2 Jasmine Donahaye, '"By Whom Shall She Arise?"', in Valman and Yosef (eds), *The Jew in Late-Victorian*, p. 163.

3 Paul Sugarman, interview with Cai Parry-Jones.

4 'The Last Jew in Merthyr', BBC Radio Wales, March 1992.

5 'The Last Jew in Merthyr'.

6 *NWC*, 7 November 1947.

7 Michael Howard, interview with Cai Parry-Jones.

8 Wendy Bellany, 'A Vanished Community', *Merthyr Historian*, 16 (2001), 101–10.

9 Harold Cairns, interview with Cai Parry-Jones, Cardiff, 17 February 2011, Hineni, 11721, Sound Archive, SFNHM.

10 Eve Pollecoff, interview with Cai Parry-Jones; Michael Howard, interview with Cai Parry-Jones.

11 Geraint H. Jenkins, *The Welsh Language and its Social Domains, 1801–1911* (Cardiff, 2000), p. 195.

12 Transcript of interview with Leo Abse for the television series 'Cymru 2000', CYM, Bangor University Archives.

13 *Evening Express*, 23 April 1901; *JC*, 19 June 1914; 28 March 1924; 23 June 1944

14 *JC*, 8 July 1983; *Jewish Telegraphic Agency*, 27 January 1982. The Welsh prayer reads as follows: 'Ein Duw a Duw ein tadau, gweddiwn hefyd dros Gymru. Diolch i ti am brydferthwch ei daear, am gyfoeth ei thraddodiadau ac am gymdeithas ei phobloedd. Boed i holl drigolion Cymru fod yn un yn eu cariad tuag atat ti ac yn eu parch i undod eu dynoliaeth, fel y rhed barn fel dyfroedd a chyfiawnder fel ffrwd gref' ('Our God and God of our fathers, we pray also for Wales. We thank you for the beauty of her land, the wealth of her traditions and the fellowship of her peoples. May all inhabitants of Wales be united in their love of you and in their respect for their common humanity, so that justice may roll down as waters and righteousness as a mighty stream'). I am grateful to Rabbi Kenneth Cohen for sending me a copy of the Welsh-language prayer together with the English translation.

15 Devra Applebaum, interview with Cai Parry-Jones, Carmarthen, 12 July 2011, Hineni, 11743, Sound Archive, SFNHM.

16 *JYB*, 1920. Jasmine Donahaye has written extensively on the life of Welsh-Jewish novelist, Lily Tobias, whose work focused on the relationship between Welshness and Jewishness; see Donahaye, 'By Whom Shall She Arise?'; Jasmine Donahaye, '"The Link of Common Aspirations": Wales in the Work of Lily Tobias', in Claire Tylee (ed.), *In the Open: Jewish Women Writers and British Culture* (Newark, 2006); Donahaye, *Whose People?*; Donahaye, *The Greatest Need*.

17 Michael Woolf, 'Negotiating the Self: Jewish Fiction in Britain since 1945', in A. Robert Lee (ed.), *Other Britain, Other British: Contemporary Multicultural*

NOTES

Fiction (London, 1996), p. 136; Donahaye, '"Gartref – bron"', in von Rothkirch and William (eds), *Beyond the Difference*, pp. 38–42; Donahaye, *Whose People?*, pp. 143–44.

18 Bernice Rubens, *Brothers* (London, 1984), pp. 203–33.

19 See, for instance, Dannie Abse, *Ash on a Young Man's Sleeve* (Cardigan, 2006); Dannie Abse (ed.), *Twentieth-century Anglo-Welsh Poetry* (Bridgend, 1997); Dannie Abse, *Welsh Retrospective* (Bridgend, 2008).

20 Dannie Abse, interview with Cai Parry-Jones, London, 14 August 2011, 11808, Sound Archive, SFNHM; *Guardian*, 15 March 2003.

21 Dannie Abse, *A Poet in the Family* (London, 1974), p. 81.

22 For more detail on her life and work, see Jasmine Donahaye, 'Jewish writing in Wales' (unpublished Swansea University PhD thesis, 2004); Donahaye, *Whose People?*; Davies, *The Chosen People*; Cai Parry-Jones, 'Judith Maro (1919–2011)', *Planet*, 205 (February 2012), 149.

23 See, for instance, Judith Maro, *Hen Wlad Newydd* (Talybont, 1974).

24 'mae'r Gymraeg yn iaith fyw ac iach. Fe adferwyd fy mamiaith, Hebraeg, gan fod y bobl yn ei harfer a'i defnyddio, yn dysgu drwyddi mewn ysgolion a phrifysgolion, yn ysgrifennu yn yr iaith. Er mor wahanol yw'r sefyllfa yng Nghymru, heb yr amgylchiadau gorfodol a symbylodd yr Israeliaid, mi welaf debygrwydd yn y dull yr wynebir y problemau. Ac felly, er gwaetha'r holl drafferthion, rwy'n cyhoeddi yn y Gymraeg, oherwydd fe ddes i garu Cymru, a pheth gwrthun i mi fuasai gweld yr hen iaith yn diflannu i grombil unffurfdod y cyfnod modern'. *Y Faner*, 19 August 1988.

25 Heini Gruffudd, *Yr Erlid: Hanes Kate Bosse-Griffiths a'i Theulu yn yr Almaen a Chymru Adeg yr Ail Ryfel Byd* (Talybont, 2012), pp. 138–43; J. Gwyn Griffiths, *Teithiau'r Meddwl: Ysgrifau Llenyddol Kate Bosse-Griffiths* (Talybont, 2004), p. 232.

26 Marion Löffler, 'Kate Bosse-Griffiths (1910–1998)', in Bernhard Maier, Stefan Zimmer and Christiane Batke (eds), *150 Jahre 'Mabinogion': Deutsch-Walisische Kulturbeziehungen* (Tübingen, 2001), pp. 170–7.

27 For more on this, see Donahaye, *Whose People?*, pp. 147–9. According to her son, Heini Gruffudd, Kate 'didn't like to talk about what happened during the war and a number of our relatives silently carried this heavy burden': *www.s4c.co.uk/ffeithiol/e_orgalon_ravensbruck.shtml*

28 'Er nad yw Kate yn ymdrin â'r pethau hyn yn ei gweithiau , mae'n sicr ei bod yn ymdeimlo'n ddwys ynglŷn a hwy ... Mae un peth yn sicr: nid oedd am wadu y rhan hon o'i phersonoliaeth ... Roedd hi'n Almaenes ac yn Iddewes', Griffiths, *Teithiau'r Meddwl*, pp. 237–9.

29 Eric Rowan 'The Visual Arts', in Meic Stephens (ed.), *The Arts in Wales 1950– 75* (Cardiff, 1979), p. 63.

30 Josef Herman, *Notes from a Welsh Diary 1944–1955* (London, 1988), p. xi.

31 Karel Lek, interview with BBC Wales, 2006: *www.bbc.co.uk/wales/arts/your-video/media/pages/karel_lek_01.shtml.* Such an engagement with Wales was in sharp contrast to the group of Jewish refugee artists and writers who passed through north Wales as part of the Bloomsbury set between the 1940s and 1960s. For more on this, see Donahaye, *Whose People?*, pp. 149–54.

32 Carol Trossett, *Welshness Performed: Welsh Concepts of Person and Society* (Tucson, 1993), p. 42. The Welsh language is an integral part of the eisteddfod and its competitions, but the festival is also open to non-Welsh speakers.

33 John T. Koch (ed.), *Celtic Culture: A Historical Encyclopedia* (Santa Barbara, 2006), p. 6.

34 *NWC*, 31 July 1849; 1 March 1851; 29 August 1863; *Rhondda Leader*, 5 April 1919.

35 The inclusion of articles relating to eisteddfods in the *JC* may also have aroused the curiosity of metropolitan Jews in London and other large Jewish centres such as Manchester and Leeds about their 'exotic' coreligionists.

36 *JC*, 21 August 1906.

37 *JC*, 24 March 1911.

38 *JC*, 24 April 1936; untitled newspaper article, XML 4558/46/129, CRO; Griffiths, *Teithiau'r Meddwl*, p. 232.

39 Simon Joseph, *My Formative Years: A Jewish Boy's Childhood in South Wales in the Early 1900s* (London, 1994), p. 61.

40 *CAJEX*, 27-2 (1977), p. 32; *JC*, 20 March, 1931.

41 *JC*, 3 May 1991.

42 *JC*, 22 June 1962; 10 August 1962.

43 Stuart Hall, 'Cultural Identity and Diaspora', in Jonathan Rutherford (ed.), *Identity: Community, Culture and Difference* (London, 1990), p. 222.

44 Hall, 'Cultural Identity', p. 225.

45 Dora Lipsett, interview with David Jacobs.

46 *Western Mail*, 5 May 1870; *Wrexham Advertiser*, 21 July 1900.

47 'The Last Jew in Merthyr'; Harry Cohen, interview with David Jacobs.

48 W. C. Elvet Thomas, 'A People Apart', in Meic Stevens (ed.), *A Cardiff Anthology* (Bridgend, 1987), p. 50.

49 Dannie Abse, interview with Cai Parry-Jones.

50 For more on this, see Gartner, *American and British Jews*, p. 57.

51 Michael Brenner, Rainer Liedtke, and David Rechter (eds), *Two Nations: British and German Jews in Comparative Perspective* (Tübingen, 1999), p. 123.

52 Naturalisation Certificate of David Priceman, 6 August 1904, HO 144/759/118816, TNA; Naturalisation Certificate of Hyman Silverstone, 28 July 1909, HO 144/907/177037, TNA.

53 'The Last Jew in Merthyr'.

54 Morris Silvergleit, interview with David Jacobs, 22 May 1978, 6017/1, Sound Archive, SFNHM.

55 John Wartski, interview with Cai Parry-Jones.

56 *NWC*, 15 November 1940.

57 Tony Fraser, interview with Colin Heyman, Cardiff, 24 November 2011, Hineni, 11757, Sound Archive, SFNHM.

58 Karel Lek quoted from: *www.atticgallery.co.uk/scripts/topicinfo.asp?t=92*

59 Anthony Grenville, 'The Integration of Aliens: The Early Years of the Association of Jewish Refugees Information, 1946-1950', in Ian Wallace (ed.), *German-Speaking Exiles in Great Britain, Vol. 1* (Amsterdam, 1999), p. 12.

60 Bill Pollock, interview with Cai Parry-Jones.

61 *JC*, 10 August 1962.

62 *CAJEX*, 19-4 (1969), p. 42.

63 Alan Llwyd, *Black Wales: A History of Black Welsh People* (Cardiff, 2005), p. 173.

64 Michael Parnell, 'Interview: Bernice Rubens', *New Welsh Review*, 3/1 (1990), 46.

65 For more on this, see Nancy Foner, *Across Generations: Immigrant Families in America* (New York, 2009).

66 *Jewish Renaissance* (October 2009), 26.

67 Hirsch, *My Llanelli*, p. 5.

68 Eve Pollecoff, interview with Cai Parry-Jones.

69 Although Tobias appears to position such xenophobic feelings as an English rather than a Welsh phenomenon (she makes it clear that the sentiments were expressed by an English schoolchild and his English father living in south Wales), the fact that some Welsh school children grinned and giggled at the remarks implies that such attitudes were also shared by a number of Welsh people; see Lily Tobias, *The Nationalists, and other Goluth Studies* (London, 1921), pp. 13–14.

70 Harold Cairns, interview with Cai Parry-Jones.

71 'Cultivating Irreverence: Leo Abse interviewed by Jasmine Donahaye', *Planet*, 160 (August/September 2003), 10–12.

72 Adam Buswell, interview with Sue Mansell, Cardiff, 22 June 2011, Hineni, 11739, Sound Archive, SFNHM.

73 Ben Soffa, interview with Cai Parry-Jones, London, 6 June 2012, Hineni, 11761, Sound Archive, SFNHM.

74 For early works on Welsh identity, see Michael Hechter, *Internal Colonialism: The Celtic Fringe in British National Development, 1536–1966* (London, 1975); Tom Nairn, *The Break-up of Britain: Crisis and Neo-Colonialism* (London, 1977). For criticism of these works, see Ralph Fevre and Andrew Thompson, *Nation, Identity and Social Theory* (Cardiff, 1999), pp. 5–13.

75 Benedict Anderson, *Imagined Communities: Reflections on the Origins and Spread of Nationalism* (London, 1983). For examples, see Fiona Bowie, 'Conflicting Interpretations of Welsh Identity', in Sharon Macdonald (ed.), *Inside European Identities: Ethnography in Western Europe* (Oxford, 1993), pp. 167–93; Charlotte Williams, 'Claiming the National: Nation, National Identity and Ethnic Minorities', in Williams, Evans and O'Leary (eds), *A Tolerant Nation: Revisiting*, pp. 331–52.

76 Graham Day and Richard Suggett, 'Conceptions of Wales and Welshness: Aspects of Nationalism in Nineteenth-Century Wales', in Gareth Rees, Janet Bujra, Paul Littlewood, Howard Newby and Teresa L. Rees (eds), *Political Action and Social identity* (London, 1985), p. 96.

77 *JC*, 1 September 1911.

78 *Bimah*, 5 (December 1995), p. 17.

79 'Cultivating Irreverence', 8.

80 'Cultivating Irreverence', 7.

81 'Cultivating Irreverence', 9. This idea that there are several versions of Wales was raised by Alfred Zimmern in 1921 and more recently by Denis Balsom; see Alfred Zimmern, *My Impressions of Wales* (London, 1921); Denis Balsom, 'The Three Wales Model', in J. Osmond (ed.), *The National Question Again* (Llandysul, 1985).

82 Leo Abse in conversation with David Parry-Jones, Wales Video Gallery, NLW. Leo's younger brother, Dannie, happily described himself as a 'Welsh Jew'. While geographical and environmental factors led Leo to reject any claims to Welshness, he also suggested that his exposure to his grandparents' Eastern European lifestyle and culture as a child played a part. By the time Dannie was born, their grandparents had either died or had aged severely and thus, in contrast to Leo, his exposure to an Eastern European way of life was minimal. See 'Cultivating Irreverence', 7–13.

83 Michael Lee, interview with Cai Parry-Jones.

84 Alwyn Pierce-Lloyd, interview with Cai Parry-Jones.

85 Harry Poloway, interview with Cai Parry-Jones.

86 Devra Applebaum, interview with Cai Parry-Jones.

87 Parnell, 'Interview: Bernice Rubens', 46.

88 *JC*, 28 November 1975.

89 D. Densil Morgan, '"The Essence of Welshness?"': Some Aspects of Christian Faith and National Identity in Wales, *c.*1900–2000', in Robert Pope (ed.) *Religion and National Identity: Wales and Scotland c. 1700–2000* (Cardiff, 2001), p. 141.

90 Paul Chambers, 'Social Networks and Religious Identity', in Grace Davie, Paul Heelas and Linda Woodhead (eds), *Predicting Religion: Christian, Secular and Alternative Futures*, p. 81; Geraint H. Jenkins, *A Concise History of Wales* (Cambridge, 2007), pp. 272–74. Nonconformity also found itself competing with alternative definitions of Welsh national identity, such as rugby. For more on this, see R. Merfyn Jones, 'Beyond Identity? The Reconstruction of the Welsh', *Journal of British Studies*, 31 (1992), 330–57.

91 Davies, *A History of Wales*, p. 621.

92 Dai Smith, *Wales: A Question for History* (Bridgend, 1999), p. 205. See, for instance, Paul Chaney and Ralph Fevre, 'Ron Davies and the Cult of Inclusiveness: Devolution and Participation in Wales', *Contemporary Wales*, 14 (2001), 21–49; Graham Day, *Making Sense of Wales: A Sociological Perspective* (Cardiff, 2002).

93 Paul Chambers and Andrew Thompson, 'Public Religion and Civil Society in Wales', in Graham Day, David Dunkerley and Andrew Thompson (eds), *Civil Society in Wales* (Cardiff, 2006), p. 217.

94 Diana Soffa, interview with Cai Parry-Jones, Cardiff, 15 June 2012, 11807, Sound Archive, SFNHM.

95 Williams, Evans and O'Leary, *A Tolerant Nation?*, p.7.

96 For a recent discussion on this, see Daniel G. Williams 'Single Nation, Double Logic: Ed Miliband and the Problem with British Multiculturalism': https://www.opendemocracy.net/ourkingdom/daniel-g-williams/single-nation-double-logic-ed-miliband-and-problem-with-british-multicu

97 Charlotte Williams, 'Claiming the National: Nation, National Identity and Ethnic Minorities', in Williams, Evans and O'Leary (eds), *A Tolerant Nation?: Revisiting*, p.347.

98 Michael Billig, *Banal Nationalism* (London, 1995).

99 Neil Evans and Paul O'Leary, 'Playing the Game', in Charlotte Williams, Neil Evans and O'Leary (eds), *A Tolerant Nation?*, p. 111.

100 Ron Silver, interview with Cai Parry-Jones, Cardiff, 7 February 2011, Hineni, 11720, Sound Archive, SFNHM; Michael Howard, interview with Cai Parry-Jones.

101 Dannie Abse, *Ash on a Young Man's Sleeve*, pp. 19–20.

102 *JC*, 3 September 1976; Geoffrey Alderman, *The Jewish Community in British Politics* (Oxford, 1983), p. 204.

103 *JC*, 27 August 1976.

104 This is in contrast to Welsh Muslims, who have produced three Plaid Cymru councillors to date. For more on this, see Paul Chambers, 'Secularisation, Wales and Islam', *Journal of Contemporary Religion*, 21, 3 (2006), 332.

105 Leo Abse in conversation with David Parry-Jones, Wales Video Gallery, NLW.

106 For examples, see *Welsh Nation*, October 1964; *Y Ddraig Goch*, Mawrth 1962; Griffiths, *Teithiau'r Meddwl*, p. 231.

107 Griffiths, *Teithiau'r Meddwl*, p. 81.

108 Alan Liss, interview with Cai Parry-Jones, Cardiff, 18 July 2012, 11827, Sound Archive, SFNHM.

109 Kenneth Cohen, email to author, 24 May 2012; Rona Hart, telephone interview with Cai Parry-Jones

110 Jasmine Donahaye, interview with Cai Parry-Jones, Aberystwyth, 30 July 2012, 11824, Sound Archive, SFNHM.

111 *JYB*, 1896-2015; Rona Hart, telephone interview with Cai Parry-Jones.

112 David Landy, 'Zionism, multiculturalism and the construction of Irish-Jewish identity', *Irish Journal of Sociology*, 16, 1 (2007), 66.

113 Deirdre Beddoe (ed.), *Changing Times: Welsh Women Writing on the 1950s and 1960s* (Aberystwyth, 2010), pp. 362–63.

114 Paul Sugarman, interview with Cai Parry-Jones.

115 Such a dilemma is expressed by Mimi Josephson in her poem, 'Which Little Land?' (1955); see, Davies, *The Chosen People*, p. 226.

116 *Bimah*, 21 (December 1999), p. 4.

117 *Bimah*, 22 (April 2000), pp. 18–19.

118 *Bimah*, 22 (April 2000), pp. 18–19; Eva Gibbor, interview with Cai Parry-Jones, Cardiff, 29 June 2012, 11823, Sound Archive, SFNHM; Jackie Altman, email to author, 7 July 2012.

119 Malka Liss, interview with Cai Parry-Jones, Cardiff, 26 September 2011, 11821, Sound Archive, 11821, Sound Archive, SFNHM.

120 *Bimah*, 22 (April 2000), p. 18; *CAJEX*, 17-1 (1967), p. 28.

121 *CAJEX*, 17-1 (1967), p. 28.

122 Grahame Davies, 'Welsh and Jewish: Responses to Wales by Jewish Writers,', in James Gifford and Gabrielle Zezulka-Mailloux (eds), *Culture and the State: Nationalisms* (Edmonton, 2004), p 219.

123 John Wartski, interview with Cai Parry-Jones.

124 Mark Avrum Ehrlich (ed.), *Encyclopedia of the Jewish Diaspora: Origins, Experiences, and Culture, Vol. 1* (Santa Barbara, 2009), p. 53.

Notes to Chapter 6

1 *JYB*, 1955–92. The 1955 edition of the *JYB* listed 3,993 Jews in Wales, while the 1992 edition listed 1,800.

2 See, for instance, Nathan Abrams, *Caledonian Jews: A Study of Seven Small Communities in Scotland* (North Carolina, 2009).

3 *JYB*, 1910–20.

4 *CAJEX*, 24/4 (1976), p. 29.

5 *JYB*, 1917–39; *JC*, 24 July 1936.

6 *JYB*, 1904–40; *JC*, 20 November 1953; 7 August 1959; 27 January 1978; letter from the Clerk of the Board of Deputies to A. Brest, honorary secretary of the Brynmawr Hebrew Congregation, 26 November 1963, ACC/3121/D02/018, LMA.

7 *JYB*, 1919–79; *JC*, 12 March 1982.

8 *JYB*, 1916–65; *CAJEX*, 11-4 (1961), p. 67; *JC*, 14 March 1975; draft letter from the Board of Trustees of the Aberavon and Port Talbot Hebrew Congregation to the Charity Commission, London, 19 March 1976, D/D SHC 23/1a, WGA.

9 *JYB*, 1924–80.

10 *JC*, 12 March 1982.

11 *JYB*, 1917–85.

12 *JYB*, 1985–99; *JC*, 17 June 1994.

13 *JC*, 13 June 1997. The building was renovated for use as a synagogue.

14 *JYB*, 1950.

15 *JYB*, 1963.

16 Letter from Israel Pollecoff to Evelyn Dresner, 17 June 1965, XM 4098/1, CRO; *JC*, 5 February 1971; 12 March 1971; profile of Kate Loewenthal: *www. jewishtelegraph.com/prof_34.html*

17 *JYB*, 1968–85. Amalgamating congregations to ensure a prolonged existence was not unique to north Wales Jewry and reflects the steps taken by many other small Jewish communities in the United Kingdom and the United States; see Weissbach, *Jewish Life*, p. 301. Blackpool's dwindling congregation merged with the neighbouring St Anne's congregation in 2012; see *JC*, 27 April 2012.

18 *CAJEX*, 5-1 (1955), p. 51; *Bimah*, 37 (December 2003), p. 31.

19 *CAJEX*, 5-1 (1955), p. 53.

20 *CAJEX*, 5-1 (1955), p. 53; *JC*, 18 February 1955. Between 1934 and 1955 a *minyan* was held in a house in Penylan to accommodate Jewish residents in the area who were unable or chose not to walk to one of the two Orthodox synagogues in the centre of Cardiff (Windsor Place and Cathedral Road) on the Sabbath.

21 Alan S. Liss, 'A short history of Reform Judaism in south Wales, 1947–1970' (unpublished certificate in education thesis, University of Wales, 1977), 15. Reform Judaism came late to Cardiff, a city noted for its Orthodoxy, with the first Reform synagogue in Britain established in London in 1840. See, for instance, Anne J. Kershen and Jonathan A. Romain (eds), *Tradition and Change: History of Reform Judaism in Britain, 1840–1995* (London, 1995). Cardiff's Reform synagogue was met with hostility from leading Orthodox functionaries in the city. For more on this, see Ursula Henriques, 'Epilogue', in Henriques (ed.), *The Jews of South Wales*, pp. 212–13.

22 *JC*, 23 July 1948; 19 September 1952.

23 *Synagogue Review*, 23/3 (1948), 37; *JC*, 23 September 1949; 7 November 1980; letter from Isadore Rapport, honorary president of the Cardiff United Synagogue to L. Corne of the CNS, 22 November 1949, in possession of the Cardiff Reform Synagogue's archivist, Stanley Soffa.

24 CNS, Summary of Annual General Meeting, 26 February 1953; CNS, Summary of Warden's Report, 18 March 1962; both documents in possession of the Cardiff Reform Synagogue's archivist, Stanley Soffa; Liss, 'A short history of Reform Judaism in south Wales', 94.

25 Ursula Henriques, 'Epilogue', in Henriques (ed.), *The Jews of South Wales*, p. 213; Diana Soffa, interview with Eve Lavine, 27 September 2011, Hineni, 11751, Sound Archive, SFNHM.

26 Constitution and Rules of the CUS, adopted on 17 May 1942, D/D JR 5/6/1, 2, GA. This rule still stands.

27 Sally Rosen, interview with Cai Parry-Jones, 25 July 2011, Hineni, 11748, Sound Archive, SFNHM.

28 *JC*, 20 October 1961; 24 August 1962.

29 *JYB*, 1995.

30 *JC*, 13 January 1989.

31 CAJEX, 28-1 (1978), p. 16; Alan Schwartz, interview with Cai Parry-Jones, Cardiff, 9 March 2011, 11803, Sound Archive, SFNHM.

32 *JC*, 17 January 1992.

33 *JC*, 17 January 1992; *www.cardiffshul.org/Kosher%20Food.htm*. A limited stock of kosher products is also made available at certain Cardiff supermarkets.

34 See, for instance, Abrams, *Caledonian Jews*; Rubinstein, *A History of the Jews in the English-speaking World*; Shevitz, *Jewish Communities on the Ohio River*; Weissbach, *Jewish Life*; Wasserstein, *Vanishing Diaspora*.

35 For more on this, see O. Morgan, *Rebirth of a Nation*, pp. 211–16; Davies, *A History of Wales*, pp. 532–5.

36 Hywel Francis and David Smith, *The Fed: A History of the South Wales Miners in the Twentieth Century* (London, 1980), p. 33.

37 D. Densil Morgan, '"The Essence of Welshness": Some Aspects of Christian Faith and National Identity in Wales, *c.*1900–2006, in Robert Pope (ed.), *Religion and National Identity: Wales and Scotland c.1700–2000* (Cardiff, 2001), p. 145.

38 K. O. Morgan, *Rebirth of a Nation*, p. 217; Gareth E. Jones, *Modern Wales: A Concise History* (Cambridge, 1994), p. 187; David Hall, *Working Lives: The Forgotten Voices of Britain's Post-War Working Class* (London, 2012), p. 225.

39 Robin Reeves, 'Multiculturality in Wales', in Eberhard Bort and Neil Evans (eds), *Networking Europe: Essays on Regionalism and Social Democracy* (Liverpool, 2000), pp. 304–5.

40 *JC*, 12 December 2008; *CAJEX*, 27-1 (1977), p. 79.

41 Henriques, 'Epilogue', in Henriques (ed.), *The Jews of South Wales*, p. 214.

42 Letter from Gustave Abrahams to J. M. Rich, Board of Deputies, 22 July 1929, ACC/3121/B/04/EA/011, LMA.

43 *CAJEX*, 24-4 (1984), p. 26.

44 *JYB*, 1919–58.

45 Examples of those who went into the family business after leaving school included Moses Stein of Amlwch (1928–97), who took over his father's drapery business in the town, and Isadore Cohen (1910–80) who ran his father's clothing store in Ammanford; see Joyce Arron, interview with Cai Parry-Jones; *Yr Arwydd*, 156 (Chwefror, 1997).

46 Charles Arron, interview with Cai Parry-Jones.

47 Eve Pollecoff, interview with Cai Parry-Jones.

48 Dave Adamson, 'Work', in Hugh Mackay (ed.), *Understanding Contemporary Wales* (Cardiff, 2010), p. 67; Martin Johnes, *Wales Since 1939* (Manchester, 2012), p. 257.

49 Adamson, 'Work', in Mackay (ed.), *Understanding Contemporary Wales*, p. 61; Johnes, *Wales*, p. 403.

50 In his 1936–9 survey of Jewish University Students, Geoffrey Block noted that 'there existed a very real problem of unemployment for all University graduates', in Wales during this period; see Geoffrey D. M. Block, 'Jewish

Students at the Universities of Great Britain and Ireland – Excluding London, 1936–1939', *Sociological Review*, 34 (July 1942), 191.

51 The industry tables of the 1951 census for England and Wales show that 69,497 people were employed in professional services in Wales, compared with 461,380 in London and the south-east of England, revealing that there were greater job opportunities for professionals in the latter region; see General Register Office, *Census 1951: England and Wales. Industry Tables* (London, 1957), p. 11.

52 *JC*, 5 March 2010.

53 *JC*, 6 November 2009; 12 May 2000; 4 June 2004.

54 Weissbach, *Jewish Life*, p. 302.

55 Ben Hamilton, interview with David Jacobs; *Bimah*, 62 (2010), p. 20; 1. *Dentists Register* (General Medical Council, 1945), 251; draft letter to the Charity Commission, 19 March 1976, D/D SHC 23/1, WGA.

56 *CAJEX*, 31/5 (1985), p. 55; *JC*, 3 May 1991.

57 *JC*, 25 January 2008; 27 May 2010; 5 July 1991.

58 *JC*, 25 March 1955.

59 Keith Kahn-Harris and Ben Gidley, *Turbulent Times: The British Jewish Community Today* (London, 2010), p. 1; Kenneth E. Collins, *Go and Learn: The International Story of Jews and Medicine in Scotland* (Aberdeen, 1988), pp. 81–97.

60 *CAJEX* 25/1 (1975), pp. 31–2; J. Ronald Williams, 'The Influence of Foreign Nationalities on the Life of the People of Merthyr Tydfil', *Sociological Review*, 28 (April 1926), 150.

61 Channah Hirsch, *My Llanelli: The Gateshead of Wales* (London, 2009), p. 75.

62 Harry Cohen, interview with David Jacobs; see also Hirsch, *My Llanelli*, p. xv.

63 Leonard Dinnerstein, *Uneasy at Home: Antisemitism and the American Jewish Experience* (New York, 1987), p. 43.

64 Leonard Minkes, 'A Jewish Boyhood in Cardiff', *Planet*, 164 (April/May 2004), p. 57.

65 Lionel Bernstein, interview with John Frances and Nicola Tucker, Hineni, 2010, 11717, Sound Archive, SFNHM.

66 Diana Leonard, *Sex and Generation: A Study of Courtship and Weddings* (London, 1980), p. 29. Such examples included Michael Glynne of Llanelli, who married Barbara Gard in London in 1958, and the engagement of Freda Landy of Llanelli to Liverpool-born Warner Bakerman in 1960; see *JC*, 13 January 1950; 15 April 1960.

67 *JC*, 9 July 1926; 25 April 1930.

68 Lionel Bernstein, interview with John Frances and Nicola Tucker; Renee Woolf, interview with Cai Parry-Jones. In the 1960s Llanelli's Jewish community numbered no more than forty individuals and its synagogue was 'rarely used'; see *JC*, 5 August 1966.

69 Harry Cohen, interview with David Jacobs.

70 One of their sons is Albert Gubay, the founder of Kwiksave; see *Daily Mirror*, 22 March 2010.

71 *JC*, 29 August 2008;

72 Shevitz, *Jewish Communities*, p.198.

73 Kershen and Romain, *Tradition and Change*, p.340.

74 Alan Schwartz, interview with Cai Parry-Jones.

75 Letter from W.Van Der Zyl to Leslie Corne, undated, document in possession of the Cardiff Reform Synagogue's archivist, Stanley Soffa; *JC*, 3 July 1987.

76 *http://www.bbc.co.uk/news/uk-wales-15103910*.

77 Quoted from the *Jewish Telegraph* website: *www.jewishtelegraph.com/prof 34.html*; Kate Loewenthal, email to author, 3 November 2011.

78 *JC*, 8 June 1984; *CAJEX*, 11/4 (1961), p. 61; Jasmine Donahaye, *The Greatest Need: The Creative Life and Troubled Times of Lily Tobias, a Welsh Jew in Palestine* (Aberystwyth, 2015), pp. 169–93.

79 Vivian Lipman, *Social History of the Jews in England 1850–1950* (London, 1954), p. 167; Laura Staetsky, Marina Sheps and Jonathan Boyd, 'Immigration from the United Kingdom to Israel', Institute for Jewish Policy Research Report (October 2013), 5; William D. Rubinstein, Michael A. Jolles and Hilary L. Rubinstein (eds), *The Palgrave Dictionary of Anglo-Jewish History* (Basingstoke, 2011), p. 213.

80 Davies, *The Chosen People*, p. 15.

81 *CAJEX*, 19/1 (1969), p. 36; 22/1 (1972), p. 29; 30/1 (1980), p. 42; 31/1 (1981), p. 42; 32/1 (1982), pp. 34–59; 32/2 (1982), p. 31; 32/3 (1982), pp. 29–83; 33/4 (1983), p. 62.

82 *JC*, 28 November 1975.

83 Rubinstein, *A History of the Jews*, p. 418.

84 ChaeRan Y. Freeze, *Jewish Marriage and Divorce in Imperial Russia* (Hanover, 2002), pp. 51–4.

85 Another reason for Jewish families being smaller may be found in the progressively diminishing influence of religious tradition in British Jewry. Judaism, in common with many other religions, traditionally fosters a high birth rate and regards fertility as a blessing. This is discussed further in Barry A. Kosmin, 'Nuptiality and Fertility Patterns of British Jewry

1850–1980: an Immigrant Transition?', in D. A. Coleman (ed.), *Demography of Immigrants and Minority Groups in the United Kingdom* (London, 1982), pp. 245–61.

86 Hannah Neustatter, 'Demographic and other statistical aspects of Anglo-Jewish population', in Maurice Freedman and James W. Parkes (eds), *A Minority in Britain: Social Studies of the Anglo-Jewish Community* (London, 1955), p. 107.

87 Hasia Diner, *The Jews of the United States, 1654–2000* (Berkeley, 2006), p. 246.

88 Kate Fisher, *Birth Control, Sex and Marriage in Britain 1918–1960* (Oxford, 2006), pp. 1–2.

89 Commenting on the Jewish community of Pontypridd in the early twentieth century, Harry Cohen noted that Jews in the town 'had large families, four, five, six, seven children, were quite commonplace'; see Harry Cohen, interview with David Jacobs.

90 Based on 1901 census returns and the Welsh returns to Hannah Neustatter's 1951 survey of the British-Jewish population, in Neustatter, 'Demographic and Other Statistical Aspects', p. 249.

91 Todd M. Endelman, *The Jews of Britain, 1656–2000* (Berkeley, 2002), p. 239.

92 *JC*, 23 November 2009.

93 Weissbach, *Jewish Life*, p. 309.

94 Weissbach, *Jewish Life*, p. 309.

95 Additionally, as mentioned in the introduction, some Jews may feel reluctant to volunteer their identity to any government list.

96 Joyce Arron, interview with Cai Parry-Jones. According to Joyce, there are forty members on the Swansea Hebrew Congregation's mailing list, but around half of the members live away from the city and retain membership for burial or sentimental reasons.

97 Harry Poloway, interview with Cai Parry-Jones. According to Harry, many of those who pay Newport's membership fee live 'out of town' and are not active congregants. Like the Swansea Hebrew Congregation, many retain membership for burial rights or sentimental reasons.

98 Harry Poloway, interview with Cai Parry-Jones.

99 *JYB*, 2001–3; *JC*, 23 December 2008; 3 September 2009; 27 May 2010.

100 Charles Arron, interview with Cai Parry-Jones.

101 Joyce Arron, interview with Cai Parry-Jones; Norma Glass, interview with Cai Parry-Jones; *JC*, 23 December 2008.

102 Charles Arron, interview with Cai Parry-Jones.

103 Charles Arron, interview with Cai Parry-Jones.; 'Jews Targeted', 7 August 2002, Newspaper Clippings, D/D SHC 20/1, WGA.

104 Joyce Arron, interview with Cai Parry-Jones; Charles Arron, interview with Cai Parry-Jones; *JC*, 9 April 1993.

105 *JYB*, 1968; census returns, 2011.

106 *Bimah*, 35 (2003), p. 20; 36 (2003), p. 35; *JC*, 15 October 2004; website of the Cardiff United Synagogue: *www.cardiffshul.org/Services.htm*.

107 *JC*, 9 September 1994; 17 December 1999; 15 October 2004; 18 May 2012.

108 *Bimah*, 21 (1999), p. 16–17; *JC*, 27 June 2003.

109 *JC*, 15 July 1988.

110 *JC*, 1 March 2002; 21 February 2014.

111 *JC*, 28 March 2014; 26 February 2016.

112 Kevin Sleight, treasurer of the Cardiff Reform Synagogue, email to author, 19 July 2013.

113 Davies, *The Chosen People*, p. 15; Paul Chambers, 'Religious Diversity in Wales', in Charlotte Williams, Neil Evans and Paul O'Leary (eds), *A Tolerant Nation?: Revisiting Ethnic Diversity in a Devolved Wales* (Cardiff, 2015), p. 126.

114 'A Shrinking Population': *www.bbc.co.uk/wales/northwest/sites/faith/pages/mike_lee.shtml*. At the time of writing, Plas Gogarth in Church Walks offers self-catering kosher accommodation for Jewish visitors to Llandudno.

115 'A Shrinking Population'.

116 *Jewish Renaissance*, 9/1 (October 2009), 3.

117 Not all Jewish academics appointed to positions in rural Welsh universities have been as proactive as Abrams, however. William Rubinstein, Professor of Modern History at the University of Aberystwyth since 1995, and Dan Cohn-Sherbok, Professor of Judaism at the University of Wales, Lampeter between 1997 and 2009 are two good examples in recent decades.

118 *JC*, 27 July 2007.

119 Quoted from the North Wales Jewish Network's website: *www.northwalesjewishnetwork.org*.

120 *JC*, 7 December 2007; 25 April 2008; 3 April 2009; 9 April 2010.

121 *JC*, 13 August 2010.

122 *JC*, 2 May 2008.

123 *JC*, 19 July 1996.

124 *JYB*, 1999; The community is called a 'group' rather than a 'congregation', as there is no dedicated place of worship and most members retain membership of the Birmingham Progressive Hebrew Congregation for burial reasons.

125 Mark Michaels, interview with Cai Parry-Jones, Montgomery, 23 April 2012, 11819, Sound Archive, SFNHM.

Notes to Conclusion

1 Todd M. Endelman, *The Jews of Britain, 1656–2000* (Berkeley, 2002), p. 12.
2 Endelman, *The Jews of Britain*, p. 4.
3 Endelman, *The Jews in Britain*, p. 12.
4 Ursula Henriques, 'The Jewish Community of Cardiff', in Ursula R. Q. Henriques (ed.), *The Jews of South Wales,* 2nd edn (Cardiff, 2013), p. 38.
5 There is evidence of Jews arriving Ireland indirectly via mainland Britain; see Cormac Ó Gráda, *Jewish Ireland in the Age of Joyce: a Socioeconomic History* (Princeton, 2006), p. 73; *JC,* 1 September 1893.
6 This was also true for many of Scotland's Jewish immigrants, but unlike the Welsh-Jewish experience, large numbers of Jewish migrants came directly to Scotland via the Scottish port of Leith; see, Nathan Abrams, *Caledonian Jews: A Study of Seven Small Communities in Scotland* (North Carolina, 2009), p. 99.
7 *JYB,* 1920–21.
8 W. D. Rubinstein, M. A. Jolles and H. L. Rubinstein (eds), *The Palgrave Dictionary of Anglo-Jewish History* (Basingstoke, 2011), pp. 96, 698.
9 Rubinstein, Jolles, and Rubinstein, *The Palgrave Dictionary*, p. 154.
10 *JYB,* 1920–39.
11 Abrams, *Caledonian Jews*, pp. 65–94.
12 D. Densil Morgan, '"The Essence of Welshness": Some Aspects of Christian Faith and National Identity in Wales, *c.* 1900–2006, in Robert Pope (ed.), *Religion and National Identity: Wales and Scotland c.1700–2000* (Cardiff, 2001), p.159.
13 Robert Liberles (ed.), *Salo Wittmayer Baron: Architect of Jewish History* (New York, 1995), p. 117.
14 Paul O'Leary, 'Foreword to the New Edition', in Henriques (ed.), *The Jews of South Wales*, p. xv.
15 Jasmine Donahaye, *Whose People? Wales, Israel, Palestine* (Cardiff, 2012), p. 160.
16 Neil Evans, 'Comparing Immigrant Histories', in Paul O'Leary (ed.), *Irish Migrants in Modern Wales* (Liverpool, 2004), p. 165.
17 W. D. Rubinstein, 'The Anti-Jewish Riots of 1911 in South Wales', *Welsh History Review*, (1997), 669.
18 Rubinstein, 'The Anti-Jewish Riots', 669.

19 See Geoffrey Alderman, 'The Jew as Scapegoat?' The Settlement and Reception of Jews in South Wales before 1914', *Transactions of the Jewish Historical Society of England*, XXVI (1974–8); 'The Anti-Jewish Riots of August 1911 in South Wales: a Response', *Welsh History Review*, 20 (2001); and Alderman, 'Into the Vortex: South Wales Jewry before 1914', JCR-UK, 1911.

20 See Rubinstein, 'The Anti-Jewish Riots'.

21 David Morris, 'The history of the Welsh Jewish communities', 1750 to the present' (unpublished PhD thesis, University of Wales, 1999), 218.

22 *JC*, 2 May 2008.

23 'Jews Targeted', 7 August 2002, Newspaper Clippings, D/D SHC 20/1, WGA; *JC*, 31 May 2013.

24 *JC*, 31 May 2013. 7 June 2013; 25 October 2013; 14 August 2015.

25 Alan Hooper and John Punter (ed.), *Capital Cardiff 1975–2020: Regeneration, Competitiveness and the Urban Environment* (Cardiff, 2006), p. 231.

Select Bibliography

Abrams, Lynn, *Oral History Theory*, 2nd edn (London: Routledge, 2016).

Abrams, Nathan, *Caledonian Jews: A Study of Seven Small Communities in Scotland* (North Carolina: McFarland and Company, 2009).

Abse, Leo, 'A Tale of Collaboration not Conflict with the "People of the Book"', *New Welsh Review* (Autumn, 1993), 16–21.

Alderman, Geoffrey, 'The Anti-Jewish Riots of August 1911 in South Wales', *Welsh History Review*, 6 (1972), 190–200.

———, 'The Jew as Scapegoat? The Settlement and Reception of Jews in South Wales before 1914', *Transactions of the Jewish Historical Society of England*, XXVI (1974–8), 62–70.

———, *Controversy and Crisis: Studies in the History of the Jews in Modern Britain* (Brighton, MA: Academic Studies Press, 2008).

———, 'The Anti-Jewish Riots of August 1911 in South Wales: A Response', *Welsh History Review*, 20 (2001), 564–71.

Allen, Richard C., and David Ceri Jones with Trystan O. Hughes (eds), *The Religious History of Wales: Religious Life and Practice in Wales from the Seventeenth Century to the Present Day* (Cardiff: Welsh Academic Press, 2014).

Baumel-Schwartz, Judith T., *Never Look Back: The Jewish Refugee Children in Great Britain, 1938–1945* (West Lafayette: Purdue University Press, 2012).

Bellany, Wendy, 'A Vanished Community', *Merthyr Historian*, 16 (2001), 101–9.

Broomfield, Stuart, *Wales at War: The Experience of the Second World War in Wales* (Stroud: History Press, 2009).

Cesarani, David (ed.), *The Making of Modern Anglo-Jewry* (Oxford: Blackwell, 1990).

Cesarani, David, and Tony Kushner (eds), *The Internment of Aliens in Twentieth Century Britain* (London: Frank Cass, 1993).

Chambers, Paul, and Andrew Thompson, 'Coming to Terms with the Past: Religion and Identity in Wales', *Social Compass*, 52/3 (2005), 337–52.

Cullen, Stephen M., 'Another Nationalism: The British Union of Fascists in Glamorgan, 1932–40', *Welsh History Review*, 17/1 (1994), 101–14.

Davies, Grahame, *The Chosen People: Wales and the Jews* (Bridgend: Seren, 2002).

Davies, John, *A History of Wales* (London: Penguin, 2007).

Dee, David, *Sport and British Jewry: Integration, Ethnicity and Anti-Semitism 1890–1970* (Manchester: Manchester University Press, 2013).

Donahaye, Jasmine, *Whose People?: Wales, Israel, Palestine* (Cardiff: University of Wales Press, 2012),

———, *The Greatest Need: The Creative Life and Troubled Times of Lily Tobias, a Welsh Jew in Palestine* (Aberystwyth: Honno, 2015).

Endelman, Todd M., *The Jews of Britain 1656–2000* (Berkeley: University of California Press, 2002).

Evans, Nicholas J, 'Indirect Passage from Europe: Transmigration via the UK, 1836–1914', *Journal for Maritime Research* (2001), 70–84.

Fevre, Ralph, and Andrew Thompson (eds), *Nation, Identity and Social Theory: Perspectives from Wales* (Cardiff: University of Wales Press, 1999).

Francis, Hywel, *Miners Against Fascism: Wales and the Spanish Civil War* (Abersychan: Warren and Pell Publishing, 2004).

Francis, Hywel, and David Smith, *The Fed: A History of the South Wales Miners in the Twentieth Century* (London: Lawrence & Wishart, 1980).

Gartner, Lloyd P., *The Jewish Immigrant in England, 1870–1914*, 3rd edn (London: Vallentine Mitchell, 2001).

———, *American and British Jews in the Age of the Great Migration* (London: Vallentine Mitchell, 2009).

Gilley, Sheridan, and William J. Sheils (eds), *A History of Religion in Britain: Practice and Belief from Pre-Roman Times to the Present* (Oxford: Blackwell, 1994).

Gould, Julius, and Shaul Esh (eds), *Jewish Life in Modern Britain* (London: Routledge and Kegan Paul, 1964).

Graham, David, Marlena Schmool and Stanley Waterman, *Jews in Britain: A Snapshot from the 2001 Census* (London: Institute for Jewish Policy Research, 2007).

Grenville, Anthony, *Jewish Refugees from Germany and Austria in Britain 1933–1970: Their Image in AJR Information* (London: Vallentine Mitchell, 2010).

Gruffudd, Heini, *Yr Erlid: Hanes Kate Bosse-Griffiths a'i Theulu yn yr Almaen a Chymru Adeg yr Ail Ryfel Byd* (Talybont: Y Lolfa, 2012).

Henriques, Ursula R. Q. (ed.), *The Jews of South Wales*, 2nd edn (Cardiff: University of Wales Press, 2013).

Hillaby, Joe, and Caroline Hillaby, *The Palgrave Dictionary of Medieval Anglo-Jewish History* (Basingstoke: Palgrave Macmillan, 2013).

Holmes, Colin, *Anti-Semitism in British Society, 1876–1939* (London: Edward Arnold, 1979).

———, 'The Tredegar Riots of 1911: Anti-Jewish Disturbances in South Wales', *Welsh History Review*, 11 (1982), 214–25.

Johnes, Martin, *Wales Since 1939* (Manchester: Manchester University Press, 2012).

Jones, Siân, Tony Kushner and Sarah Pearce (eds), *Cultures of Ambivalence and Contempt: Studies in Jewish-non-Jewish Relations* (London: Vallentine Mitchell, 1998).

Jordan, Glen, Colin Heyman, Eve Lavine, Cai Parry-Jones, Diana Soffa and Chris Weedon (eds), *Hineni: Life Portraits from a Jewish Community* (Cardiff: Butetown History and Arts Centre, 2012).

Kahn-Harris, Keith, and Ben Gidley. *Turbulent Times: The British Jewish Community Today* (London: Continuum, 2010).

Kushner, Tony, 'Horns and Dilemmas: Jewish Evacuees in Britain during the Second World War', *Immigrants and Minorities*, 8 (1988), 273–91.

———, *The Persistence of Prejudice: Anti-Semitism in British Society during the Second World War* (Manchester: Manchester University Press, 1989).

——— (ed.), *The Jewish Heritage in British History: Englishness and Jewishness* (Abingdon: Routledge, 1992).

Kushner, Tony, and Katherine Knox (eds), *Refugees in an Age of Genocide: Global, National and Local Perspectives during the Twentieth Century* (London: Frank Cass, 1999).

Kushner, Tony and Hannah Ewence (eds), *Whatever Happened to British Jewish Studies?* (London: Vallentine Mitchell, 2012).

Langham, Raphael, *The Jews in Britain: A Chronology* (Basingstoke: Palgrave Macmillan, 2005).

Leighton-Langer, Peter, *The King's Own Loyal Enemy Aliens: German and Austrian Refugees in Britain's Armed Forces, 1939–1945* (London: Vallentine Mitchell, 2006).

Lipman, Vivian D., *Social History of the Jews in England: 1850–1950* (London: Watts, 1954).

———, *A History of the Jews in Britain since 1858* (Leicester: Leicester University Press, 1990).

Liss, Alan S., 'A short history of Reform Judaism in south Wales, 1947–1970' (unpublished thesis for certificate in education, University of Wales, 1977).

Llwyd, Alan, *Cymru Ddu/Black Wales: A History* (Cardiff: Hughes a'i Fab, 2005).

Mars, Leonard, 'Immigration and Anglicization: Religious Education as an Issue in the Swansea Hebrew Congregation, 1894–1910', *Jewish Journal of Sociology*, 39/1–2 (1997), 76–86.

Morgan, Kenneth O., *Rebirth of a Nation: Wales 1880–1980* (Oxford: Oxford University Press, 1982).

Morris, David, 'The history of the Welsh Jewish Communities: 1750–present' (unpublished PhD thesis, University of Wales, Aberystwyth, 1999).

Morris, Henry, *We Will Remember Them: A Record of the Jews who Died in the Armed Forces of the Crown from 1939* (London: AJEX, Association of Jewish Ex-Servicemen and Women, 1989).

Mosse, Werner E., and Julius Carlebach (eds), *Second Chance: Two Centuries of German-Speaking Jews in the United Kingdom* (Tübingen: Mohr, 1991).

Neilson, Janet M., 'The History and Influence of Swansea's Jewish Community, 1730–2006', *Minerva: The Journal of Swansea History*, XIV (2006), 23–36.

Newman, Aubrey, *Provincial Jewry in Victorian Britain: Papers for a Conference at University College, London Convened by the Jewish Historical Society of England* (London: Jewish Historical Society of England, 1975).

O'Kane, Martin, and John Morgan-Guy (eds), *Biblical Art from Wales* (Sheffield: Sheffield Phoenix Press, 2010).

O'Leary, Paul, 'Anti-Irish Riots in Wales, 1826–1882', *Llafur*, 5/4 (1991), 27–36.

———, 'Film, History and Anti-Semitism: Solomon and Gaenor (1999) and the Representations of the Past', *North American Journal of Welsh Studies*, 7 (2012), 38–52.

Parry, Jon, 'The Tredegar Anti-Irish riots of 1882', *Llafur*, 3/4 (1983). 20–3.

Perks, Robert, and Alistair Thomson (eds), *The Oral History Reader*, 3rd edn (Abingdon: Routledge, 2015).

Pollins, Harold, *Economic History of the Jews in England* (New Jersey: Fairleigh Dickinson University Press, 1982).

———, 'The Jewish Community of Brynmawr, Wales', *Jewish Journal of Sociology*, L, 1–2 (2008), 5–32.

———, 'The Swansea Jewish Community – The First Century', *Jewish Journal of Sociology*, 1/2 (2009), 35–9.

Pope, Robert (ed.), *Religion and National Identity: Wales and Scotland c.1700–2000* (Cardiff: University of Wales Press, 2001).

Roth, Cecil, *The Rise of Provincial Jewry: The Early History of the Jewish Community in the English Countryside, 1740–1840* (London: Jewish Monthly, 1950).

Rubinstein, William D., *A History of the Jews in the English-Speaking World: Great Britain*. (London: Macmillan Press, 1996).

——, 'The Anti-Jewish Riots of 1911 in South Wales: A Re-examination', *Welsh History Review*, 18 (1997), 667–99.

Rubinstein, William D. and Hilary L. Rubinstein, *Philosemitism: Admiration and Support in the English-Speaking World for Jews, 1840–1939* (New York: St Martin's Press, 1999).

Rubinstein, William D., Michael A. Jolles and Hilary L. Rubinstein (eds), *The Palgrave Dictionary of Anglo-Jewish History* (Basingstoke: Palgrave Macmillan, 2011).

Saunders, Neville H., *Swansea Hebrew Congregation, 1730–1980* (Swansea: Swansea City Council, 1980).

Skinner, Patricia (ed.), *The Jews in Medieval Britain* (Woodbridge: Boydell Press, 2003).

Smith, Dai, *Wales: A Question for History* (Bridgend: Seren, 1999).

Sperber, Haim, 'Philanthropy and Social Control in the Anglo-Jewish Community during the Mid-nineteenth Century (1850–1880)', *Journal of Modern Jewish Studies*, 11/1 (2012), 85–101.

Stephenson, David, 'Jewish Presence in, and Absence from, Wales in the Twelfth and Thirteenth Centuries', *Jewish Historical Studies*, 43 (2011), 7–20.

Sugarman, Martin, *Fighting Back: British Jewry's Military Contribution in the Second World War* (London: Vallentine Mitchell, 2010).

Thompson, Paul, *Voice of the Past: Oral History*, 3rd edn (New York: Oxford University Press, 2000).

Weindling, Paul, 'Medical Refugees in Britain and the Wider World, 1930–1960: Introduction', *Social History of Medicine*, 22/3 (2009), 451–9.

Weissbach, Lee S., *Jewish Life in Small-Town America: A History* (New Haven: Yale University Press, 2005).

Wiener, Abraham, 'An Episode in South Wales: How Dr Moses Hyamson Lost the British Chief Rabbinate', *Menorah Journal* (Autumn, 1951), 134–50.

Williams, Charlotte, Neil Evans and Paul O'Leary (eds), *A Tolerant Nation?: Exploring Ethnic Diversity in Wales* (Cardiff: University of Wales Press, 2003).

Williams, Charlotte, Neil Evans and Paul O'Leary (eds), *A Tolerant Nation?: Revisiting Ethnic Diversity in a Devolved Wales* (Cardiff: University of Wales Press, 2015).

Williams, E. Wynne, 'Jewish Refugees at Gwrych Castle', *Abergele Field Club and Historical Society Review*, 1 (1982), 2–5.

Williams, J. Ronald, 'The Influence of Foreign Nationalities on the Life of the People of Merthyr Tydfil', *Sociological Review*, 28 (1926), 148–52.

Index

Aronson, John and Maria 21, 119
Aronson, Solomon 21
Arron, Bennett 145
Arron, Charles 95
Arron, Joyce 57
art 116, 118–20; *see also* émigré artists Herman,
   Josef; Koppel, Heinz; Lek, Karel; Neuschul,
   Ernest
Ashkenazi Jews 12, 38, 86, 121, 127, 169,
   187n.129
assimilation 11, 47–9, 56, 63, 86, 118, 124, 126–8,
   150, 153, 195n.119
Auban, Reuben 86

Balfour Declaration 100
Balsom, Denis 218n.81
Bangor 7, 11, 14; Aronson family 21, 36, 119;
   Bolloten family 115; charity 63; *cheder* 56–7,
   60; eisteddfod 119; foundation of Jewish
   community 37; Hyman brothers 21; kosher
   meat 62, 78; Freemasonry 95; Jewish
   involvement in local politics 93; Jewish
   professionals 146; migration to 21, 23, 36–7;
   North Wales Jewish Network 156–7, 164;
   numerical decline of Jewish community 140,
   152; Pollecoff family 95, 114; religious
   leadership 51–4, 80, 92; Second World War 78,
   80–1, 87; Shafran family 80, 87, 98; synagogue
   38, 42–3, 90; toleration 91, 97–8, 101; Wartski
   family 37, 40, 60, 91, 93, 101, 124, 136
Bangor University 37, 60; evacuation of
   students to, 80; anti-Israel activity, 111;
   Jewish academic staff, 140, 151, 156
Baptists 73, 79, 81, 100–101, 103–104; *see also*
   Nonconformity
Bargoed: Barnett family 95, 144; foundation of
   Jewish community 35; Jewish involvement
   in sport 95; numerical decline of Jewish
   community, 139, 144
Barnett, Joseph and Hannah 20
Barnett, Louis 46
Barnett, Phyllis 95
Barnett, Solomon 34
Barry 31, 120
bar mitzvah 72, 79–80, 150, 154
Barsky, Abraham 34
Barth, Anneliese 72
bat mitzvah 116
Bechhöfer, Susi and Lottie 73

Bellany, Wendy 114
Benjamin, Israel P. 84
Berg, Joseph 72
Bernfeld, Werner 67, 125
Bernstein, Bernard 114
Bernstein, Lionel 149
Bernstein, Ronald 83, 146
Berry, Revd Emmanuel 53, 57
Beth Hamedrash and Talmud Torah (Cardiff)
   47, 191n.63
Bevan, Rita, Nia and Ffion 116
Bick, Bernd Israel 76
Billig, Michael 131
Birmingham 53, 55, 78, 143, 157, 190n.35,
   227n.124
Black, Monty 114
Bloch, Revd Solomon 12
Board of Deputies of British Jews 131, 144,
   207n.33
Boer War 103, 106, 108
Bolloten, Joseph 115
Boone, Mordecai 35, 144
Bosse-Griffiths, Kate 86, 118, 120, 133
Boston 27
Braham, Peter 26
Bridgend: burials 45; *cheder* 57; foundation of
   Jewish community 36; numerical decline of
   Jewish community 139; religious leadership
   52; synagogue 42
Brill, Otto 70
Brinks, Gerald 146
Bristol 17–18, 155
British Medical Association 67–8
British Union of Fascists (BUF) 92–3
Brodie, Morris 38
Brothers 116–17; *see also* Rubens, Bernice
Bruck, Werner F. 68
Brynmawr burials, 45; *cheder* 56; formation of
   Jewish community 35, 40–1; marriages 149;
   mikvah 43; numerical decline of Jewish
   community 139; pawnbroking 33; religious
   leadership 51, 53; synagogue 40–1, 43, 90,
   153; vandalism of Jewish cemetery 111;
   Yiddish 122
Buckley 34
Builth Wells 81
Burns, Lena and Leslie 57
Burial Acts 44
Buswell, Adam 127